I0814103

DFW DECO

Detail, **Texas and Pacific passenger station and office building, Fort Worth**
1931, Wyatt C. Hedrick, Inc.

JIM PARSONS AND DAVID BUSH

Fort Worth, Texas

Library of Congress Cataloging-in-Publication Data

Names: Parsons, Jim, 1977- author. | Bush, David, 1957- author.
Title: DFW deco : modernistic architecture of north Texas / Jim Parsons and David Bush.
Other titles: Dallas-Fort Worth deco
Description: Fort Worth, Texas : TCU Press, [2017] | Includes bibliographical references.
Identifiers: LCCN 2017011519 | ISBN 9780875656359 (alk. paper)
Subjects: LCSH: Art deco (Architecture)--Texas. |
Architecture--Texas--History--20th century. | Dallas (Tex.)--Buildings,
structures, etc. | Fort Worth (Tex.)--Buildings, structures, etc.
Classification: LCC NA730.T5 P37 2017 | DDC 720.9764/0904--dc23
LC record available at https://urldefense.proofpoint.com/v2/url?u=https-3A__lccn.loc.
gov_2017011519&d=DQIFAg&c=7Q-FWLBTAxn3T_E3HWrzGYJrC4RvUoWDrzTlit-
GRH_A&r=O2eiy819IcwTGuw-vrBGiVdmhQxMh2yxeggw9qlTUDE&m=SacpGC5lUEAwg-
d7xCkp5NHLQ-kVRIrRxkV60WLd5GbQ&s=QCiTVdOOIi5VrpzGeS9re2MaDo6kUvHGKX-
e22SDgW2E&e=

TCU Box 298300
Fort Worth, Texas 76129
817.257.7822
www.prs.tcu.edu
To order books: 1.800.826.8911

Designed by Bill Brammer
www.fusion29.com

To Melinda Esco, whose guidance, friendship,
humor, and patience made this project possible.

Detail, **State of Texas Building, Fair Park, Dallas**
Texas Centennial Architects, Associated, and Donald Barthelme, Sr., architects
1936

Foreword

ART DECO IS A TRANSITIONAL STYLE, BRIDGING long-held traditions of classicism and what is sometimes described as "modernistic" influences from the Modern Movement that began in the early twentieth century. As the Modern Movement espoused a design dogma associated with a "new" way of thinking about architecture, art, and design that placed high value on innovation, analytical and formal explorations, functionality, mass production, and the machine-made, the Art Deco style was able to remain connected aesthetically to previous styles of architecture while also pursuing the intentions of modernity. The tradition can be found in the symmetry and subtle classical forms and in the craftsmanship and artistic treatment of ornamentation. The modernity can be found in the abstracted classical forms, the use of new materials, and in the stepped shapes that responded to new zoning setbacks. I have always appreciated Art Deco for its "style," the very distinctive characteristics that are recognizable in the decorative and fine arts as well as architecture. However, it is the ornamentation that excites me the most; it is the thing that attracts people to Art Deco and causes them to be drawn in, to linger, and to look more closely.

Ornamentation is delightful for purely aesthetic reasons, but it is also used to communicate, allowing the visitor to "read" the building, and thus to engage with it. This traditional architectural component is best known by the French term *architecture parlante*, or "architecture that speaks." Ornamentation can tell stories, expressing a building's purpose, its location, or the architect's design intent. A great building that exemplifies this idea, and is well described in this book, is the Hall of State in Dallas, originally the State of Texas Building of the Texas Centennial Exposition of 1936. This building's principal purpose is to communicate with the visitor about Texas. With stories of the state's origins, history, native building materials, flora and fauna, people and industry, the building speaks clearly. The names of Texas heroes are carved into the stone entablature, and allegorical murals describe the history of the state in the central hall, all with the purpose of celebrating the state's ample resources. Once Louis Sullivan's "form follows function" and Adolf Loos's "ornament and crime" mantras and other design tenets of the Modern Movement took hold after World War II, that kind of building—architecture that speaks—was out of favor.

Also traditional is the use of artists, artisans, and craftsmen—the human hand. This direct connection between a building and the human beings who made it is another way ornamentation engages the visitor. During Art Deco's peak period of popularity in the late 1920s and in the 1930s, hands were not that hard to come by. And during the Great Depression, building projects provided necessary work for the underemployed. Incorporating craft was not only popular, but was also encouraged during this period, as the federal government financially supported public art and mural programs that provided work for artists. In a similar way, architectural design that incorporated ornamental metals, decorative painting, and bas-relief panels provided work for metalworkers, decorative painters, sculptors, masons, tile makers, and others. Art Deco was the last architectural style to have the full benefit of the artist's and craftsman's labor-intensive contributions. Later architecture would focus instead on the machine-made systems that avoided expression of man's participation in order to express a new age.

While the use of ornamentation and the craft that produced it are traditional, the appearance of the ornament in Art Deco was meant to be modernistic. Hence, designers created the abstracted and geometric forms and patterns such as the chevron that are so strongly associated with the style. A true hybrid of the past and future, Art Deco aspired to be new without letting go of the past. As described in the 1925 *Handbook of the Exposition Internationale des Arts Décoratifs et Industrials Modernes:*

> Works admitted to the Exposition must show new inspiration and real originality. They must be executed and presented by artisans, artists, and manufacturers who have created the models, and by editors whose work belongs to modern decorative and industrial art. Reproductions, imitations, and counterfeits of ancient styles will be strictly prohibited.

Both the modernity and tradition come through in Jim Parsons and David Bush's fourth book on Art Deco architecture in Texas. The authors have used their collective talents in the areas of architectural history, photography, writing, and historic preservation to present this style in a way that will satisfy both the professional looking for a resource book with facts and connections to the region's architectural history and the lay person who will be delighted by the beauty of the style's forms, materials—and, especially, the ornamentation.

— Nancy T. McCoy, FAIA, FAPT

Preface

THE FOCUS OF *DFW DECO* WAS ORIGINALLY to be Art Deco architecture in the Dallas-Fort Worth Metroplex. But as work progressed, it became evident that significant modernistic buildings existed over a much broader area. A more precise description of the region represented would be North Central Texas and Northeast Texas, the territory where Dallas- and Fort Worth-based architects did the majority of their work.

Most of the buildings in this book are grouped according to their original uses. Chapters are devoted to commercial, institutional, and residential buildings, as well as buildings associated with travel and transportation and entertainment. Skyscrapers are in a separate chapter defined by form rather than function. The exposition buildings constructed for the 1936 Texas Centennial celebrations are described in their own chapter as well.

Buildings are referred to by their original names as referenced in newspaper articles, telephone directories, and city directories of the period; later names are included where appropriate and known. Buildings and artworks are listed in chronological order based on the year of completion or the year in which a building was remodeled in modernistic style. In a few instances, photos of related buildings are shown together for comparison, e.g., the J.B. Pope Building (1929) and the New Pope Building (1935). Each chapter begins with a featured building or complex that may be presented out of chronological order.

The names of architects and contractors and the years of completion were determined from a variety of sources, including cornerstones and plaques, architectural drawings and period newspapers, professional journals, city directories, and telephone directories.

The final chapter of the book is composed of biographical sketches of the architects, designers, and artists whose work is featured in *DFW Deco*. In some cases, previously published works about these projects and the lives and careers of these men and women conflict with information in materials from the period. When in doubt, we have based our writing on primary sources, including archived newspaper and journal articles, professional directories and city directories, public records, and the architects and artists' own accounts.

We owe a debt of gratitude to Judith Singer Cohen for her book *Cowtown Moderne: Art Deco Architecture of Fort Worth, Texas*, which was published in 1988 after a decade of research. The book offers an excellent examination of the economic, social, and aesthetic forces that shaped Art Deco architecture in the Panther City. *DFW Deco* covers many of the same buildings Cohen wrote about, but *Cowtown Moderne* includes information and details gleaned from interviews and correspondence with some of the people who helped design and build them—people who are now gone. The book is an invaluable resource.

We hope that *DFW Deco* opens readers' eyes to the rich modernistic heritage of the region the same way that *Cowtown Moderne* did for Fort Worth.

— Jim Parsons and David Bush

Mural detail, **United States Post Office, Farmersville**
1941, Jerry Bywaters

CHAPTER 1

INTRODUCTION

Detail, **Sinclair Building**.

"In the New World we have the pyramids of the mighty Mayan civilization in Yucatan and Guatemala, the design of which, with only slight modification, might well serve as models for the set-back skyscrapers of New York and other American cities."

Alfred C. Bossom
Fellow, Royal Institute of British Architects
in the *New York Times*
August 16, 1925

OPPOSITE
Sinclair Building at dusk, Fort Worth
1930, Wiley G. Clarkson & Co.

BY THE TIME ARCHITECT ALFRED BOSSOM began promoting Mesoamerican pyramids as viable models for American skyscrapers, the basic form for tall buildings had been established. New York City's 1916 zoning resolution encoded the "setback principle" that was designed to prevent tall buildings from blocking air movement and light, and in 1922, Eliel Saarinen's proposal for the Tribune Tower in Chicago showed how setbacks could be combined with sweeping vertical lines to create graceful tapering towers. During the construction boom of the 1920s, setback skyscrapers came to define the skylines of the nation's largest cities. Although the stepped profiles were not really necessary on tall buildings in either Dallas or Fort Worth—both had ample light and air—they reinforced the image of a modern, progressive city. Before floodlights ever illuminated the Mayan-inspired crown of Fort Worth's Sinclair Building, North Texas architects, developers, and contractors were regularly touring the newest buildings in New York, Chicago, and Detroit to bring the latest ideas in modernistic design back home.[1]

The stepped pyramid wasn't the only aspect of Mesoamerican architecture that designers found appropriate for modern American buildings. Bossom noted that the hard, white light and uninteresting shadows of the Yucatan had inspired the Maya to "evolve an architecture of simple surface decorations without cornices but with a strong emphasis on verticality." The lighting conditions Bossom described certainly fit the Lone Star State, and the use of reliefs and surface ornamentation on the facades of classic Art Deco buildings provided interest through the interplay of light and shadow.[2]

Although Art Deco was the height of modernity in the 1920s and '30s, buildings constructed in the style were not described as Deco when they were built; instead, they were called *modern* or *modernistic*. The term *Art Deco* was not coined until the 1960s, when a new appreciation of the style emerged after decades of disdain. British art historian Bevis Hillier popularized the expression, which was adapted from the *Exposition Internationale des Arts Décoratifs et Industriels Modernes*, the official name of the Paris Exposition of 1925 that was meant to

Entrance, **Sinclair Building**

reestablish France as a leader in luxury goods and proved to be the pinnacle of European Art Deco design.[3]

In the United States, Art Deco refers to the concurrent styles of architecture, decorative arts, fine art, fashion, and industrial design that were popular from the 1920s through World War II. With such a broad scope, Deco is an imprecise term that can suggest anything from the Chrysler Building to flapper dresses, streamlined locomotives, and the sets of Hollywood musicals.

Besides its wide range of applications, Art Deco also spanned the extravagance of the Jazz Age and the austerity of the Great Depression. There are bound to be contradictions in a movement that provided the backdrop for such extremes. Proponents described Art Deco as a completely contemporary style with no historical precedents, yet it borrowed heavily from ancient, medieval, and indigenous sources. Initially designed to appeal to the elite, the style was popularized in the movies and became part of American consumer culture. A celebration of individuality that depended on mass production, Art Deco was thoroughly modern.

Deco defined

In this book, the terms *Deco* and *modernistic* are used interchangeably to describe the architectural style that helped shape the built environment in Texas from the late 1920s through about 1950. These umbrella terms encompass the three subtypes of American modernistic architecture: *Art Deco*, *Art Moderne*, and *PWA Deco*, also known as *WPA Deco*.

Art Deco

Art Deco is the classic, highly ornamented architecture of the late 1920s and early 1930s. Sometimes called *Zigzag Deco* or *Zigzag Moderne*, the style is recognizable for its vertical orientation, angular profile, and frequent use of zigzag patterns and chevrons as decorative elements. Art Deco buildings are usually symmetrical and commonly feature geometric interpretations of natural forms or stylized ornamentation inspired by classical and Gothic architecture. Decoration is frequently in the form of low reliefs. Ancient and indigenous influences, including motifs from Egyptian, Mayan, Pueblo, and Aztec culture, often serve as the inspiration for the decoration on Art Deco buildings. (In addition to the Sinclair Building's adaptation of Mayan design, Fort Worth alone boasted elaborate Egyptian Deco in the Worth Theater and the colorful "Aztec Princes" on the Aviation Building. Unfortunately, both the Worth and the Aviation Building have been demolished.)

Detail, customer service lobby,
Dallas Gas Company Building
1931, Lang & Witchell

Art Deco is also known for its rich materials. Finely detailed metalwork, often executed in innovative alloys, is common, particularly around building entrances. Interiors often incorporate elaborate metal grilles and banisters, murals, reliefs, and highly polished wood and stone, as well as intensely colored terra cotta, glass, mosaic tile, and terrazzo. Pyramidal or stepped roofs with pinnacles, lanterns, or beacons are typical of the style, particularly on tall buildings; even low-rise Art Deco structures often use strong vertical lines and elaborate finials to suggest height. In North Texas, Art Deco design is usually found on commercial buildings and skyscrapers built before 1931, as well as a small number of public buildings designed before the onset of the Great Depression.

Art Moderne

Often called *Streamline Moderne*, the architecture of the later 1930s was inspired by industrial design, particularly the ocean liners, airplanes, and aerodynamic locomotives that were revolutionizing travel. Moderne buildings are recognizable for their smooth surfaces, curved corners, horizontal orientation, flat roofs, and comparative lack of ornamentation. Facades are usually asymmetrical and commonly feature metal casement windows that wrap around corners. Materials with industrial applications, such as aluminum, stainless steel, and glass block, are frequently incorporated into Moderne design. Sculptural elements are not uncommon, but are used in a much more restrained fashion than on Art Deco buildings. White is usually the predominant color in streamlined buildings; accent colors tend to be muted.

Art Moderne design is found in a wider range of buildings than Art Deco. The streamlined styling was used for industrial and commercial projects, especially retail stores, theaters, and manufacturing plants; it was also favored for service stations, diners, motels, and other automobile-oriented structures. In addition, Art Moderne was the style most often used for modernistic houses. The smooth surfaces and industrial inspiration of the relatively unornamented Art Moderne helped pave the way for the International Style.

Detail, **Greyhound Union Bus Terminal, Dallas**
1948, Grayson Gill

Detail, **Van Zandt County Courthouse, Canton**
1937, Voelcker & Dixon

PWA Deco

PWA Deco, also known as WPA Deco, is the architecture of post offices, courthouses, schools, and city halls that were designed and built by the federal government or with federal assistance during the Great Depression. The style's names refer to two of the largest economic stimulus programs that were part of President Franklin Delano Roosevelt's New Deal.

Congress authorized the creation of the Public Works Administration (PWA) in 1933 to stimulate business and reduce unemployment as the Depression deepened. The PWA eventually invested more than six billion dollars in such federal projects as highways, bridges, and dams, and local projects including schools, county courthouses, hospitals, city halls, streets, and sewage systems. Local projects were funded with PWA grants that usually covered at least half of the costs, with state, county, or municipal governments providing the remaining portion. Private businesses bid on the contracts and carried out the work.[4]

The Works Progress Administration (WPA) was the largest New Deal program. Renamed the Work Projects Administration in 1939, the WPA directly employed millions of Americans in cooperation with state and local governments that provided a portion of project funding. Most WPA projects involved building infrastructure, but the program's diverse efforts also included historic preservation, social science research, and theater, publishing, and art. The legacy of the PWA and WPA includes thousands of post offices and federal buildings, as well as libraries, schools, and recreation buildings in every state of the union.[5]

PWA Deco is sometimes called "stripped classicism" or, more pejoratively, "starved classicism" for its use of simplified classical detailing stylized along modernistic lines. PWA Deco combines the angular profile and symmetry of Art Deco design with Art Moderne's horizontal orientation, clean lines, and flat roofs. PWA Deco uses less ornamentation than Art Deco, but more than Art Moderne.

Public art was an important component of many New Deal projects. The Public Works of Art Project was the first federal art program and was designed to give unemployed professional artists meaningful work. The PWA and WPA also supported public art programs, as did the US Treasury Department. The most familiar products of these efforts are the murals painted in public buildings, particularly post offices, in cities and small towns across Texas and around the United States.

PWA Deco is the most common style of architecture for Depression-era federal buildings, post offices, and county courthouses. As a result of changing tastes and attitudes and new economic realities, these projects became the last iteration of the neoclassical government buildings that had symbolized stability and security for generations of Americans.

Deco in North Texas

The spread of modernistic architecture in North Texas can be mapped as three expanding areas, each of them influenced by a different world-changing event.

The smallest area encompasses the cities of Dallas and Fort Worth, which enjoyed rapid growth as a result of the general prosperity of the 1920s and the ongoing population shift from farms and small towns to cities. At the turn of the twentieth century, both Dallas and Fort Worth were mercantile centers and rail hubs, each prospering from a different mainstay of the Texas economy: cotton in Dallas and cattle in Fort Worth.

In the years before and after World War I, major petroleum discoveries west and northwest of Fort Worth transformed the city into a regional oil center. At about the same time, three army airfields opened to train pilots and ground crews for combat in Europe. In addition to flooding the city with thousands of servicemen and many of their dependents, the airfields laid the groundwork for the aviation industry that would be a focal point of Fort Worth's development in the decades to come. In 1928, the Fort Worth Association of Commerce adopted the Five-Year Work Program to promote the city's future growth and prosperity. The Association's efforts to attract new businesses in-

Postcard, **Fort Worth City Hall and Public Library**
early 1940s

fluenced the development of the modernistic buildings that rose in the city in the late 1920s and early 1930s.[6]

While Fort Worth looked to the West, much of the Dallas economy was focused on the cotton-growing regions of East Texas. The city was the world's largest inland cotton market and an important wholesale market. Banking and insurance were major industries, and a strong manufacturing base grew to include automobiles and ready-to-wear clothing. The discovery of the great East Texas Oil Field in October 1930 made Dallas a center for petroleum financing when local bankers became the first in the nation to lend money to oil companies using oil reserves in the ground as collateral.[7]

Most of the traditional Art Deco or Zigzag Deco architecture in the region exists in Dallas and Fort Worth, particularly the ornate setback skyscrapers that define the period. The stock market crash of October 1929 effectively brought this era to end, although construction continued on projects that were already underway.

To the east and southeast of Dallas, exploitation of the East Texas Oil Field transformed the agricultural economy and sparked significant construction projects. The largest oil reservoir in the contiguous United States covered 198 square miles—forty miles from north to south and between four and eight miles from east to west. As the population exploded in towns and cities across the region, architects from Dallas, Fort Worth, and Houston, along with local designers and builders, produced modernistic buildings for what had been modestly sized county seats and small rural communities. In Kilgore, for example, the population grew from 650 in 1930 to more than 12,000 by 1936. In addition to building the houses, schools, and churches these new residents required, contractors had to replace almost all of Kilgore's commercial buildings, which had been demol-

Esplanade of State, Fair Park, Dallas 1936

ished when oil was discovered under the original townsite. The result was a new, largely modernistic business district.[8]

The economic stimulus programs instituted by President Franklin D. Roosevelt as part of the New Deal spread the pared-down classical architecture that came to be called PWA or WPA Deco over the widest area. The PWA and the WPA helped construct federal buildings, post offices, county courthouses, schools, and recreational facilities in communities ranging from very small rural towns to large urban centers. Both Dallas and Fort Worth used federal funding to embark on extensive expansion and improvement of their public education systems. With the notable exception of North Side High School, Fort Worth constructed school buildings in traditional architectural styles, while Dallas tended to favor modernistic schools.

In the midst of the Great Depression, the public was also exposed to modernistic architecture during two popular celebrations of the one hundredth anniversary of Texas's independence from Mexico: the Texas Centennial Exposition in Dallas and the Texas Frontier Centennial in Fort Worth. Both events were held in 1936, and each featured major permanent exhibition and entertainment facilities.

The United States' entry into World War II and its accompanying restrictions on civilian construction brought Art Deco architecture's most prolific era to an end, though the economic boom that followed the conflict resulted in a surge of suburban commercial buildings and movie theaters that carried modernistic design through the end of the 1940s.

CHAPTER 2

COMMERCIAL

Relief, **Western Union Building**

"A trip through the new building, on the northwest corner of Third and Main Streets, is a revelation of the newest and fastest in wire telegraphy . . . the new plant will take care of Fort Worth's needs for 30 years."

Fort Worth Star-Telegram
August 30, 1931

OPPOSITE
Western Union Telegraph Co. Building
312-314 Main Street, Fort Worth
James B. Davies, architect
1931

At 5 P.M. SATURDAY, AUGUST 29, 1931, employees at the Western Union Telegraph Company threw a series of switches that rerouted Fort Worth's telegraph service to the company's new downtown building without interrupting transmissions. As with most of the projects completed during Fort Worth's Five-Year Work Program, the new Western Union building was designed to meet current needs and to serve the much larger city that was on the horizon.[1]

The renderings of the Western Union building produced by Fort Worth architect James B. Davies show a four-story facility with traditional Art Deco ornamentation. It is not clear when or why it was decided to construct a three-story building, but Davies's original design elements were maintained on the shorter structure. The continuous pattern that gives Art Deco its Zigzag nickname is evident on stringcourses and lintels, while chevrons and patterned brick distinguish the modernistic interpretation of a castellated parapet. The subtle use of color highlights decorative relief panels as well as the peaks of the zigzags and chevrons.

Descriptions of the Western Union plant make the building's design sound both innovative and quaint. The most distinctive aspect of the new structure was how quiet it was inside. Telegraph equipment and cables were relegated to the third floor, well above the bank-like lobby where customers could send telegrams from a marble counter under rows of clocks. The telephone bureau occupied the second floor, where messages could be called in to Western Union operators.

Messengers had their own quarters, which included a lounge with playing cards and games, a shower room, and a room to change into uniform. As Western Union faced increased competition from the Bell System of telephone companies, the bike messengers began providing services other than delivering telegrams. In the early 1930s the Fort Worth branch instituted the Western Union Radio Service in cooperation with Fakes & Company, a downtown furniture store that also sold radios. Western Union messengers would deliver replacements for burned-out radio tubes day or night for thirty-five cents plus the price of the tube.[2]

Roofline, **Western Union Building**

At the same time Western Union was constructing its new facility, the Southwestern Bell Telephone Company was building three new telephone exchanges in Fort Worth. When Exchange No. 7 on Pershing Avenue went into service at midnight on March 1, 1931, almost three thousand telephones were transferred to "dial machines" that allowed customers to place calls without an operator. Fort Worth received all-automatic telephone service at midnight April 30, 1932, when Exchange No. 4 on West Bowie Street and Exchange No. 6 on Chestnut Avenue were activated.[3]

Many of the Southwestern Bell buildings were designed by Irvin R. Timlin, the company's in-house architect, who worked from corporate headquarters in St. Louis. The Fort Worth exchanges were comparatively small buildings that did not look out of place in residential neighborhoods: either one or two stories tall, they featured modernistic details, but subdued them with a virtually monochromatic palette of buff brick and light cast stone. Ornamentation was limited to the entrances, windows, and cornices, and typically took the form of low reliefs, zigzags, and decorative masonry grilles and panels.

Longview's new telephone office and exchange opened in 1935 with updated switchboards for operator-assisted service. The detailing was much more restrained than on the Fort Worth exchanges; spandrels were brick rather than cast stone, and the main entrance included a lintel with a zigzag motif that might have looked somewhat dated when the building was completed.

The telephone exchanges are still in use, and all have been enlarged at least once. Early additions were usually architecturally compatible with the original construction—workers went to the trouble of reusing one of the distinctive skyline reliefs when Fort Worth's Exchange No. 6 on Chestnut Avenue was enlarged, for example—but most of the later expansions had very little character. Some of them even covered or eliminated original detailing, marring what are otherwise well-preserved examples of a distinctive genre of Art Deco corporate architecture.[4]

Southwestern Bell Telephone Exchange No. 7
later Pershing Exchange Building
5400 Pershing Avenue, Fort Worth
Irvin R. Timlin (St. Louis), architect
William H. Southwell Construction Co., contractors
1931

The original one-story building had ornate ornamentation at the roofline; those decorative elements were lost when the second floor was added.

Lantern, **Exchange No. 7**

Relief, **Exchange No. 7**

Southwestern Bell Telephone Exchange No. 4
later Wilson Exchange Building
1414 West Bowie Street, Fort Worth
Irvin R. Timlin (St. Louis) with
Lang & Witchell (Dallas), architects
1932

The original modernistic building labors beneath an ungainly mansard roof, the result of an unfortunate later addition.

Southwestern Bell Telephone Exchange No. 6
later Market Exchange Building
2401 Chestnut Avenue, Fort Worth
1932

Skyline relief, **Exchange No. 6**
Exchange No. 6 includes a unique detail: a set of relief panels depicting a cityscape backed by a modernistic sky. One of the panels appears to have been saved and repositioned when the building was expanded to the north.

Southwestern Bell Telephone Exchange No. 8
later Valley Exchange Building
1128 Eagle Drive, Fort Worth
1947

Southwestern Bell Telephone Co. Office and Exchange
308 North Fredonia Street, Longview
Eckert-Burton Construction Co. (Dallas), contractors
1935

Southwestern Bell
Haskell Exchange Building, 1930
later Southwestern Bell Long Distance Building
4100 Bryan Street, Dallas
Irvin R. Timlin (St. Louis), architect
1930

In 1929, Southwestern Bell announced plans to rebuild its Haskell Exchange in East Dallas to handle all long-distance calls in Texas as well as telephone traffic from Mexico, Latin America, the Far East, and other parts of the United States. It was estimated that the new facility, completed in 1930, would rank Dallas second only to New York in the routing of long-distance calls.[5]

The Haskell Exchange, which later came to be known as the Long Distance Building, was expanded five times between 1930 and 1970. The building today bears virtually no resemblance to the original design, although some detailing from the 1930 portion remains visible on the Haskell Avenue facade.[6]

Irvin R. Timlin was one of many in-house architects designing at a time when corporations dealing in consumer goods and services were developing a national presence. Some firms understood that good architecture could also be good business, and company architects put that idea to work. Edward F. Sibbert designed distinctive modernistic 5¢-to-25¢ stores for S. H. Kress & Company from corporate headquarters in New York. Theodore H. Stueber played the same role in Dallas as company architect for Wyatt Food Stores, an unusual position in a local chain.

Retailers' dependence on promoting fashionable images has taken a heavy toll on modernistic commercial design, which itself was often used to update buildings constructed in earlier architectural styles. Nevertheless, classic Art Deco and Art Moderne stores, banks, and industrial buildings can be found in big cities, suburban neighborhoods, and small towns throughout North Texas, with especially significant concentrations of modernistic commercial buildings along Jefferson Boulevard in the Oak Cliff section of Dallas and in downtown Kilgore.

Haskell Exchange Building, 2017

Relief panel, **Haskell Exchange Building**

Retail

F. B. Pope Building
111-119 North Kentucky Street, McKinney
Lang & Witchell (Dallas), architects
J. Ed Michael, contractor
1929

Prominent businessman Fletcher B. Pope razed the original Pope Building in 1929 and replaced it with a modern retail and office building. Skillern's Drug Store, which opened in the corner space in 1929, and the J. C. Penney Company department store, which opened in 1935, operated out of the Pope Building for decades.[7]

Detail, **F. B. Pope Building**

Welcome to
HISTORIC
Downtown
McKINNEY
SHOP. DINE. ENJOY.
feeds our soul
KEEP McKINNEY BEAUTIFUL
Welcome to
HISTORIC
Downtown
McKINNEY
SHOP. DINE. ENJOY.
P

New Pope Building
116-118 East Louisiana Street, McKinney
1935

At the time of its completion, the New Pope Building was described as being constructed of white stone. The McKinney Dry Goods Company was at street level, with medical and dental offices on the second floor. The local newspaper praised the developer: "If we had a few more builders like F. B. Pope, this old town would blossom like a Green Bay Tree on the river's brink."[8]

Busch-Kirby Building, Annex
1511 Main Street, Dallas
Lang & Witchell, architects
1930

The annex allowed the A. Harris department store, which occupied the lower floors of the Busch-Kirby Building, to add ten ladies' fitting rooms and a trousseau room as well as expanded drapery, candy, and mail order departments and a larger lunch counter and soda fountain. The addition also included a women's restroom with a lounging room that offered "a welcome opportunity to rest to the woman weary with shopping."[9]

Detail, **Busch-Kirby Building**

OPPOSITE

Blackstone Café and Postal Telegraph Co.
100-100a East Main Street, Kilgore
1931

Historic photos indicate that the doorways on the facade are in the same positions as when the original businesses opened. The telegraph office occupied 100a, the narrow space on the left.

Safeway Stores No. 113
113 East Jefferson Boulevard, Dallas
1932

Detail, **Safeway Stores No. 113**

CasaSelect
101 E. Jefferson
CasaSelect
Bus Stop
Red Tag Sale

The Great Atlantic & Pacific Tea Co.
A&P Grocery Stores No. 49
101-107 East Jefferson Boulevard, Dallas
1933

Detail, **A&P Grocery Stores No. 49**

RODDEN
DECORACIONES
Dulces
Sueños

Rodden Building
3723-3725 West Marshall Avenue
(US Highway 80), Longview
1933
1935, addition

When the Rodden Building was completed in 1933, the *Longview Daily News* noted that it housed the Hall-Wren Pharmacy and the newly established Greggton post office, which was located at the back of the drugstore. The building was expanded to the west two years later when the post office was enlarged. Longview annexed Greggton in 1959.

Detail, **Rodden Building**

La Mode
demolished
1708-1712 Elm Street and
1801-1805 Main Street, Dallas
Remodeled 1934

The women's ready-to-wear store extended through its downtown Dallas block, offering entrances on both Elm and Main streets. It is not clear which storefront this photo depicts. The street plan of downtown Dallas is not a regular grid; despite the irregular numbering, 1708 Elm and 1801 Main are part of the same block.

Sexton Building
130 North Commerce Street, Overton
1934

Bert Barber's Book Store
215 West Eighth Street, Fort Worth
Remodeled c. 1935

Entrance, **Bert Barber's Book Store**

FAR LEFT
Grille, **Bert Barber's Book Store**

213–217 East Main Street, Kilgore
c. 1935

Detail, **215-217 East Main Street**

Hall Furniture Co.
118 West Lamar Street, Sherman
Remodeled 1936

This building was constructed as two adjoining commercial buildings sometime between 1875 and 1885; the structures were altered and connected over the years leading to a 1936 Art Deco remodeling. The new design incorporated opaque structural glass, a product that was invented in 1900 but did not become popular until the late 1920s. The material was used extensively in the 1930s and 1940s to modernize storefronts. Hall Furniture Company operated from this location from 1892 to 1992.[10]

Detail, **Hall Furniture Co.**

S. H. Kress & Co.
604 Main Street and 603 Houston Street,
Fort Worth
Edward F. Sibbert (New York), architect
W. H. Bowen Co. (El Paso), contractors
1936

Dime-store magnate Samuel H. Kress used distinctive architecture to distinguish his chain of 5¢-to-25¢ stores. Company architect Edward F. Sibbert is particularly known for his modernistic designs of Kress stores built between 1929 and 1941.

Detail, Main Street facade, **S. H. Kress & Co.**

Cokesbury Book Store
demolished
1908-1910 Main Street, Dallas
Mark Lemmon, architect
W. C. Henger, contractor
1937

The Methodist Publishing House (later United Methodist Publishing House) opened its first store in 1898 in Dallas and the first Cokesbury Book Store in 1925 in Dallas. Growing sales prompted construction of a new five-story building. The air-conditioned store was faced in Georgia marble with bronze door trim and detailing. Shelves and interior fixtures were of primavera wood, also known as blonde mahogany.

The first floor was devoted to retail sales. School supplies and interdenominational church supplies were sold on the second floor, which also housed the mail order department. Mailing and stock rooms were on the third floor, with general offices on the fourth. Meeting rooms and the two-hundred-seat Cokesbury Auditorium occupied the fifth floor. The auditorium was available for public use by application.[11]

Although it later sold only religious works, for many years Cokesbury advertised that it carried books from all publishers. In 1944, the store's newspaper advertisements noted that readers were demanding "big best sellers" and announced Cokesbury would be carrying *Strange Fruit* by Lillian Smith, a controversial novel about miscegenation that was soon banned by Boston censors and the US Post Office. At the time, *Strange Fruit* was also available from the Baptist Book Store in Dallas.[12]

WASHATERIA
123
WASHATERIA
WASH & DRY

OPPOSITE

Cabell's Dairy Shop No. 3
123 East Jefferson Boulevard, Dallas
1938

The three Cabell brothers opened their first ice cream shop in Dallas in 1932. The success of their five-cent double-dip ice cream cones spurred the opening of stores throughout the city.[13]

RIGHT

McCrory's 5¢-10¢-25¢ Store
901-905 Houston Street, Fort Worth
Wiley G. Clarkson & Co., architects
Remodeled 1938

S. H. Kress & Company leased this building from 1910 to 1936, when the five-and-dime moved to a new location a few blocks north. McCrory's, a Kress competitor, opened its store after the property had undergone a modernistic update. The building has been significantly altered since this photo was taken.[14]

Safeway Stores No. 66 and Neil-Simpson Drug Co. No. 2
310-314 West Rusk Street, Tyler
1938

S. H. Kress & Co.
2508 Lee Street, Greenville
S. H. Kress & Co. Architectural and Construction Department (New York), architects
Bowen Construction Co. (Dallas), contractors
1939

Detail, **S. H. Kress & Co.**

Boedecker's Bowling
309 East Jefferson Boulevard, Dallas
1939

The ninety-thousand-dollar facility was sanctioned by the American Bowling Congress and opened with sixteen lanes, summer and winter air conditioning, and a suction unit to remove tobacco smoke. Future Hall of Fame bowler Buddy Bomar (1916-1989) managed the lanes when Boedecker's opened for business.[15]

TAURANT
Deep In The Heart of
TEX-MEX
EL CORAZON
VINTAGE TEX MEX

OPPOSITE
Wyatt Food Stores No. 24
110 West Davis Street, Dallas
Theodore H. Stueber, architect (attributed)
1940

Theodore H. Stueber was the in-house architect for Wyatt Food Stores from 1931 to 1961, when the Kroger Company acquired the Wyatt grocery chain. Wyatt Cafeterias remained an independent company after the acquisition. The cafeteria chain had its start in 1932 with a small steam table and lunch counter in one of the grocery stores; by 1938, Wyatt Food Stores featured prepared food departments with restaurant seating.[16]

ABOVE
W. T. Grant Co.
611-615 Houston Street, Fort Worth
Alfred S. Alschuler (Chicago), architect
Remodeled 1939

The W. T. Grant chain of variety stores opened its Fort Worth location at 611-615 Houston Street in 1922 and operated continuously from the same address until 1964. Research suggests that the original building was extensively remodeled in 1939. Early in August of that year, the W. T. Grant Company received a construction permit for a two-story building at Sixth and Houston and was advertising specials in its new store by mid-November, an extremely rapid turnaround even by 1930s standards. The streamlined building remains substantially unchanged, but its Houston Street facade is obscured by trees.[17]

Park Cities Home & Auto Supply
later Park Cities Animal Hospital
4365 West Lovers Lane, Dallas
1947

2624 Elm Street
Deep Ellum, Dallas
Remodeled c. 1948

In 1948 and 1949, this building, as well as those at 2810 and 2550-2552 Elm Street, were advertised in the *Dallas Morning News* as having Vitrolite storefronts. Only 2624 Elm has retained its distinctive facade. Vitrolite was a brand of opaque structural glass that was popular for updating commercial buildings in the 1930s and 1940s. The product was originally manufactured by the Vitrolite Company, which was later purchased by the Libby-Owens-Ford Glass Company.

Roy White Paint Co.
later Tim's German Auto
2632 White Settlement Road, Fort Worth
A. W. Flint, contractor
Remodeled 1947

Detail, **Roy White Paint Co.**

Meyer Building
420 North Green Street, Longview
1948

Although a plaque on the facade dates the building to 1947, the *Longview Daily News* reported that construction was completed early in 1948. At the time, the building contained two commercial spaces on the ground floor and an apartment upstairs.[18]

Financial Institutions

Texas State Bank
later Jacksonville City Hall
301 East Commerce Street, Jacksonville
S. W. Ray, architect
1931

Relief, **Texas State Bank**

1511

OPPOSITE

Dallas Bank & Trust Co. Annex
later The Joule
1511 Commerce Street, Dallas
Herbert M. Greene, LaRoche & Dahl, architects
Jopling Construction Co., contractors
1933

The annex was built following the merger of Dallas National Bank and Dallas Bank & Trust. It extended what had been Dallas National Bank's Main Street building through the block to provide an entrance on Commerce Street.[19]

RIGHT

Jacksonville Building and Loan Association
314 South Main Street, Jacksonville
Remodeled 1933

The large red object on the sidewalk is a concrete tomato. Jacksonville was dubbed "Tomato Capital of the World" during the first half of the twentieth century, when the town was the primary shipping point for the area's abundant tomato crop.[20]

Detail, **Jacksonville Building and Loan Association**

First National Bank, Plano
later A.R. Schell & Son Agency
1001 East Fifteenth Street, Plano
Abe Cain, designer and builder
Remodeled 1936

This building was constructed in 1896 and shared by Plano National Bank and the Odd Fellows Lodge. In 1931, Plano National Bank and Farmers National Bank consolidated as First National Bank. The updated design from 1936 features black Carrara Glass, a structural pigmented glass made by the Penn-American Glass Company. Carrara Glass had been manufactured since 1900, but did not become popular until the late 1920s.[21]

OPPOSITE
Equitable Building & Loan Association
demolished
401 West Seventh Street, Fort Worth
Butcher & Sweeney Construction Co., contractors
1937

Equitable's curved, four-color neon sign attracted as much attention as the company's new location. The *Fort Worth Star-Telegram* reported that the Acers Sign Company had custom fit each unit of neon tubing on what was believed to be the only sign of its kind in the Southwest. Equitable was the first tenant in a streamlined commercial building that included storefronts from 401 through 409 West Seventh Street.[22]

EQUITABLE
BUILDING & LOAN
ASSOCIATION
HOME
LOANS
INSURED
SAFETY
FOR YOUR
SAVINGS

Kilgore National Bank
later The Long Trusts
118 South Kilgore Street, Kilgore
James L. Downing (Henderson), architect
1937

Kilgore National Bank moved forward on plans for a new building when the owner of the land beneath the bank's original location acquired a drilling permit and announced his intention to place an oil well on the site in downtown Kilgore.[23]

Detail, **Kilgore National Bank**

Longview National Bank
demolished
108 South Fredonia Street, Longview
Noah L. Peters, architect
C. S. Lambie & Co. (Amarillo), contractors
1940

The institution was called Rembert National Bank when its new building was announced, but the name had changed by the time construction was completed. Plans called for the two-story building to be clad in Indiana limestone above a five-and-a-half-foot base of Minnesota rainbow granite.[24]

Office Buildings

Arnold Building
109 North Jackson Street, Henderson
Arthur E. Thomas (Dallas), architect
J. O. Everett Co. (Dallas), contractors
1931

New Arnold Building
111-115 North Jackson Street, Henderson
c. 1935

M. Kangerga & Brother
102 East Main Street, Henderson
1931

In September 1931, the Kangerga building became the headquarters for the civilian officials responsible for enforcing state laws regulating production in the East Texas Oil Field. Three weeks earlier, Governor Ross S. Sterling had declared Gregg, Rusk, Smith, and Upshur counties "in open insurrection against the conservation laws of the state" and placed them under martial law.[27]

The governor called up eight hundred troops from the Texas National Guard to halt all oil production in East Texas, a controversial action that helped stabilize the price of crude oil. At the time martial law was declared, it was possible to purchase a barrel of oil for as little as five cents; within nineteen days of the shutdown, the price of crude oil had risen to sixty-eight cents a barrel.[28]

OPPOSITE
Crim Office Building
111 North Kilgore Street, Kilgore
1931

On May 6, 1931, a *Dallas Morning News* correspondent stationed on the roof of the new Crim building in downtown Kilgore reported on the successful effort to extinguish an oil well fire that had been burning since the previous week.[25]

The oil derricks behind the Crim Office Building are a recreation of the "World's Richest Acre," a 1.195-acre tract in downtown Kilgore that held twenty-four producing oil wells. At one point in the city's history, downtown Kilgore held the greatest concentration of oil wells in the world.[26]

Communications

Longview News & Journal Building
demolished
312-314 East Methvin Street, Longview
Zimmerman & Morgan, architects
J.W. Lawless, contractor
1936

To celebrate the opening of its new building, the *Longview Daily News and Morning Journal* published the largest single issue of a newspaper to that date: the May 31, 1936, *East Texas Edition*, which contained 350 pages. After the new tubular printing press was installed, the paper described the crowd in front of the building's plate-glass window as "a veritable rendezvous of lovers of machinery" as passersby stopped to watch press runs of thirty thousand sixteen-page newspapers per hour. The press had not yet been installed when this photo was taken.[29]

KFJZ Radio/Texas State Network Building
later Hair Restoration Institute of DFW
1201 West Lancaster Avenue, Fort Worth
Joseph R. Pelich, architect
1939

In May 1938, Mr. and Mrs. Elliott Roosevelt, President Franklin D. Roosevelt's son and daughter-in-law, announced plans for KFJZ, Mrs. Roosevelt's recently purchased radio station in Fort Worth. The improvements included construction of a new building for the station's studios and business offices.

When the facility was completed, it also housed the Texas State Network (TSN), which Elliott Roosevelt founded in 1938 to provide daily programming and live news coverage to twenty-three radio stations across Texas. Many TSN programs originated from the new KFJZ studios.[30]

KRLD Radio Transmitter Plant
Saturn Road, Garland
1939

KRLD's new transmitter house and 475-foot towers allowed the station to increase its signal to fifty thousand watts, the highest power authorized for AM radio stations. At the time, KRLD was owned by the *Dallas Times Herald* and had its studios in the Adolphus Hotel. The station was one of the Columbia Broadcasting System's sixteen original affiliates.[31]

WFAA, the radio station owned by the *Dallas Morning News*, had completed an Art Deco transmitter house in 1929 near Grapevine. Architect George Dahl of Herbert M. Greene, LaRoche & Dahl designed the building. Fort Worth's KGKO finished its own modernistic transmitter house outside Arlington in 1938. Both the WFAA and KGKO buildings have been demolished.[32]

Soft Drink Plants

Although soft drink production dropped by half from 1929 to 1932, the industry recovered rapidly as improvements in manufacturing, bottling, and distribution kept costs low while innovative marketing campaigns drove demand. Many of the plants built during the era featured plate-glass windows that allowed passersby to see the modern, hygienic equipment involved in the bottling process.[33]

Longview Coca-Cola Bottling Co., 1935
later Geo Logic Environmental Services
340 West Tyler Street, Longview
Percy E. Zimmerman, architect
C. S. Lambie & Co. (Amarillo), contractors
1935

Bottling operations and the company's offices were located on the first floor; the second floor was used for storage. The tower on the east end of the building housed the freight elevator.[34]

Longview Coca-Cola Bottling Co., 2016

Greenville Dr. Pepper Bottling Co.
3201 Washington Street, Greenville
1937

Greenville's Dr. Pepper plant was expanded in 1939 to accommodate new bottling equipment and provide additional storage space. At the time, the plant's reception room and office were decorated in silver, red, and green, the company colors. The building was later converted into a private home.[35]

When this building was constructed, the soft drink was still called "Dr. Pepper." The period in the logo was not dropped until the 1950s.

Coca-Cola Syrup Plant
6445 Lemmon Avenue, Dallas
Jesse M. Shelton (Atlanta), architect
1938

Fort Worth Dr. Pepper Bottling Co., 1938
later Trinity Pain Medicine Associates,
The Institute of Age Management and
Regenerative Medicine
1401 Henderson Street, Fort Worth
Hubert Hammond Crane, architect
Thomas S. Byrne, Inc., contractors
1938

"Drink-a-bite-to-eat," Dr. Pepper's slogan from the 1920s to the mid 1940s, encouraged customers to maintain their energy through the day by having a Dr. Pepper at ten in the morning and again at two and four o'clock in the afternoon. In the historic photo, the lanterns and railings at the Fort Worth building's entrance feature the company's 10-2-4 logo.

The numbers 10, 2, and 4 were also prominently displayed on the clocks on either side of the building's tower. Chimes in the tower rang every day at 10 a.m., 2 p.m., and 4 p.m. At those times, Dr. Pepper employees across the country paused to refresh themselves with the company's soft drink. During the holiday season, a special program of chimes and Christmas carols played from the tower every evening at half past seven.[36]

Fort Worth Dr. Pepper Bottling Co., 2015

Marshall Coca-Cola Bottling Co.
later 511 Technology Center
511 North Washington Street, Marshall
Neild-Somdal-Neild (Shreveport), architects
C. S. Lambie & Co. (Amarillo), contractors
1938

Edward F. Neild, Neild-Somdal-Neild's founding partner, designed Marshall's Coca-Cola bottling plant. He later served as one of the architects on President Harry S. Truman's restoration and rebuilding of the White House and as lead architect on the Harry S. Truman Library and Museum (1957) in Independence, Missouri.

Entrance, **Marshall Coca-Cola Bottling Co.**

Detail, **Marshall Coca-Cola Bottling Co.**

Dr. Pepper Syrup and Bottling Plant
demolished
5523 East Mockingbird Lane, Dallas
Thomas, Jameson & Merrill,
architects and engineers
Inge Construction Co., contractors
1949

Although the name of the building highlights its industrial purpose, this massive facility also served as the national headquarters of the Dr. Pepper Company. The general and executive offices and boardroom were on the top floor above the syrup factory, bottling plant, and shipping department. Visitors were welcomed in an elaborate lobby that featured murals depicting the story of carbonation.

The streamlined pylon atop the building held clock faces with the numbers 10, 2, and 4 highlighted in keeping with the company's slogan that encouraged consumers to drink Dr. Pepper three times during the day.[37]

Industrial

Merchants' Exchange Building, 1952
later Gaston Building
demolished
901 Commerce Street, Dallas
Charles Stevens Dilbeck, architect
Fred McQueen, contractor
Remodeled 1934

Banker and investor William H. Gaston (1840-1927) constructed the Merchants' Exchange Building in 1884 and renamed it the Gaston Building in 1891.

In 1934, the Lorch Manufacturing Company signed a ten-year lease on the property and the Gaston Estate carried out renovations that converted the office building into a dress factory. The *Dallas Morning News* reported that the exterior remodeling incorporated a design scheme used for new ready-to-wear manufacturing plants on the East Coast.[38]

Lorch held an open house in January 1935 and invited the public to see "a model, modern factory in operation" as well as the display room for the company's line of College Campus Frocks.[39]

Merchants' Exchange Building, c. 1895

401
401
SHABAN INDUSTRIES INC.

Universal Mills Office Building
later Shaban Industries, Inc.
401 North Beach Street, Fort Worth
Charles M. Davis, designer and engineer
1940

Relief, **Universal Mills Office Building**
Dwight C. Holmes, sculptor

Crown Machine & Tool Co.
later Thrifty Nickel Want-Ads
2800 West Lancaster Avenue, Fort Worth
Fooshee & Cheek (Dallas), architects
1944

Crown Machine & Tool Company manufactured 81-millimeter mortar shells for the US Army during World War II in a plant located behind the firm's office building. After the war, the company developed, designed, and built machinery to produce disposable polystyrene cups. By 1956, Crown Plastic Cup Company was shipping eight million cups per month from West Lancaster Avenue.[40]

Detail, **Crown Machine & Tool Co.**

Nocona Boot Co.
901 US Highway 82, Nocona
Haynes & Kirby (Lubbock), architects
Burford Construction Co. (Dallas), contractors
1948.

This $250,000 boot factory realized the ambition of Enid Justin (1893-1990), the founder, president, and general manager of the Nocona Boot Company. "Miss Enid" established the firm in 1925 when her older brothers moved the family's boot-making business from Nocona to Fort Worth.

The new facility allowed Nocona Boots to double its output to four hundred pairs per day. Radio stations in Fort Worth and Wichita Falls carried the plant's opening ceremonies live, while a plane flew overhead trailing a banner that read, "Congratulations, Miss Enid." In 1981, Enid Justin sold her shares in Nocona Boot to Justin Industries, which had grown from her brothers' boot company. Justin closed the Nocona plant in 1999.[41]

CHAPTER 3

SKYSCRAPERS

Dallas Power & Light Building at night, 1931

"Four major office buildings in any one year is something to write home about, but four buildings in 'the year of the great heebie-geebies,' that is an act of God."

Ralph Bryan, architect
in the *Dallas Morning News*
February 1, 1931

THE OPENING OF DALLAS POWER & LIGHT'S new headquarters in late 1931 made headlines not only because it represented an addition to the Dallas skyline, but also because the building's completion capped a year in which five major construction projects were wrapped up downtown (the four mentioned by *Dallas Morning News* achitecture columnist Ralph Bryan plus the DP&L building, which was completed late in the year). As Bryan noted, it was a remarkable year given the economic outlook at the time.[1]

There was another reason to take notice of the downtown building boom, at least for those interested in architectural trends. Four of the new structures, DP&L's tower, the Dallas Gas Company Building, the central YMCA, and the Tower Petroleum Building, were designed in the modernistic style, a significant departure from the classically inspired skyline Dallas reared in the preceding decades. "In the years to come, [these buildings] will be looked upon as standing for just as distinct an architectural period as was marked by the courthouse, the late Oriental Hotel, and the Wilson Building," Bryan wrote.[2]

Indeed, Lang & Witchell's modern design for the light company building—attributed to the firm's chief designer, Dudley Green—drew a sharp contrast with its traditional neighbors, including the landmark Magnolia Petroleum Company Building (1922, Alfred C. Bossom) down the block. DP&L's building was composed as a sparsely ornamented buff brick tower rising nineteen stories through a series of setbacks. Deep-set vertical window channels exaggerated the building's height and created a striking effect when floodlights switched on at dusk, washing the structure in light that cycled between red, white, and amber.[3]

The tower was set on the largest part of the DP&L property, occupying the corner of Jackson and Browder streets; Lang & Witchell took advantage of a relatively narrow strip of land sandwiched between two existing buildings to give DP&L frontage on busy Commerce Street.

Although the Commerce Street wing was built at the same time as the tower, it read as a separate building thanks to its limestone facing and distinctive detailing. Beneath an enormous stained-glass window depicting the Norse god

Dallas Power & Light Building, 2016
later Texas Utilities Building, DPL Flats
1506 Commerce Street, Dallas
Lang & Witchell, architects
C. L. Shaw & Co., contractors
1931

Commerce Street Annex, Dallas Power & Light Building

The Commerce Street Annex of the Dallas Power & Light Building includes the building's major integrated artwork. At the top left and right corners of the facade are engaged portrait busts of Thomas Edison and Charles Proteus Steinmetz, the pioneers of direct and alternating current, respectively.

Above the entrance, a large stained-glass window designed by Georgia Jensen and Roger McIntosh of the Pittsburgh Plate Glass Company depicts the Norse god Thor rising above a cityscape, electric transmission lines descending from his fists. He is flanked by panels showing dynamos, high-voltage transmission towers, lightning bolts, and illuminated light bulbs.[4]

Thor creating electric light, a set of bronze-framed glass doors led from Commerce into a showroom where the latest electric products were displayed, serving as the main entrance for most visitors to the building. The showroom gave onto the tower's marble-lined elevator lobby and a hundred-foot-square room where Dallasites could pay their bills and arrange for electric service.

More interesting were areas dedicated to lighting demonstrations. In the basement, rooms designed for the use of merchants and manufacturers offered a variety of lighting fixtures and types that could be used to test the effect of light in shops, offices, and other business buildings; nearby, a model storefront was used to show off innovations in retail display lighting. On the second floor was a similar area where homeowners, architects, and interior designers could use a range of lighting to evaluate window treatments, upholstery, and color schemes. As one description put it, "the demonstration hall has been designed and equipped to afford what might be best termed a housewives' and home builders' laboratory."

Also on the second floor, an area designed to resemble a Spanish courtyard, complete with a vaulted ceiling painted and lit to look like a bright blue sky, led to one of the more novel features of the building: a fully electric model home. Its rooms were decorated in a variety of styles to showcase different lighting effects, while a fully equipped laundry room and kitchen demonstrated the "unlimited possibilities"

Thor window, **Dallas Power & Light Building**

Charles Proteus Steinmetz portrait bust,
Dallas Power & Light Building

Thomas Edison portrait bust,
Dallas Power & Light Building

Browder Street entrance,
Dallas Power & Light Building

The exterior of DP&L's office tower is embellished with terra cotta panels bearing typical Art Deco fountain and foliage designs, while the entrances facing Browder and Jackson streets are outlined in black granite featuring reliefs of allegorical figures and workers generating electricity.

Browder Street entrance relief,
Dallas Power & Light Building

Detail, **Dallas Power & Light Building**

Upper levels of tower,
Dallas Power & Light Building

The top two floors of the tower originally housed club and meeting rooms for employees. The penthouse structure was added when the building underwent a residential conversion in 2008.[5]

Elevator lobby,
Dallas Power & Light Building

Although the building's ground-floor spaces have been subdivided, many original features remain intact. Changes have apparently included painting over the vaulted elevator lobby ceiling, which was originally "decorated to produce a metallic effect suggesting precious metals," as well as the loss of allegorical murals in the lobby.[6]

Elevator surround detail,
Dallas Power & Light Building

Detail, lobby staircase,
Dallas Power & Light Building

Lobby staircase,
Dallas Power & Light Building

of electric appliances. Unfortunately, the model home no longer exists, though several portions of the ground-floor public spaces remain largely intact.[7]

With its high-profile setting, modern lines, and dazzling floodlights, the DP&L Building was one of the premier Art Deco skyscrapers that went up in North Texas—but it was far from the only one. Fort Worth built several modernistic skyscrapers that remain landmarks today, including the Blackstone Hotel and the Sinclair Building. Perhaps the most surprising Deco skyscraper in the region is the People's National Bank Building in Tyler, which opened in 1932; the striking building, with its original public interiors intact, remains one of the city's tallest structures.

More modest, yet equally modern, mid-rises were built in smaller cities, reflecting growing oil fortunes. The editors of the *Longview Daily News* admitted that the six-story buildings completed in 1935 could not be called skyscrapers, but told their readers that by looking up, "you'll get a perspective of the future Longview. . . . you'll see a skyline in the making."[8]

Telephone Building
later Three Bell Plaza, Three AT&T Plaza
308 South Akard Street, Dallas
Lang & Witchell with Irvin R. Timlin (St. Louis), architects
Henger & Chambers, contractors
1928

When it was built, Southwestern Bell Telephone Company's Texas headquarters was the largest telephone building in the South. In addition to administrative offices and room for five telephone exchanges, the building contained a marble-lined business office, a power plant, a fully equipped emergency hospital, and an auditorium. Plans were revised before construction began to provide more space for the region's growing telephone operations; although a large addition was expected to be built relatively quickly, officials declared that it would not be necessary for at least five years.[9]

In fact, the expansion was not begun until 1961. That work, completed in 1963, consisted of a twenty-three-story annex and the addition of ten floors to the 1928 building, dramatically altering its original massing. Almost all the Art Deco detailing was removed or covered at that time. AT&T, Southwestern Bell's corporate successor, continues to occupy the building.[10]

Across the street is the vaguely modernistic 311 South Akard (1949, E. V. McCright), which the telephone company purchased and heavily remodeled in the 1970s.[11]

Blackstone Hotel
later Hilton Hotel, Courtyard Downtown Fort Worth/Blackstone
601 Main Street, Fort Worth
Mauran, Russell & Crowell (St. Louis) with Elmer G. Withers Architectural Co., architects
Bellows-Maclay Construction Co., contractors
1929

Fort Worth's Blackstone Hotel opened October 10, 1929, two weeks before "Black Thursday" and the great Wall Street crash. The twenty-two-story hotel boasted three hundred rooms, eighteen suites—some with private terraces overlooking the city—and a dining room with a floor "especially constructed for dancing."

Luxuries in each guest room included ice water on tap, private baths, and ceiling fans, but one of the most heavily advertised amenities was the "Centralized Radio," a system developed by RCA. Each room was outfitted with a built-in loudspeaker that allowed guests to enjoy two programs produced especially for the hotel; the Blackstone was the first hotel in the South with such a system.[12]

In 1952, the Hilton Hotel Corporation took a ten-year management lease of the Blackstone, branded the hotel as a Hilton, and began an extensive remodeling that replaced the original black marble-lined second-floor lobby with a new lobby at street level. The hotel reverted to local management in 1962 and closed twenty years later. A restoration was completed in 1999, when the hotel reopened as a Courtyard by Marriott.[13]

Blackstone Hotel, 1929

Blackstone Hotel, 2016

Detail, **Blackstone Hotel**

The architects designed the Blackstone with a series of setbacks crowned by large terra cotta pinnacles bearing stylized floral designs. Most of the setbacks created private terraces for hotel suites; a large loggia on the fourteenth floor was available for the use of all guests.[14]

Frieze detail, **Blackstone Hotel**

None of the original lobby existed when restoration work began in the late 1990s. The decision was made not to recreate the space; instead, a new lobby was built on the ground floor and embellished with decorative elements that were made using casts of the exterior terra cotta ornamentation.[15]

Gas Building, c. 1940
later Fort Worth City Hall Annex
908 Monroe Street, Fort Worth
Wyatt C. Hedrick, Inc., architects
C. L. Hudgens, contractor
1929
Wyatt C. Hedrick, Inc., architects
1957, top three floors

Black granite distinguishes the entrance to the Gas Building, which was constructed as the headquarters of the Fort Worth Gas Company. The decorative frieze, exterior cladding, and classically inspired elements are Indiana limestone.

The structure was designed so that more stories could be added; in its ad announcing the building's opening, Fort Worth Gas estimated it would need six more floors by 1940. The addition of three floors designed by architect Wyatt C. Hedrick was announced in 1956; the somewhat jarring result was completed in 1957.[16]

The Lone Star Gas Company, a natural gas transmission firm, purchased and liquidated the Fort Worth Gas Company in 1931; subsequently the building was often referred to as the Lone Star Gas Building.[17]

LEFT
Gas Building, 2016

Teller counter, customer service lobby, **Gas Building**

Entrance detail, **Gas Building**

Frieze detail, **Gas Building**

Customer service lobby, **Gas Building**

The ornate lobby where customers transacted business reflects Spanish and Gothic influences. The decorative tile was imported from Valencia, Spain, and the trim is black marble. The *Fort Worth Star-Telegram* noted that the new Gas Building was located near the Water Department in City Hall, the telephone company's office, and the power company's building, making it more convenient for customers to pay their various utility bills.[18]

Aviation Building
later Commercial Standard Building,
Trans-American Life Building
demolished
105 East Seventh Street, Fort Worth
Wyatt C. Hedrick, Inc., architects
James T. Taylor Construction Co., contractors
1930

A major office building dedicated entirely to aviation interests may have seemed like an unusual idea in 1929—but not in Fort Worth, which by that time had become an aviation center. Builder A. P. Barrett announced plans for the Aviation Building that summer; his Southern Air Transport Company (which later became American Airlines) would occupy space in the building along with "the aviation interests of the city."[19]

Barrett hired Wyatt C. Hedrick's firm to design the building. Initial drawings showed a 275-foot skyscraper tapering through cutaways and setbacks to a Gothic-inspired crown, its facade clad in brick that gradually became lighter in shade as the building ascended. As actually built, the Aviation Building was less elaborate, yet still impressive. Hedrick's chief designer, Herman P. Koeppe, gave the sixteen-story building bold Aztec- and Mayan-inspired reliefs and a lobby decorated with black and gold marble, travertine, and Monel, a nickel alloy. Perhaps the best-known element was the main entrance, which was flanked by two oversized guardian figures in polychrome cast concrete; locals dubbed them the "Aztec Princes." The speed with which the building went up was noteworthy as well, with steelwork completed in thirty days and the entire construction taking only five months and twenty-three days from start to finish.[20]

When the building was demolished in 1978 to make way for a new skyscraper, Art Deco enthusiast Judith Singer Cohen led an effort to save some of the detailing, including the Aztec Princes. The figures were removed and stored at Texas Christian University; plans were announced in 1986 to reassemble them in a public park, but it seems that did not occur.[21]

Sinclair Building
512 Main Street, Fort Worth
Wiley G. Clarkson & Co., architects
Harry B. Friedman, contractor
1930

The Sinclair Building, Fort Worth's best example of a modernistic setback skyscraper, was meant to be the last word in office building design when oilman Richard O. Dulaney announced the project in 1929. Dulaney and his contractor, Harry Friedman, toured modern buildings in Chicago, Detroit, and cities on the East Coast to gather inspiration for their tower; when the building opened, Dulaney declared it "the most perfect type of modernistic architecture in the Southwestern States." Dulaney initially intended to name the building for himself, but plans changed when the Sinclair Oil Company signed a lease to occupy six floors as its Southwestern headquarters in the summer of 1930.

Architect Wiley G. Clarkson used recessed window channels outfitted with green cast-stone spandrels to emphasize the building's vertical lines, which rose through two set-backs to a series of pinnacles decorated with abstracted scrollwork. Concealed floodlights accented the setbacks after dark, a relative rarity in Fort Worth at the time.[22]

Eagle finials, **Sinclair Building**

Distinctive stylized eagles keep watch over the skyline from the Sinclair Building's first setback.

Entrance grille, **Sinclair Building**

Lobby ceiling detail, **Sinclair Building**

Storefront reliefs, **Sinclair Building**

Elevator doors, **Sinclair Building**

Lobby, **Sinclair Building**

A shopping arcade lined with rich green marble led from the Main Street entrance to the elevator bank. This area was drastically remodeled at some point in the building's history; in her 1988 book *Cowtown Moderne*, Judith Singer Cohen wrote that the elevator doors and mailbox were the only original details still visible. When restoration work began later that year, workers discovered fragments of the elaborate plaster ceiling and some original marble still in place behind partitions. The arcade was returned to its 1930 appearance, although modern hanging light fixtures were added to supplement the original indirect lighting.[23]

Foyer ceiling, **Sinclair Building**

Storefronts and the building's main entrance are designed with Mayan-influenced stepped arches. The metal screen at the main entrance and the dramatic stepped ceiling in the foyer behind it were both removed in the late 1950s; they were recreated as part of a restoration completed in 1990.[24]

Sinclair Building, 1930

Dallas Gas Company Building
later Lone Star Gas Company Building,
TXU Gas Company Building,
Atmos Energy Building, Lone Star Gas Lofts
301 South Harwood Street, Dallas
Lang & Witchell, architects
Jopling Construction Co. contractors
1931

The Dallas Gas Company's headquarters building was one of five major construction projects completed in downtown Dallas in 1931. Unlike the others, however, the gas company's building was only a portion of what was expected to be a larger facility. Plans called for ten stories to be added to the building at a later date, which would have resulted in a slender tower rising above a rather solid base. However, the extra floors were never built, and the gas building remains more substantial than soaring.[25]

Lang & Witchell's chief designer, Dudley Green, gave the building an exterior of light-colored brick and buff cast-stone trim, which Dallas Gas boasted would stay clean thanks to the city's widespread use of "smokeless" natural gas. The company also bragged that virtually all the materials used in construction came from a hundred-mile radius of Dallas.[26]

The Lone Star Gas transmission company purchased Dallas Gas in 1927, just as it would later do with the local utility in Fort Worth; the Dallas Gas building was built next door to Lone Star's headquarters. The Dallas Gas name was dropped in 1943, and it was apparently then that the building was renamed the Lone Star Gas Company Building.[27]

Spandrel panels,
Dallas Gas Company Building

The exterior ornamentation is relatively spare. Notable features include elaborate bronze lanterns at the building's entrances and bold allegorical figures in the spandrel panels.

Harwood Street entrance,
Dallas Gas Company Building

Detail, **Dallas Gas Company Building**

Customer service lobby,
Dallas Gas Company Building

The ground-floor customer lobby's subdued color scheme of black, cream, and bronze was originally offset by a brilliantly colored ceiling that seems to have caught some early observers off guard. "About the ceiling, we don't quite know," architect Ralph Bryan wrote in his newspaper column. "We sort of think it is the kind of thing that might grow on one." Unfortunately, the ceiling decoration has not survived.

Gas appliances were displayed in basement showrooms reached via a black marble staircase that descended from the customer lobby. The basement also contained a women's lounge attended by a maid, as well as gas-powered electricity generators and equipment that air conditioned the building's public rooms.[28]

Writing desk, customer service lobby,
Dallas Gas Company Building

OPPOSITE
Reliefs, customer service lobby,
Dallas Gas Company Building

Detail, customer service lobby,
Dallas Gas Company Building

Offices in the customer service area were divided by wooden partitions with modernistic detailing.

Clock, elevator lobby,
Dallas Gas Company Building

Ceiling, elevator lobby, **Dallas Gas Company Building**

Elevator lobby,
Dallas Gas Company Building

The elevator lobby featured some of the building's most exuberant detailing, with walls of black and silver rising two stories to a ceiling extravagantly painted with stars, rays, and geometric patterns. Elevator doors and a wall clock decorated with black and silver floral and fountain motifs add glamour to one of Dallas's most sophisticated Art Deco spaces.

Elevator doors,
Dallas Gas Company Building

Tower Petroleum Building
1907 Elm Street, Dallas
Mark Lemmon, architect
Henger & Chambers, contractors
1931

In June 1930, the *Dallas Morning News* reported that the architect, contractor, and developer of the Tower Petroleum Building were leaving for New York and Chicago to inspect recently completed skyscrapers and the design features of contemporary offices. It had already been decided that the twenty-two-story Dallas building would be "of the modern American setback architecture."

When the building was completed, forty-six floodlights illuminated the upper two setbacks in yellow light, creating the illusion that the top five floors were not attached to the rest of the building. Architect and columnist Ralph Bryan described the effect as "some sort of mirage or fairy castle just floating by and likely to be blown over to Fort Worth or somewhere else if it comes up a strong enough wind."

The modernistic Tower Theater (1937, W. Scott Dunne, demolished) was later constructed at the rear of the Tower Petroleum Building. Patrons entered the theater from Elm Street through the ground floor of the office building.[29]

Details, **Tower Petroleum Building**

Modernistic motifs decorating the base of the building are echoed in the setbacks near the top of the tower.

Dallas YMCA Central Branch
demolished
605 North Ervay Street, Dallas
Anton F. Korn, architect
Nathan Wohlfield, contractor
1931

Dallas's fifteen-story downtown YMCA housed a surprising number of facilities, including a soda fountain and grill, meeting and banquet rooms, a law library, club rooms for local newsboys (complete with a replica log cabin), a health spa, an indoor swimming pool, and residential rooms for 260 men. Although the exterior detailing was Gothic-inspired, architect Anton F. Korn gave the building a modern setback profile borrowed from taller Art Deco skyscrapers. Ralph Bryan, architecture columnist for the *Dallas Morning News,* was effusive in his praise of the design, complimenting the "honest, straightforward mass" and pleasantly decorated bedrooms "that might inspire more letters home to mother."

After serving downtown for a half century, the building was demolished to make way for the Lincoln Tower office development.[30]

People's National Bank Building
later People's Petroleum Building
102 North College Avenue, Tyler
Alfred C. Finn (Houston), architect
American Construction Co. (Houston), contractors
1932
Alfred C. Finn (Houston), architect
Hugh E. White, contractor
1936, addition

The People's National building, built in 1932 by businessman Samuel A. Lindsey, reflects Tyler's position as a center of activity during the East Texas oil boom. With about seventeen thousand residents, Tyler was already the largest city in its area when oil was discovered nearby in 1930. As more wells came in across the region, drillers, geologists, refiners, oil field suppliers, surveyors, and others associated with the oil industry flocked to Tyler because of its business and banking facilities and attractive neighborhoods.

Lindsey's skyscraper was built not only to provide space for People's National Bank, but also to meet the growing demand for office space in Tyler. The building proved so popular that a six-story addition was built atop its low west wing in 1936.[31]

After World War II, downtown Tyler's dominance as the region's business center began to slip. Tenants moved out of the People's National building, and the bank itself decamped to a new building next door in the early 1980s, leaving the historic tower almost completely vacant. However, new owners Garnett and Tim Brookshire and Andy Bergfeld have refurbished tenant floors, restored public areas, and recreated lost features using Finn's original drawings, making the building a vibrant part of downtown Tyler once again.[32]

People's National Bank Building
from North College Avenue, 1932

Entrance, **People's National Bank Building**, 1932

Houston architect Alfred C. Finn's design relied on setbacks, contrasting spandrel panels, and stylized ornaments at the top of each window bay to emphasize the building's verticality, making it appear to tower even higher over the low-rise commercial buildings of downtown Tyler. The original casement windows were replaced with fixed panes, and the sills and spandrels were covered with tinted glass when the building was air conditioned in 1969. The streamlined ornaments seem to have been eliminated at that time, as were original street-level windows and doors; the entrance's metal grille may have been removed then as well.[33]

Banking hall,
People's National Bank Building, 1932

The second-floor banking hall is the most notable interior in the building, and one of the most remarkable in Tyler. The room's main features, including rounded, gold-leafed columns, marble wainscoting, and streamlined light fixtures, remain intact, although the original teller stations and writing tables are gone. The historic photo shows that the mezzanine was added after the building opened.

FAR LEFT
Lobby, **People's National Bank Building**

Lobby staircase, **People's National Bank Building**, 1932

Original marble, terrazzo, and aluminum survive in the ground-floor lobbies. Historic photos indicate that the ceiling in this space was originally painted in a geometric pattern.

Detail, banking hall,
People's National Bank Building

Banking hall, **People's National Bank Building**

Reliefs, banking hall, **People's National Bank Building**

A series of reliefs in the banking hall represent some of the agricultural products for which the Tyler area was known: lumber (represented by pine boughs), tomatoes, corn, and roses. Roses were particularly important. The local rose industry took off after a peach blight ended fruit production in the region; by the 1940s, more than half of America's rose bushes were grown near Tyler. The city still bills itself as the "Rose Capital of the World."[34]

Glover-Crim Building
140 East Tyler Street, Longview
Zimmerman, Peters & Strange, architects
C. S. Lambie & Co. (Amarillo), contractors
1933
Peters, Strange & Co., architects
C. S. Lambie & Co. (Amarillo), contractors
1935, top four floors

The Glover-Crim Building was constructed as a two-story building with retail space on the ground floor and twenty-one offices upstairs. The structure was designed to support four additional floors of offices, which were added in 1935.[35]

Detail, **Glover-Crim Building**

McWilliams Building
later Southwest Reserve Life Building, Cargill Tower, Weaver Building
208 North Green Street, Longview
Martin T. Clements with Voelcker & Dixon (Wichita Falls), architects
T. L. James & Co., Inc. (Ruston, Louisiana), contractors
1935

Longview's first air-conditioned office building was constructed for the McWilliams Hardware & Furniture Company. The McWilliams store occupied the first three floors with leased office space on the remaining three stories. When the construction contracts were awarded, the planned office entrance on North Green Street was described as "exceptionally impressive." While a relatively ornate entrance is partially visible in images of the building through the 1950s, photos from 1980 forward indicate that the original detailing on the entry was either removed or covered when the street-level storefronts were updated.[36]

Blackstone Building
315 North Broadway, Tyler
Preston M. Geren (Fort Worth), architect
Hugh E. White, contractor
1938

Tyler businessman Edmond P. McKenna and associates developed the city's first fully air-conditioned office building in response to the oil industry's continuing demand for space. The Blackstone Building stood adjacent to McKenna's Blackstone Hotel and Annex (1922, 1931, demolished), Tyler's largest and best hotel and a center of social and business activity.[37]

Entrance detail, **Blackstone Building**

Crowdus Building
later Continental Building
1512 Commerce Street, Dallas
1904
Whitson & Roberts, architects and contractors
1935, sixth floor
1940, top eight floors

The J. W. Crowdus Drug Company built the first section of this building as its store and warehouse in 1904. By 1935, the major tenant was the Continental Supply Company, an oil and gas equipment firm; a sixth story was added that year. Eight additional floors were built and the various sections of the building were unified beneath a modern limestone and brick facing in 1940.

Dallas Power & Light, the Continental Building's neighbor, purchased the building around 1980 and occupied it until 2003. The building has been repurposed as residential lofts.[38]

Ceiling detail, main waiting room,
Texas and Pacific passenger station

CHAPTER 4

TRAVEL & TRANSPORTATION

"See to it that Fort Worth does become a city of one million people."

John C. Lancaster,
president of the Texas and Pacific Railway at a banquet celebrating the opening of the Texas and Pacific terminal complex
November 3, 1931

OPPOSITE
Texas and Pacific terminal complex
Passenger station and office building
later Texas & Pacific Lofts
221 West Lancaster Avenue, Fort Worth
Wyatt C. Hedrick, Inc., architects
Armin Helfensteller,
construction superintendent
1931

LOOKING BACK, LANCASTER'S CHALLENGE to Fort Worth leaders seems a bit outlandish. The city was growing in 1931, but its population stood at just under 165,000, and the worsening economy was dampening the outlook for most of the nation. Yet there was plenty of cause for optimism in Cowtown: Livestock, oil, cotton, and trade had driven significant expansion in Fort Worth since the beginning of the twentieth century, and the city was in the midst of a transformative building boom. Some twenty million dollars in major construction had been completed in the previous two years alone, and projects totaling another eleven million dollars were on the drawing board.[1]

The opening of the Texas and Pacific's new terminal complex at the south end of the business district only reinforced local confidence. The railroad had announced plans for the project in the spring of 1929, promising that it would invest up to eight million dollars in new passenger and freight buildings and associated trackage, platforms, streets, and underpasses. "We are spending a lot of money here in the belief that Fort Worth is one of the principal distribution centers of the Southwest," T and P President Lancaster said. "These improvements will do more for Fort Worth, in our opinion, than any other thing."[2]

Architect Wyatt C. Hedrick and his chief designer, Herman P. Koeppe, were hired to design the various terminal structures, including a skyscraping passenger station and office building, a baggage annex, and separate warehouses for inbound and outbound freight. The most elaborate detailing was reserved for the showpiece of the complex, the thirteen-story passenger station and office tower, which welcomed travelers with an imposing Art Deco facade and an elaborately decorated three-story main waiting room. "There is nothing quite so fine in the United States and no building in the South to compare with the new Texas and Pacific passenger terminal," Hedrick told reporters as the station opened.[3]

The freight warehouses, located a block west of the passenger building, were designed in a complimentary yet utilitarian style. It was the warehouses' size that really made an impression—especially the vast Inbound Freight

T&P
TAVERN

Main waiting room,
Texas and Pacific passenger station, 1931

The passenger station's main waiting room and ticketing hall were lavishly decorated with marble floors and wainscoting, plaster walls scored to resemble stone, and a ceiling embellished with gilded and enameled chevrons, rays, and medallions. Thirteen chandeliers trimmed in aluminum and nickel hung over specially designed mahogany benches where passengers waited for trains to arrive and depart. A restaurant and separate waiting rooms for women and African Americans opened off the central space.[4]

Chandelier, main waiting room,
Texas and Pacific passenger station

Main waiting room, **Texas and Pacific passenger station**

Detail, **Texas and Pacific passenger station and office building**

Grille, main waiting room,
Texas and Pacific passenger station

Among the passenger station's innovations was a public address system that was used to announce arriving and departing trains. Loudspeakers concealed behind modernistic grilles broadcast to the station's waiting rooms, restaurant, and concourse. "Passengers are somewhat mystified when they hear the trains being announced in a clear, resonant voice—a voice coming from nowhere," the *Fort Worth Star-Telegram* marveled. "There is no train caller in sight, and—here is one for Ripley—every word is distinct and understandable."[5]

Detail, **Texas and Pacific passenger station and office building**
Lavishly carved limestone panels on the passenger and office building feature geometric and floral designs, eagles, stylized compass roses, and occasional Gothic and Egyptian motifs. Towers at the building's corners housed machinery and water tanks.[6]

Warehouse, which could accommodate the simultaneous loading and unloading of ninety railcars and forty-eight motor trucks and could store an estimated 3,500 carloads of goods in more than eleven acres of floor space.[7]

The scale of the complex prompted the editors of the *Dallas Morning News* to remember the opening of the T and P's previous Fort Worth station in 1899, and to marvel at Fort Worth's rapid growth. "They were saying that the T. & P. had then built 'fifty years ahead of the town,'" they wrote. "Within thirty-two years the building, which was then amazing, is now merely obsolete. The man who has built anything fifty years ahead of Fort Worth has yet to be born."[8]

Although the Texas and Pacific complex was a vote of confidence in the dominance of rail, it opened just as automobile travel and air transportation began to seriously challenge that dominance. Traffic through the T and P station built to a peak during World War II, then began a rapid decline. Adding insult to injury, an elevated highway was built along Lancaster Avenue in front of the passenger station in the late 1950s, effectively cutting it off from downtown Fort Worth. Passenger operations at the T and P station ended in 1967, after which the office section of the building was rented to various non-railroad organizations while passenger areas sat unused. A restoration of the passenger terminal and office building was completed in 1999, and commuter rail service to Dallas was launched from the station in 2001. The magnificent waiting room was repurposed as an event venue, the former office spaces above as residential lofts.

Detail, elevator lobby, **Texas and Pacific passenger station and office building**

Detail, elevator door, **Texas and Pacific passenger station and office building**

Elevator lobby, **Texas and Pacific passenger station and office building**

Upper levels of the passenger building contained offices for the Texas and Pacific Railway, other railroads, various freight and transfer lines, and district offices for various state and federal agencies.[9]

Passenger station baggage and commissary annex,
Texas and Pacific terminal complex
Wyatt C. Hedrick, Inc., architects
Ball Construction Co., contractors
1931

The baggage annex adjoining the passenger station was built with street-facing loading docks where cars and trucks could drop off and pick up luggage and packages. Motorized baggage carts and elevators transferred items between the docks and the train platforms.[10]

Inbound Freight Warehouse,
Texas and Pacific terminal complex
West Lancaster and Jennings Avenues
Wyatt C. Hedrick, Inc., architects
Bellows-Maclay Construction Co., contractors
1931

The passenger and office building was the public face of the T and P terminal complex, but the massive Inbound Freight Warehouse got just as much attention in the press. The 611-foot-long building included areas for dry and cold storage on each of its nine levels, and it boasted heat and humidity control throughout, as well as an automatic fire alarm and sprinkler system. Goods ranging from eggs to automobiles were shuttled around the warehouse using a fleet of rubber-tired tractors and enormous high-speed elevators. Strong vertical lines on the building's exterior helped offset its length; zigzag detailing was executed in brick and tile rather than carved stone.[11]

Detail, **Texas and Pacific terminal complex Inbound Freight Warehouse**

Detail, **Texas and Pacific terminal complex Inbound Freight Warehouse**

ABOVE
Awning detail,
Texas and Pacific terminal complex Inbound Freight Warehouse

The freight warehouses also fell into disuse by the late 1970s, the victims of increased shipping by truck and airplane. The smaller outbound warehouse was demolished; the inbound warehouse stands unoccupied. Various plans for its redevelopment have not come to fruition.[12]

The same forces that drew traffic away from the T and P terminal helped to build a variety of structures across North Texas dedicated to other modes of transportation. A rapidly improving highway system meant that more people could take to the roads, leading to the construction of modernistic bus stations in some towns. More common were the new dealerships and service stations built for the growing number of car-owning Texans. Auto traffic even led Dallas to create two of its best-known features—Dealey Plaza and the Triple Underpass, both designed to give motorists a grand new entrance to downtown.

Service Stations

Jenkins-Harvey Super Service Station and Garage
124 South College Avenue, Tyler
James P. Baugh, architect
1929

The Jenkins-Harvey building is a surprisingly urban facility for what was at the time a moderately sized county seat. Gasoline pumps and auto service were located on the first floor, along with the business office and restrooms. A ramp led to the second-floor parking garage, which was built with spaces for eighty-five cars. A fire pole provided a quick connection for attendants between the parking area and the gas pumps.[13]

Detail, **Jenkins-Harvey Super Service Station and Garage**

Humble Service Station No. 172
500 East Methvin Street, Longview
John F. Staub (Houston), architect
c. 1930

Although he was best known for designing traditional homes for affluent clients, John F. Staub was hired in 1929 to create the prototype for Humble Oil & Refining Company service stations. Many Staub stations survive in varying states of preservation.[14]

Detail, **Humble Service Station No. 172**

Detail, **Good Luck Service Station No. 5**

Good Luck Service Station No. 5
903 Cadiz Street, Dallas
1939

The Good Luck Oil Company (GLOCO) operated a chain of Dallas service stations. Three of GLOCO's distinctive "super-service stations" were built; the location on Cadiz Street at South Lamar is the only remaining example. The glass-enclosed area was originally the station's canopy where the gas pumps were located.

Lyles & Seelye Gulf Service Station
301 North Locust Street, Denton
P. R. L. Hogner (Pittsburgh), architect (attributed)
Service Station Supply Co. (Fort Worth), contractor
1939

P. R. L. Hogner, the Gulf Oil Corporation's chief architect from 1933 to 1955, designed the company's standard Automotive Garage in 1934.

Automobile Dealerships

Holley Motor Co. (Dodge)
236 South Broadway, Tyler
1939

Packard-Dallas, Inc.
demolished
2222 Ross Avenue, Dallas
Pitzinger-Lane Associates, architects
1939

Packard encouraged its dealers to build elegant, custom-designed showrooms to display the company's line of luxury automobiles. The air-conditioned Dallas dealership featured indirect lighting and soundproofing, with the cars shown against photographic murals of Texas. The Dallas Board of Education purchased the building in August 1941 for use as a defense training school.[15]

Tyler Nash Co.
616 West Erwin Street, Tyler
1947

Edwards Motor Co. (Chevrolet)
112 East Wise Street, Bowie
Charles T. Freelove (Fort Worth), architect
1948

J. P. 'PUNK' McN
2400 JOHNSON ST
ONE WAY
DO NOT ENTER

J. P. "Punk" McNatt Motor Co. (Oldsmobile-Cadillac)
2401 Johnson Street, Greenville
1948

Bus Terminals

Intercity bus lines prospered during World War I and grew with the expanding Texas highway system in the 1920s. The need for reliable, affordable transportation between sometimes isolated oil boomtowns helped the state's motor carriers survive the Great Depression. The industry reached its peak during World War II, when buses carried military personnel as well as civilians impacted by tire and gasoline rationing. Many bus lines used their wartime profits to upgrade terminals, but postwar ridership dropped in the face of competition from automobiles and airlines.[16]

Airline Bus Terminal
later Greyhound Bus Station
214 East South Street, Kilgore
1939

Airline Motor Coaches was an important bus line in East Texas from 1930 to 1946, when it was acquired by Dixie-Sunshine Motor Corporation.[17]

Bowen Bus Center
demolished
106 West Lancaster Avenue, Fort Worth
Edward L. Wilson, architect
1941

Bowen Motor Coaches built its flagship bus center across Lancaster Avenue from Fort Worth's landmark Texas and Pacific passenger terminal. The Bowen station was known for its large, well-equipped USO recreation room.

West facade, Union Bus Station, mid 1950s
later Greyhound Bus Terminal
303 North Bois d'Arc Street, Tyler
Remodeled 1946

An examination of historic photos, city directories, and Sanborn Fire Insurance Maps indicates the Dixie-Sunshine Motor Corporation created its Tyler depot by remodeling the c. 1933 building that housed Eisen's French Market & Delicatessen. The company's buses operated under the name Dixie-Sunshine Trailways.

South facade, **Union Bus Station**, mid 1950s

Union Bus Station
Remodeled 1975

In 1975, the *Tyler Courier-Times* enthusiastically reported that the city's newly updated bus terminal featured "an attractive stucco and bronze metal exterior" and a "carpeted waiting room [with] brightly colored yellow, orange, and red-toned wall coverings."[18]

Greyhound Union Bus Terminal
205 South Lamar Street, Dallas
Grayson Gill, architect
Arch Munn & Sons, contractors
1948

Greyhound's Dallas terminal replaced the Cotton Belt passenger depot from 1903. The bus station was constructed in two parts. Greyhound moved into half of the former railroad depot; the vacant portion of the depot was demolished, and construction began on the first section of the bus terminal. When the first half of the Greyhound terminal was completed, bus operations moved into the new section of the building; the rest of the railroad station was demolished, and the final section of the bus terminal was built.[19]

Infrastructure

Union Terminal Co. Underpass
(Triple Underpass)
Elm, Main, and Commerce Streets, Dallas
Austin Road & Bridge Co., contractors
1936

Engineers from the State Highway Department and the Texas and Pacific Railway designed the million-dollar Union Terminal Company Underpass (commonly called the Triple Underpass from the time of its completion) on the west side of downtown Dallas to connect three major cross streets with State Highway 1. The underpass allowed drivers to avoid several sets of railroad tracks and provided a gateway to downtown Dallas for motorists arriving from Fort Worth.

The structure's completion was a point of great pride for local residents, who turned out by the thousands to celebrate the opening of the underpass in May 1936. Before the traditional speeches, two parades passed beneath the viaduct. One procession approached from the east and the other from the west, and they somehow combined into a single parade that passed through the "mammoth portal."

Even more people arrived that evening for a square dance contest and band competition in the glow of the illuminated underpass. In the midst of the celebrations, a member of the Bonehead Club, a surprisingly prominent group of pranksters, was arrested for "christening" the underpass with a bottle of ketchup.[20]

ABOVE
Commerce Street tunnel,
Union Terminal Co. Underpass

Signage and lighting on the Triple Underpass still look as they did when the structure opened in 1936.

LEFT
Detail, **Union Terminal Co. Underpass**

Dealey Plaza rendering
Main and Houston Streets, Dallas
Hare & Hare (Kansas City),
landscape architects
1941

As the Triple Underpass was being planned, Dallas officials were considering options for beautifying the city's new gateway from the west. The Dallas Park Board acquired two blocks of land adjacent to the underpass in 1934. Triple Underpass Park was renamed Dealey Plaza in 1935 to honor *Dallas Morning News* publisher George Bannerman Dealey (1859-1946) for his promotion of city planning.

Several projects were carried out over the years, including the installation of concrete pylons and the planting of a variety of shrubs. In 1939, the city authorized Kansas City landscape architects Hare & Hare to develop a comprehensive plan for Dealey Plaza, and work began the following year. The $92,000 project was carried out with support from the Work Projects Administration and included a complete landscaping program, grading, the installation of curved sidewalks, and the construction of classically inspired pergolas, peristyles, and shelters.

Dealey Plaza and the Triple Underpass are part of the Dealey Plaza National Historic Landmark District, the site of President John F. Kennedy's assassination in 1963.[21]

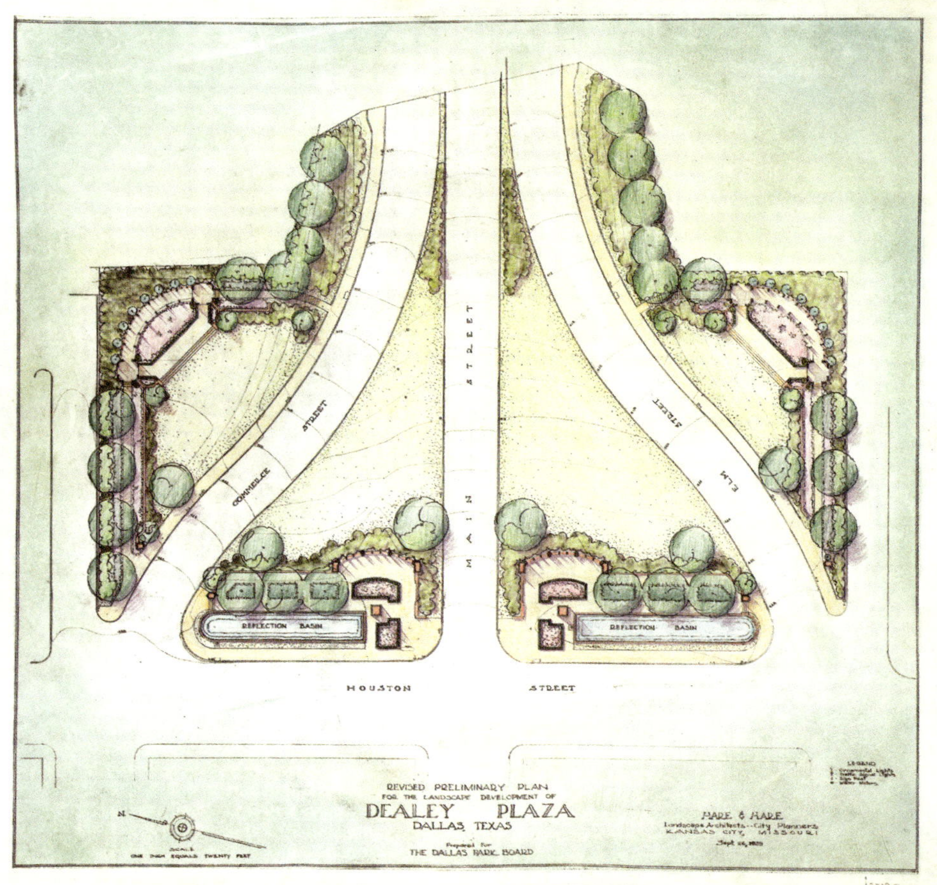

Site plan, **Dealey Plaza**

Detail, **Dealey Plaza**

Fountain basins and a pair of twenty-five-foot obelisks flanking Main Street were among the first improvements to Dealey Plaza. The basins and obelisks were designed by Dallas architect George L. Dahl and completed in 1937; the $15,000 cost was shared by the city and the National Youth Administration. A statue of George Bannerman Dealey replaced one of the obelisks in 1949.[22]

Peristyle detail, **Dealey Plaza**

RIGHT
South pergola, **Dealey Plaza**

Lodging

Hotel Kilgore
demolished
Albert H. Boren (Dallas) with Noah L. Peters (Longview), architects
T. L. James & Co., Inc. (Ruston, Louisiana), contractors
1936

The tallest building in Kilgore boasted an air-cooling system plus ice water and "radio connections" in each of its sixty-five rooms.[23]

Res-Mor Courts
700 West Upshur Avenue (US Highway 80),
Gladewater
1950

For a time, US 80 was dubbed the "Main Street of Texas" because of the number of tourists driving in from the east. Elvis Presley stayed at Res-Mor Courts in 1954 and 1955 when he played the now-demolished Mint Club in Gladewater.[24]

Belmont Motor Hotel
901 Fort Worth Avenue, Dallas
Charles Stevens Dilbeck, architect
Burford Construction Co., contractors
1947

The Belmont's architect described the seventy-five-room facility as the first "California-style" motor hotel in Texas. The resort-inspired complex contains one- and two-story buildings grouped on three levels of a sculpted hilltop on the former Fort Worth highway.[25]

Guest rooms, **Belmont Motor Hotel**

Guest rooms, **Belmont Motor Hotel**

ABOVE
Main building, **Belmont Motor Hotel**

Aviation

Although Dallas and Fort Worth each boasted aviation pioneers, Fort Worth took an early lead in the industry's development, thanks in part to the presence of three military airfields where American and Canadian pilots and ground crews trained during World War I.

In 1925, when the federal government mapped airmail routes for commercial airlines, Fort Worth was the transfer point where the east-west Atlanta-to-Los Angeles service crossed the north-south Kansas City-Houston-San Antonio route. Guaranteed income from postal contracts was intended to promote the development of commercial passenger service throughout the United States.

ABOVE RIGHT
American Airways Hangar and Administration Building
later American Aero FTW
201 Aviation Way, Meacham Field, Fort Worth
A. Epstein (Chicago), designers and structural engineers
Thomas S. Byrne, Inc., contractors
1933

American Airways was established in 1930; the administration building housed the executive offices of the company's southern division along with radio operations and pilot rooms. American Airways was renamed American Air Lines in 1934 and American Airlines later that same year. The restored building is a unique historic resource from this early period of commercial aviation.[26]

Entrance detail, **American Airways Hangar and Administration Building**

The 1933 version of the American Airways logo appears on the building in metal and stone reliefs. Goodrich Murphy, a traffic manager for the airline, designed the logo—which featured an eagle astride a globe, its beak aligned with the beam of a searchlight—in 1931. American's logo retained elements of Murphy's design until 2013.[27]

Relief, **American Airways Hangar and Administration Building**

Municipal Airport Terminal and Administration Building
demolished
Meacham Field, Fort Worth
Wiley G. Clarkson & Co., architects
Quisle & Andrews, contractors
1937

By 1936, when construction began on Fort Worth's new municipal air terminal, the city was the nation's third-busiest aviation center after Chicago and Newark. That year, American Airlines established the first coast-to-coast sleeper service using the new Douglas Sleeper Transport, a DC-3 airliner with fourteen seats that could be converted into berths—in essence, a flying Pullman car. American's eighteen-hour overnight flights between New York and Los Angeles stopped in Fort Worth to change pilots.[28]

Architect Wiley G. Clarkson and designer Charles O. Chromaster planned the new facility, which officially opened on June 19, 1937, with an air parade over the city and an air show at Meacham Field. The air-conditioned terminal included a coffee shop, lounges, and a barbershop, as well as radio traffic control for the region. The final cost of $150,000 was funded with municipal bonds and grants from the federal Public Works Administration.[29]

Terminal and Administration Building
demolished
Love Field, Dallas
Thomas D. Broad, architect
Wood & Scurlock, contractors
1940

Dallas dedicated its new air terminal with more traditional ceremonies than had opened Fort Worth's airport three years earlier. Along with the usual speeches, the event included performances by local junior high school bands and visiting Canadian bagpipers, drills by air cadets, and songs by the Braniff Airways Troubadours.[30]

The floor of the central concourse contained the building's most striking feature: a colorful terrazzo map depicting the nations and major cities of the Western Hemisphere that lie north of the equator. The terminal's facilities included a public dining room with views of the airfield, a barbershop, men's and women's lounges, and private quarters for pilots and air hostesses. Local bonds and Public Works Administration grants covered the building's $210,000 cost.[31]

CHAPTER 5

ENTERTAINMENT

Relief, **Warner Brothers Film Exchange**

"A film exchange is a department store offering everything from super productions to news reels and Western pictures."

Ned Depinet
district manager,
Universal Film Exchange
in the *Dallas Morning News*
October 14, 1923

OPPOSITE
Warner Brothers Film Exchange
508 Park Avenue, Dallas
Weiss, Dreyfous & Seiferth (New Orleans), architects
Stearman & Son, contractors
1930

When the Warner Brothers Film Exchange opened in 1930, the facility provided one-stop shopping for exhibitors interested in showing the Hollywood studio's latest productions. The building housed the regional offices of the company's major subsidiaries: Vitagraph (distribution), Vitaphone (short subjects and cartoons), First National Pictures (contemporary comedies, dramas, and crime films), and Warner Brothers Pictures (prestige motion pictures, costume dramas, and musicals). Theater chain booking agents and independent theater owners could preview the studio's offerings in the building's penthouse screening room.[1]

During the first half of the twentieth century, film exchanges were an integral part of a sophisticated system that produced and distributed movies on an industrial scale. Before the advent of television, theater owners might show several films a week to keep audiences coming back and seats filled. Motion picture studios and independent agencies set up film exchanges in rail hubs across the country to meet their exhibitors' needs. Every year, exchange employees were responsible for ensuring hundreds of motion pictures and related advertising materials were shipped on a timely basis to thousands of theaters across the United States.[2]

Despite its distinctive Art Deco facade, the Dallas exchange was a utilitarian building shaped by the needs of the motion picture industry and local ordinances addressing the hazards associated with storing and handling highly flammable cellulose nitrate film. As early as 1915, Dallas had laws requiring that silent films be stored in metal cabinets or fireproof vaults and banning film exchanges in buildings that were partially used for residential purposes. The local ordinances were strengthened in 1922 after a spectacular fire destroyed several buildings on "Film Row," the blocks of Commerce and Main Streets between Ervay and Harwood where most of the film exchanges were located.[3]

When the alarm came in at 10 p.m. on December 10, 1921, every fire station in the city was called into action. A blaze in one of the film exchanges had spread to adjacent buildings, and explosions in the exchanges on the south side of Commerce Street sent burning reels of nitrate

508
PARK
AVENUE

Kingfisher relief, **Warner Brothers Film Exchange**

Aeolus relief, **Warner Brothers Film Exchange**

This relief is believed to depict Aeolus, ruler of the winds in Greek mythology. His daughter Alcyone and her husband were transformed into halcyon birds (kingfishers) by Zeus. Aeolus calms the winds during the "halcyon days" of winter so the kingfishers can nest.

film flying into buildings on the north side of the street, spreading the fire. Traffic came to a standstill as Saturday night audiences poured out of downtown vaudeville theaters and silent movie houses to watch the far more exciting live show. By the time the flames were extinguished, the fire had destroyed the movie inventories, contracts, receipts, and equipment in six film exchanges and gutted the Western Auto Supply Company and Skillern Bros. Drug Store No. 2.[4]

The Dallas fire commissioner demanded a ban on storing films downtown, but city officials settled for allowing downtown exchanges built according to an amended city ordinance. The new measures required the installation of vent pipes in each film vault to allow the escape of accumulated gases. All film had to be stored in vaults at night, and employees were prohibited from working in basements.[5]

In its original configuration, the Warner Brothers exchange included shipping and receiving facilities, fireproof film storage vaults, freight and passenger elevators, and the company's regional offices. The architects ornamented the building's facade with custom cast-stone reliefs and detailing of black Belgian marble; the small lobby had a plaster ceiling finished in a color called "aluminum bronze" and a polished marble floor in a zigzag pattern that hinted at Hollywood glamour. Fire safety was the overriding concern, however. The structure was built of reinforced concrete with brick and hollow-tile infill, and the ornate marble surround on the main entrance framed kalamein fireproof doors. The floors in most of the building were painted cement, there was a sprinkler system throughout, and even the apertures on the screening room's projection booth were fitted with metal safety shutters.[6]

When the building was completed, the third floor was occupied by Brunswick Radio, a Warner Brothers acquisition that was soon renamed Brunswick Records. In the late 1930s, field producer Don Law set up a makeshift recording

Lobby, **Warner Brothers Film Exchange**

studio in the Brunswick offices for sessions with legendary bluesman Robert Johnson and Western swing innovators Bob Wills and His Texas Playboys, among many others.[7]

Warner Brothers eventually sold its Dallas facility to Glazer's Wholesale Drug Company, which occupied the property for many years. By the turn of the twenty-first century, the derelict building was facing demolition before it was rescued and revitalized by First Presbyterian Church of Dallas as part of the institution's Encore Park community outreach project.

In addition to film exchanges, Film Row was home to the general offices or the booking offices of several large theater chains. Interstate Theaters, Jefferson Amusement Company, Robb & Rowley Theaters, and Phil Isley Enterprises all had representatives in Dallas and commissioned theaters from the city's architects. W. Scott Dunne, Jack Corgan, and Pettigrew, Worley & Company were among the most prolific designers of movie houses.[8]

The region's modernistic downtown movie palaces did not survive. Fort Worth's classic Art Deco Hollywood Theater (1930, Alfred C. Finn with Wyatt C. Hedrick) is partially demolished, its 1,700-seat auditorium now used as a parking garage; in Dallas, the Art Moderne Tower Theater (1937, W. Scott Dunne), with its lobby aquarium, neon handrails, and seating for 1,400, is just a memory. Fortunately, a number of theaters in residential areas and smaller cities and towns provide a glimpse of the film industry's heyday.[9]

Palace Theater
later Western Auto
101 North Jackson Street, Henderson
Emile Weil, Inc. (New Orleans), architects
1929

Emile Weil's design for Henderson's Palace Theater incorporates subtle Art Deco details along with classically inspired elements befitting his Beaux Arts training. Weil also created movie palaces in Texarkana and Marshall, Texas, and Shreveport, Louisiana.[10]

Harlem Theater
demolished
2407 Elm Street, Dallas
1934

The Harlem Theater was built on the site of the Palace Theater, which was destroyed by fire in September 1933. Both theaters served Dallas's African American community.[11]

National Theater
522 Oak Street, Graham
Corgan & Moore (Dallas), architects
Remodeled 1934

Entrance, **National Theater**

Texas Theater
later Fine Arts Theater
115 North Elm Street, Denton
W. Scott Dunne (Dallas), architect
Geo. P. O'Rourke Construction Co. (Dallas), contractors
Remodeled 1935

Palace Theater
demolished
113 East Seventh Street, Fort Worth
Geo. P. O'Rourke Construction Co. (Dallas), contractors
Remodeled 1936

Fan dancer Sally Rand was one of the luminaries on hand to open the remodeled Palace Theater in 1936. The theater originally opened in 1908 as Byers's Opera House and was renamed the Palace when it was converted to a silent picture house in 1919. The Palace brought talking pictures to Fort Worth when Al Jolson's *The Jazz Singer* opened at a midnight showing on March 15, 1928.[12]

The Palace is remembered for the carbon-filament light bulb that burned backstage from September 21, 1908, until March 18, 1977, when it was carefully removed before the theater's demolition. The famous bulb was featured in *Ripley's Believe It or Not* and the *Guinness Book of World Records* before going on display at the Stockyards Museum in Fort Worth, where it remains lit.[13]

New Isis Theater
2401 North Main Street, Fort Worth
W. Scott Dunne (Dallas), architect
1936

Grand Theater
21 Lamar Avenue, Paris
J. Harvey "Jake" Elder (Dallas),
construction engineer
Geo. P. O'Rourke Construction Co. (Dallas),
contractors
1937

Lakewood Theater
1825 Abrams Road, Dallas
H. F. Pettigrew, architect
Geo. P. O'Rourke Construction Co., contractors
1938

The Lakewood was the first theater built with the signature pylon sign that marked Interstate Theaters' most significant suburban locations.

Marquee detail, **Lakewood Theater**

Pylon, **Lakewood Theater**

Overton Theater
210-212 East Henderson Street, Overton
1938

State Theater
200 East California Street, Gainesville
Raymond F. Smith (Dallas), architect
Remodeled 1938

OPPOSITE
Crim Theater
112 South Kilgore Street, Kilgore
Llewellyn W. Pitts (Beaumont), architect
1939

CRIM
CITY OF STARS
KILGORE
Cable TV
High-Speed Internet

Kessler Theater
1230 West Davis Street, Dallas
Raymond F. Smith, architect
1942

Granada Theater
3524 Greenville Avenue, Dallas
1946

Circle Theater
later Carnaval Night Club
2711 Storey Lane, Dallas
Pettigrew, Worley & Co., architects
Geo. P. O'Rourke Construction Co., contractors
1947

The thousand-seat Circle Theater was named for its location near Tom Field Circle, popularly "The Circle," a traffic rotary that no longer exists. Advertisements for Interstate Theaters' newest suburban location trumpeted its "Symphonic Sound • Pushback Seats • Year 'Round Weather."[14]

Entrance, **Circle Theater**

FAR RIGHT
Circle Theater, 1969

This 1969 image shows the Circle with its original exterior lighting: a series of neon circles that chased across the building's facade.

Inwood Theater
5458 West Lovers Lane, Dallas
1947

Ticket booth, **Inwood Theater**

LAKE COUNTRY PLAYHOUSE
LAKE COUNTRY PLAYHOUSE
SELECT
SELECT
MAX PG
FRI SAT SUN
MAX PG
FRI SAT SUN

Forest Theater
1918 Martin Luther King Jr. Boulevard, Dallas
Pettigrew, Worley & Co., architects
Geo. P. O'Rourke Construction Co., contractors
1949

The Forest Theater was named for its location on Forest Avenue (later Martin Luther King Jr. Boulevard) at Harwood Street and the planned Central Expressway. The three-sided pylon sign was designed to be seen from all three thoroughfares. Interstate Theaters' largest suburban location could seat 1,500 patrons. The theater featured a spun-glass screen for clear images and "Acousticon" earphones for hearing-impaired patrons.[15]

When the Forest Theater opened in 1949, the surrounding neighborhood was predominately white and had a significant Jewish population. By 1956, the area was largely African American. The theater's last show for white audiences was held on Saturday, February 25, 1956. The Forest reopened on Friday, March 2, as a theater serving black patrons.[16]

OPPOSITE
Select Theater
later Lake Country Playhouse
114 North Johnson Street, Mineola
Remodeled 1948

CHAPTER 6

INSTITUTIONAL

Detail, **United States Court House, Fort Worth**

"The massive buildings and gorgeous trimmings will certainly be missed. A postoffice will never be the same without the . . . space and weight and impractical magnificence we're used to in such edifices."

Editorial in the
Kokomo (IN) Tribune
August 6, 1934

OPPOSITE
United States Court House, Fort Worth
later Eldon B. Mahon
United States Courthouse
501 West Tenth Street, Fort Worth
Paul Philippe Cret (Philadelphia)
with Wiley G. Clarkson & Co., architects
James L. Barnes (Logansport, Indiana), contractor
1934

THE *KOKOMO TRIBUNE*'S ELEGY FOR "IMPRACTICAL MAGNIFICENCE" was a reaction to an announcement that US Treasury Secretary Henry Morgenthau had made a few days earlier. Noting the limited amount of funds available to build a growing list of federal facilities, Morgenthau said that expensive materials and grand interiors had to go. Uncle Sam, he declared, would build "no more mausoleums." That fall, federal architects began substituting plaster and iron for marble and bronze in buildings from coast to coast. Exterior ornamentation was pared down, too, ushering in the rather austere federal style sometimes called "starved classicism."[1]

In many ways, Fort Worth's United States courthouse—which was nearly finished when Morgenthau made his announcement—represents the end of an era. Although it is not as sophisticated as contemporary government buildings in larger cities, the Fort Worth structure's detailing and richly appointed courtrooms are an impressive example of public architecture in the early days of the Depression.

The Fort Worth courthouse began with a $1.2 million government appropriation in the summer of 1930. It was, newspapers noted, the result of a twenty-year effort to replace the city's overcrowded 1896 federal building and post office. Philadelphia architect Paul Philippe Cret was tapped to draw up plans for the courthouse; the *Fort Worth Star-Telegram* reported that local architect Wiley G. Clarkson would then produce working drawings. When planning began, Clarkson promised that the new building would be "one of the most pretentious structures of its type in the nation."[2]

The architects designed the courthouse with distinctly modern lines, but based it on the Beaux Arts classicism that had been the norm in federal architecture for decades. The principal facade, facing north onto Burnett Park, featured a limestone-clad base supporting a row of eleven stacked window bays alternating with limestone piers, creating the Art Deco equivalent of a classical colonnade. A closer look would reveal a wealth of modernistic detailing, including stylized aluminum lanterns and metalwork embellished with modified Mayan and Egyptian patterns. "The general design of the building is modern in that it does not follow the prescribed

UNITED STATES COURT HOUSE
W 10th St
500

ABOVE
Lantern, **United States Court House, Fort Worth**

North entrance, **United States Court House, Fort Worth**, 1934

The West Tenth Street entrance was intended to lead to a branch post office and postal savings bank. Although signage and post boxes were installed, research by the General Services Administration, which manages the courthouse, indicates that the branch post office never actually operated in the building.

Fort Worth's central postal operations were handled from a new main post office that was built at approximately the same time as the courthouse. Wyatt C. Hedrick designed the neoclassical post office building, which opened in 1933 on Lancaster Avenue.[3]

The north entrance facing Burnett Park is virtually unaltered from the time the courthouse opened. Above the doors, aluminum screens are decorated with zigzags and a variety of exotic details, including Plains Indian arrows and Egyptian lotus leaves.[4]

lines of any of the old schools of architecture," Clarkson explained.[5]

Cret and Clarkson were hired to design the Fort Worth federal building under an agreement reached between the federal Office of the Supervising Architect (OSA) and the American Institute of Architects (AIA), a professional organization for architects in private practice. The OSA, an agency of the US Treasury Department, was established in 1852 to design federal buildings across the country. Beginning in 1915, the OSA produced standardized sets of plans to reduce the cost and construction time of federal projects. Although some design variation was allowed, the standard plans meant that the same building, more or less, might be built in a number of different cities.[6]

In late 1930, a year into the Great Depression, the AIA began criticizing the OSA for its inability to work quickly and for mass-produced designs that "must inevitably narrow and stereotype our national architecture." A year later, the AIA drafted federal legislation that would require the OSA to hire private architects and relegate its own staff to supervisory roles. "The government of the United States is no more qualified to design our buildings than to paint our pictures or write our books," one architect sniffed. (Little did he know that a few years later, the government would fund the creation of both paintings and books through New Deal programs.)[7]

In the end, the Treasury Department agreed to use private architects for projects costing more than sixty thousand dollars, including the Fort Worth federal building. Smaller federal facilities, such as the post offices in Graham and Mineola, were built according to standard OSA plans. Government officials increasingly retained private architects until the OSA was dissolved in 1939.[8]

There was little such drama when it came to the design of public facilities and other institutional buildings for Texas counties and municipalities. Instead, private architects and contractors bid on projects as they were announced, resulting in a diverse group of buildings that more directly represented the taste and wealth of their communities than did those built with the architectural oversight and financial backing of the federal government.

Court of Appeals, **United States Court House, Fort Worth**

The fourth-floor Court of Appeals is one of the most dramatic spaces in the building, with walls paneled in American black walnut rising twenty-two feet to a ceiling embellished with geometric designs and a central medallion featuring the scales of justice.

Detail, Court of Appeals, **United States Court House, Fort Worth**

RIGHT
Mural, **United States Court House, Fort Worth**
Texas Rangers in Camp
Frank Albert Mechau
(Colorado Springs, Colorado), artist
1940

BELOW RIGHT
Mural, **United States Court House, Fort Worth**
The Taking of Sam Bass

In January 1938, the Treasury Department's Section of Painting and Sculpture (later the Section of Fine Arts) invited artists in Texas and sixteen Western states to submit mural proposals for a number of public buildings across Texas and the western United States. Colorado artist Frank Mechau was chosen that December to execute three murals for the Court of Appeals in Fort Worth's federal courthouse, for which he was paid $2,900.[9]

Mechau picked the Texas Rangers as the subjects of his two principal murals. In one panel, the Rangers mount their horses in camp; in the other, they prepare for a gunfight with the outlaw Sam Bass. Bass and his gang held up stagecoaches and trains in the Midwest and North Texas in 1877 and 1878, prompting a special unit of Texas Rangers to track them. A member of Bass's posse informed on him in the summer of 1878, leading to the confrontation on July 19 at Round Rock, near Austin, which Mechau painted. The Rangers wounded Bass in the melee, and he died in Round Rock two days later. Mechau's smaller third mural depicts the flag and seal of Texas along with Rangers' riding gear.[10]

ABOVE

Federal District Court, **United States Court House, Fort Worth**

Although smaller than the Court of Appeals, the Federal District Court room has an equally high level of decoration. Walls are paneled in oak with inlaid chevrons, while the entry doors are covered in leather. The twenty-one-foot-high ceiling includes plasterwork in geometric designs and a border of swirling flowers, leaves, and pineapples. The gallery's original green rubber tile floor, long covered, has been restored.

FAR RIGHT

Corridor detail, **United States Court House, Fort Worth**

Broad, marble-trimmed corridors on the upper levels of the federal building led to courtrooms, judges' chambers, and offices for a variety of government agencies, including the local branch of the Internal Revenue Service, a grain inspection laboratory, and the Fort Worth weather bureau. Many original hallway details, including marble drinking fountains, remain intact.[11]

Detail, Federal District Court, **United States Court House, Fort Worth**

Federal

United States Post Office, Jacksonville
later Landmark Event Center
402 East Rusk Street, Jacksonville
James A. Wetmore, US Supervising Architect
Sanford Brothers Construction Co.
(Montgomery, Alabama), contractors
1933

Jacksonville's post office was built from a standard plan created by the Office of the Supervising Architect that incorporates Art Deco and Art Moderne ornamentation on a classically inspired facade. The post office was expanded in 1967, but the one-story addition was designed in keeping with the rest of the building. The US Postal Service vacated the facility in 2000.[12]

Detail, **United States Post Office, Jacksonville**

Detail, **United States Post Office, Jacksonville**

Relief, **United States Post Office, Jacksonville**

Detail, **United States Post Office, Jacksonville**

United States Post Office, Graham
later Old Post Office Museum & Art Center
510 Third Street, Graham
Louis A. Simon, US Supervising Architect
Neil A. Melnick, contractor
1936

Lantern, **United States Post Office, Graham**

Mural, **United States Post Office, Graham**
Oil Fields of Graham
Alexandre Hogue, artist
1939

The Graham post office murals were created under the Section of Fine Arts (originally the Section of Painting and Sculpture), a New Deal program administered by the US Treasury Department that commissioned artists to create high quality works to decorate federally owned buildings. The program awarded commissions competitively, based on artistic merit. The Section, as it was usually called, made possible the creation of more than eleven hundred murals and three hundred sculptures from 1934 to 1942.[13]

United States Post Office, Mineola
later Mineola Historical Museum
114 North Pacific Street, Mineola
Louis A. Simon, US Supervising Architect
1937

Relief, **United States Post Office, Mineola**

Detailing on post offices built in the 1930s according to standardized plans from the Office of the Supervising Architect often dealt with various ways in which the mail has been delivered. This relief represents airmail service with an airplane engine and propeller before folded wings.

United States Post Office
Terminal Annex, Dallas
later Terminal Annex Federal Building
207 South Houston Street, Dallas
Lang & Witchell, architects
A. J. Rife Construction Co., contractors
1937
Lang & Witchell, architects
Algernon Blair (Montgomery, Alabama), contractor
1940, top two floors

The building, commonly known as the Terminal Annex, was constructed as a parcel post facility. In 1940, two floors were added and additional federal offices were moved into the building. The Terminal Annex is part of the Dealey Plaza National Historic Landmark District (see page 126).[14]

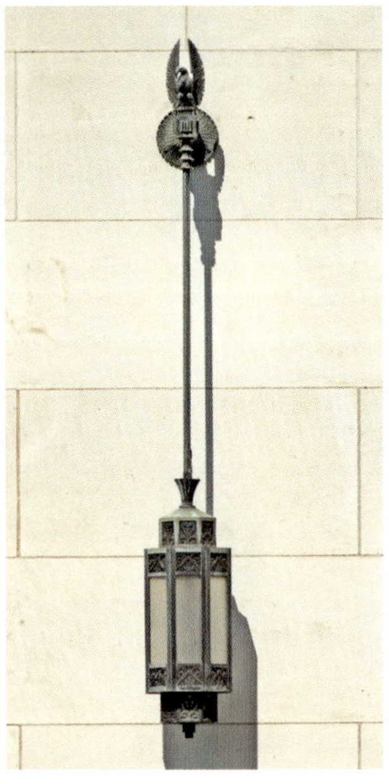

Lantern, **United States Post Office Terminal Annex, Dallas**

Relief, **United States Post Office Terminal Annex, Dallas**

ABOVE
Mural, **United States Post Office Terminal Annex, Dallas**
Pioneer Home Builders
Peter Hurd (San Patricio, New Mexico), artist
1940

New Mexico artist Peter Hurd's mural designs were selected from among 144 proposals to decorate the lobby of the Terminal Annex in the same January 1938 competition that chose Frank Mechau as muralist for the Fort Worth federal courthouse. Hurd and his assistant, Ernesto Burciaga, completed two of three proposed Terminal Annex murals, but construction in the building delayed work on the third. The last mural was to feature a stagecoach arriving with the mail; it was never painted.[15]

RIGHT
Mural, **United States Post Office Terminal Annex, Dallas**
Airmail Over Texas

United States Post Office, Kilgore
later Old Post Office History & Art Center
224 South Kilgore Street, Kilgore
Louis A. Simon, US Supervising Architect
Wyatt C. Hedrick, Inc. (Fort Worth), architects
1938

BELOW
Mural, **United States Post Office, Kilgore**
Contemporary Youth

Mural, **United States Post Office, Kilgore**
relocated to the East Texas Oil Museum
1100 Broadway Boulevard, Kilgore
Pioneer Saga
Xavier Gonzalez (Alpine, Texas), artist
1941

The Kilgore Historical Preservation Foundation restored four post office murals and relocated them for display in the East Texas Oil Museum in 1999.

RIGHT

Mural, **United States Post Office, Farmersville**
203 McKinney Street, Famersville
Soil Conservation in Collin County
Jerry Bywaters (Dallas), artist
1941

BELOW

Mural, **United States Post Office, Longview**
201 East Methvin Street
Rural East Texas
Thomas M. Stell Jr. (San Antonio), artist
1942

Stell won a regional competition to paint the Longview mural in June 1941, making it one of the last post office murals commissioned in Texas by the US Treasury Department's Section of Fine Arts.[16]

County

Anderson County Jail
704 Avenue A, Palestine
Theo. S. Maffitt, architect
Campbell & White (Tyler), contractors
1932

Young County Courthouse
516 Fourth Street, Graham
Withers & Thompson (Fort Worth), architects
James T. Taylor Construction Co.
(Fort Worth), contractors
1932

Work on the courthouse was delayed several months when Young County residents petitioned to stop the project until an election could be held to decide whether the county seat should be moved from Graham to Newcastle. The Texas Supreme Court eventually allowed construction to continue.[17]

Reliefs, **Young County Courthouse**

The Young County Courthouse reliefs depict scenes from the North Texas plains, including cattle ranching and buffalo hunting, as well as typical iconography such as American eagles.

BELOW
Lantern, **Young County Courthouse**

LEFT
Light fixture, **Young County Courthouse**

Interiors of the Young County Courthouse combine modernistic fixtures with elaborate stenciling.

Gregg County Courthouse
101 East Methvin Street, Longview
Voelcker & Dixon (Wichita Falls), architects
C. S. Lambie & Co. (Amarillo), contractors
1933

Detail, **Gregg County Courthouse**

Lantern, **Gregg County Courthouse**

Rusk County Jail
later Rusk County offices
West Charlevoix and North Van Buren Streets, Henderson
DeFee & White, architects
Rogers Hale Construction Co., contractors
1933

FAR LEFT
South entrance detail, **Rusk County Jail**

LEFT
West entrance, **Rusk County Jail**

Upshur County Courthouse
100 West Tyler Street, Gilmer
Elmer G. Withers Architectural Co. (Fort Worth), architects
1937

The "debt-free" Upshur County Courthouse was one of the few Depression-era Texas courthouses built without federal aid. A special tax levied on oil properties allowed the county to pay for the $200,000 construction project without issuing bonds.[18]

The Upshur courthouse bears a strong resemblance to Withers & Thompson's Young County Courthouse (1932) in Graham. The basic form of both buildings is the same, although the courthouse in Graham is much more ornate.

Detail, **Van Zandt County Courthouse**

Van Zandt County Courthouse
121 East Dallas Street, Canton
Voelcker & Dixon (Wichita Falls), architects
1937

The $210,000 courthouse was proudly described as "debt-free" when it was dedicated. A special county tax provided $125,000 and a grant from the federal Public Works Administration covered the balance. The modern building included a home demonstration kitchen in the basement and a "breakproof" jail on the top floor.[19]

Gregg County Community Building
later The Gladewater Museum
116 West Pacific Avenue, Gladewater
C. H. Leinbach (Dallas), architect
J. W. Sherman, contractor
1938

Jack County Courthouse
100 North Main Street, Jacksboro
Voelcker & Dixon, Co. (Wichita Falls), architects
Eckert-Fair Construction Co. (Dallas), contractors
1940

In August 1940, the *Dallas Morning News* published Texas folklorist J. Frank Dobie's syndicated column lamenting the loss of nineteenth-century courthouses and calling to task the builders of the "ultramodernistic" Jack County Courthouse for failing to appreciate the "honest, natural architecture" of the native sandstone buildings around it.[20]

LEFT
Entrance, **Jack County Courthouse**

Longview Community Center
500 East Whaley Street, Longview
Zimmerman & Morgan, architects
McKinley Bros. Construction Co., contractors
1940

Gregg County provided the Federation of Women's Clubs a gift of $30,000 to complete the $39,000 building. In return for contributing $9,000 and furnishing the building, the county leased the community center to the federation for twenty years with the stipulation that the building be maintained for public use.[21]

When completed, the community center included a theater with an orchestra pit and seating for 300, club and reception rooms, and a banquet hall that could seat up to 310.[22]

Rockwall County Courthouse
101 East Rusk Street, Rockwall
Voelcker & Dixon (Wichita Falls), architects
J. W. Sherman (Gladewater), contractor
1942

The courthouse was built with labor provided by the federal Work Projects Administration, which also furnished $44,609 of the $96,275 cost. Rockwall County and the Rockwall City Chamber of Commerce contributed the balance of the funding. The building no longer serves as the county courthouse.[23]

Detail, **Rockwall County Courthouse**

Municipal

Fort Worth Central Fire Station and Signal Alarm Station
later Fire Station No. 2
1000 Cherry Street, Fort Worth
Wyatt C. Hedrick, Inc., architects
R. F. Ball Construction Co., contractors
1930

Firefighters moved into the new station during the last days of 1930, but the building was not formally dedicated until April 1931 because delivery of the fire signal equipment had been delayed. Designer Herman P. Koeppe's exterior remains largely unaltered.[24]

Siren tower, **Central Fire Station**

Fort Worth Public Market
1400 Henderson Street, Fort Worth
B. Gaylord Noftsger (Oklahoma City), architect
Quisle & Andrews, contractors
1930

The City of Fort Worth encouraged Oklahoma developer John J. Harden to construct a market that would allow farmers to sell directly to consumers and clear the streets of parked produce wagons. Opening advertisements announced that the facility included an A&P grocery store, café, soda fountain, delicatessen, pet shop, beauty salon, and barbershop as well as fish, poultry, and meat markets. Farmers could rent any of 145 stalls for thirty-five cents a day. The market operated through 1934, but by 1936 "the old Public Market building" was serving as the rainout location for dog shows.

In January 1941, the Farmers & Consumers Company began seeking new concessionaires and reopened the market as a cooperative in May. Food sales continued and shoppers could also rent frozen food storage lockers. In May 1942, ads announcing the sale of the Public Market's fixtures appeared in the *Fort Worth Star-Telegram*.[25]

Municipal Bathhouse
later Bath House Cultural Center
West Lawther Drive at T&P Hill,
White Rock Lake Park, Dallas
Carsey & Linskie, architects
1930

The City of Dallas dammed White Rock Creek in 1910 to create a reservoir to help address the increasing demand for water. Calls to build recreational facilities around White Rock Lake began as early as 1915, but active development of the lakeshore as a municipal park did not start until the late 1920s.[26]

Entrance, **Municipal Bathhouse**

White Rock Boathouse
521 East Lawther Drive,
White Rock Lake Park, Dallas
Carsey & Linskie, architects
Bailey, Burns & Fitzpatrick, contractors
1930

Detail, **White Rock Boathouse**

Setback pinnacles and a zigzag frieze in cast concrete enliven the low-slung boathouse.

Paul Laurence Dunbar Negro Branch, Dallas Public Library
demolished
2721 Thomas Avenue, Dallas
Bryan & Sharp, architects
1931

At the time, architect Ralph Bryan told the *Dallas Morning News* he had specifically rejected the popular Southern Colonial style for the African American branch library because "it is really the architecture of his masters in the days of slavery." Bryan said the modernistic design of the Dunbar library "was governed by simplicity in the mass, the lines and in the materials, without resorting to any of the accepted architectural styles."[27]

The library was named for Paul Laurence Dunbar (1872-1906), one of the first African American poets to gain national recognition.

Henderson Fire Department
109 South Marshall Street, Henderson
1934

Historic photographs show the storefronts were originally bays for Henderson's fire trucks.

Detail, **Henderson Fire Department**

Mural, **Carnegie Library, Tyler**
later Carnegie History Center
125 South College Avenue, Tyler
Industrial and Agricultural Development of East Texas
James Douthitt Wilson (Fort Worth), artist
1934

Public art was an important part of the Roosevelt administration's employment programs. The mural series in Tyler was funded through the Public Works of Art Project (PWAP), a six-month trial effort designed to give meaningful work to professional artists. PWAP murals were painted in new and existing public buildings.[28]

BELOW
Mural, **Carnegie Library, Tyler**

Mural, **Carnegie Library, Tyler**

Mural, **Paris Public Library**
326 South Main Street, Paris
The 1916 Paris Fire
Jerry Bywaters (Dallas), artist
1934

The federal Public Works of Art Project commissioned Jerry Bywaters to create murals for the Paris library. The first panel depicts residents trying to save their possessions from the fire that destroyed blocks of houses and the city's central business district on March 21, 1916.[29]

FAR RIGHT
Mural, **Paris Public Library**
Rebuilding Paris

The second panel shows citizens rebuilding after the 1916 fire. "Smile," the city's unofficial motto in the aftermath of the blaze, could be seen on signs throughout Paris.

Mural, **Dallas Municipal Building**
lost
106 South Harwood Street, Dallas
Passing of the Frontier
Alexandre Hogue and Jerry Bywaters, artists
1934

Alexandre Hogue and Jerry Bywaters painted their mural series in Dallas's 1914 city hall with funding from the Public Works of Art Project. The ten murals showed scenes from the history of Dallas, beginning with the construction of pioneer John Neely Bryan's cabin in 1841 and ending with depictions of modern innovations such as radio-dispatched police cars and the Cadiz Street Viaduct over the Trinity River.[30]

An expansion of city hall was completed in 1956, prompting a renovation of the 1914 building. Because the murals had been painted directly onto the building's plaster walls, the city said they would have to be destroyed as the old building was reconfigured and equipped with central air conditioning. Dallas leaders apparently felt no sentiment for the paintings: "They date from the Depression, a period we all want to forget," one official told the *Dallas Morning News*. ("It is perhaps fortunate that the ancient Indian paintings on the bluff near Paint Rock in Concho County are not the property of the city of Dallas," historian Sam Acheson quipped. "They are even more primitive looking.")[31]

For the next sixty years, it was assumed that the murals were completely lost. However, workers preparing the former Municipal Building for a new tenant in 2015 were surprised to find that fragments of some of the panels had survived behind drywall and drop ceilings, although the vast majority of the mural cycle had indeed been removed. A version of the lost murals exists at Dallas Area Rapid Transit's Union Station light rail stop, where Dallas artist Philip Lamb used Hogue and Bywaters's work as the basis for terrazzo panels that he created in 1996.[32]

Mural, **Dallas Municipal Building**
Water

Mural, **Dallas Municipal Building**
Viaducts Bridge the Trinity

Mural, **Dallas Municipal Building**
Radio Equipped Police Cars

Hogue and Bywaters sometimes painted around existing building features including windows, doors, and even a fire hose, which they incorporated into this mural celebrating modern municipal services. The man pictured at bottom right is Henry "Dad" Garrett, a Dallas inventor whose innovations included radio-dispatched police cars (1921) and automatic traffic lights (1924).[33]

Fort Worth City Hall
later A. D. Marshall
Public Safety & Courts Building
1000 Throckmorton Street, Fort Worth
Wyatt C. Hedrick, Inc. and Elmer G. Withers
Architectural Co., architects
James T. Taylor Construction Co., contractors
1939

On January 4, 1929, the Association of Commerce kicked off the new year by recommending Fort Worth build a new city hall "in keeping with the size and prestige of the municipality." It would be almost ten years to the day before the recommendation became a reality in this crisply composed building, the work of Wyatt C. Hedrick's chief designer, Herman P. Koeppe.[34]

The cornerstone for the new city hall was laid on May 5, 1938, and construction was completed by the end of the year. City Hall formally opened on January 5, 1939, when Fort Worth's City Council met in the new building for the first time. The official dedication ceremony was held March 25 after furnishings were installed in the building. The federal Public Works Administration provided almost half of the building's $500,000 cost. The structure served as Fort Worth City Hall until 1978.[35]

RIGHT
Detail, **Fort Worth City Hall**

FAR RIGHT
Lantern, **Fort Worth City Hall**

OPPOSITE
Fort Worth City Hall, c. 1939

The name "City Hall" in distinctive Moderne typography was removed after 1978.

CITY HALL

Fort Worth Public Library
demolished
915 Throckmorton Street, Fort Worth
Joseph R. Pelich, architect
A. Farnell Blair (Lake Charles, Louisiana), contractor
1939

Fort Worth's library was built on a triangular plot diagonally across the street from the new city hall. Even the *Dallas Morning News* described the library as one of the best equipped in the Southwest and predicted the building would become Fort Worth's "center of activity for arts, letters, music, and drama."[36]

The facility included two soundproof rooms: one where blind patrons could listen to "talking books" over loudspeakers, and one with a piano where students could practice pieces from the library's substantial music collection. The Fort Worth Art Association's collection of paintings, the genesis of the Modern Art Museum of Fort Worth, was displayed in a pentagonal gallery on the library's third floor.[37]

The library building was vacated in 1978 and later sold to private developers. It was demolished in 1990.[38]

Greenville Municipal Building, 1940s
2821 Washington Street, Greenville
William R. Ragsdale, architect
Eckert-Fair Construction Co. (Dallas), contractors
1939

Greenville Municipal Building, 2016

Tyler City Hall
212 North Bonner Avenue, Tyler
T. Shirley Simons, architect
A. M. Campbell & Co., contractors
1939

RIGHT
Entrance, **Tyler City Hall**

FAR RIGHT
Staircase, **Tyler City Hall**

Mineola City Hall and Fire Station
115 West Kilpatrick Street, Mineola
1941

Construction began on the fire station portion of the building in 1930, but the city did not have enough money to complete the project. City Hall was finished eleven years later with funding from the federal Public Works Administration. The building no longer houses city hall or the fire department.[39]

Henderson Municipal Building
400 West Main Street, Henderson
James L. Downing, architect
Rogers Hale Construction Co., contractors
1948

Education

During the Great Depression, the Dallas and Fort Worth school districts embarked on significant public school construction and rehabilitation projects with assistance from the federal Public Works Administration and Works Progress Administration. Both programs also helped build modern schools in rural areas and supported the development of junior colleges.

The new Dallas public schools, in particular, featured modernistic designs. Although usually planned and built on abbreviated schedules, these schools have proven to be extremely well constructed and functional when regularly maintained. Decades later, many of these buildings continue to serve their communities.

Peacock Military Academy
later Urban Park Elementary School
6901 Military Parkway, Dallas
Lang & Witchell, architects
F. A. Mote, contractor
1930

Two weeks before the 1929 stock market crash, San Antonio-based Peacock Military Academy announced plans to build a new campus just east of Dallas. Construction began on the administration building as the first effects of the Great Depression were being felt. Peacock sold its Dallas branch in 1933 and the facility operated for one semester as North Texas Military Academy. Pleasant Mound Independent School District purchased the abandoned property in 1938 and opened Pleasant Mound School in 1939. Dallas Independent School District annexed Pleasant Mound after World War II.[40]

Relief, **Peacock Military Academy**

Relief, **Peacock Military Academy**

Robert E. Lee Grammar School
later Robert E. Lee Elementary School
2911 Delmar Avenue, Dallas
DeWitt & Washburn, architects
Eckert-Burton Construction Co., contractors
1931

Lee School made news because it was built of cast concrete, with all decorations and reliefs created by the formwork used when the concrete was poured. Contractor A. E. Eckert toured concrete schools in Los Angeles and San Francisco to study the construction technique.[41]

Detail, **Robert E. Lee Grammar School**

Maple Lawn School
later Maple Lawn Elementary School
3120 Inwood Road, Dallas
Flint & Broad, architects
1932
Danna & Welch, architects
Norgaard & Shaw, contractors
1950, addition

ABOVE
Reliefs, **Maple Lawn School, 1932**

Relief, **Maple Lawn School, 1932**
Allie Tennant, sculptor

Reliefs, **Maple Lawn School, 1950**
Jose Martin, sculptor

The reliefs flanking the entrance to Maple Lawn's 1950 addition depict a group of girls learning "The Star Spangled Banner" and a group of boys studying geography.

Kilgore College Administration Building
1101 South Henderson Boulevard, Kilgore
Phelps & Dewees (San Antonio), architects
1936

North Side Senior High School
2211 McKinley Avenue, Fort Worth
Wiley G. Clarkson & Co., architects
Harry B. Friedman Co., contractors
1937

Clarkson's designer Charles O. Chromaster planned North Side Senior High School to take advantage of its location on a hilltop facing an open vista to the southwest. The Works Progress Administration supported an extensive landscaping project for the school grounds; the park-like area has been largely built over.[42]

RIGHT
Auditorium, **North Side Senior High School**

BELOW
Detail, **North Side Senior High School**

Fort Worth sculptor Evaline Sellors supervised the production of the cast-stone architectural ornaments for the school building.[43]

Rusk School
later Braly's Ace Hardware
420 West Palestine Avenue, Palestine
Theo. S. Maffitt, architect
Kraus Brothers, contractors
1938

Farrington Field
1501 University Drive, Fort Worth
Preston M. Geren, architect
1939

When planning began in 1937, the 18,500-seat athletic facility was called Fort Worth Public School Stadium; on completion it was dedicated as Farrington Field in memory of E. S. Farrington, long-time athletic director for Fort Worth's high schools. Two-thirds of the $240,000 cost was covered by the Works Progress Administration, which was also asked to provide labor and building materials. The Fort Worth Independent School District paid the remaining expenses with income from ticket sales to football games, track meets, and other sporting events. Designers A. George King and Everett L. Frazior were responsible for the stadium's modernistic look.[44]

Reliefs, **Farrington Field**
Evaline Sellors, sculptor

Dallas High School Athletic Field
later P. C. Cobb Stadium
demolished
Stadium Road, Dallas
Hoke Smith, architect
1939

Dallas celebrated the opening of its new public high school stadium on October 4, 1939, with what newspapers called a "monster football party": three ten-minute exhibition games featuring the six Dallas high schools followed by a demonstration by the schools' massed bands and pep squads, a group that totaled about a thousand members. The stadium, which seated 23,457, was designed to serve all of Dallas's public high schools; an adjacent field house contained locker rooms, offices, hospital facilities, and a gym with a seating capacity of three thousand. A grant from the Works Progress Administration covered about three-quarters of the complex's $800,000 construction cost.[45]

The stadium was commonly known as "Dal-Hi Stadium"; it was later named for P. C. Cobb, the athletic director of Dallas schools. The stadium and field house were demolished in 1981 to make way for the Infomart.[46]

Relief, **Dallas High School Athletic Field**

One of the stadium's most memorable features was a relief band depicting students engaged in various athletic activities. Fragments of the reliefs survive in city storage.[47]

J. W. Ray School
later J. W. Ray Elementary School
2211 Caddo Street, Dallas
Christensen & Christensen, architects
Morris-Quillin, contractors
1939

The new facility was originally to be called North Dallas Negro Elementary School. Before the school opened, the Board of Education renamed the campus in honor of J. W. Ray, the first principal of Dallas Negro High School (later Booker T. Washington High School).[48]

Detail, **J. W. Ray School**

Alex W. Spence Junior High School
later Alex W. Spence Middle School
4001 Capitol Avenue, Dallas
Mark Lemmon, architect
Nathan Wohlfeld, contractor
1940

The *Dallas Morning News* reported the new Spence Junior High was "as streamlined as the modern textbook," particularly noting the number and size of the windows, the extra-wide corridors with soundproofing material on the ceilings, and the special rooms for teaching metalworking, woodworking, art, and music. The school is named for a former president of the Dallas Board of Education.[49]

Detail, **Alex W. Spence Junior High School**

Auditorium entrance,
Alex W. Spence Junior High School

The Spence auditorium had a seating capacity of six hundred and a professional-quality movie projection booth. The band room, located above the auditorium's entrance, featured oak block floors and an acoustically treated ceiling.[50]

Stonewall Jackson School
later Stonewall Jackson Elementary School
5828 East Mockingbird Lane, Dallas
C.H. Griesenbeck and John B. Danna, architects
Russell J. Brydon, contractor
1939
Meers Construction Co., contractors
1952, second floor

Entrance, **Stonewall Jackson School**

Auditorium entrance, **Stonewall Jackson School**

Paris Junior College Administration Building
2400 Clarksville Street, Paris
Will H. Lightfoot, architect
1941

John Tyler High School Auditorium
later D. K. Caldwell Auditorium
301 South College Avenue, Tyler
T. Shirley Simons, architect
1941

Fraternal

Masonic Temple, Fort Worth
later The Masonic Center
1100 Henderson Street, Fort Worth
Wiley G. Clarkson & Co., architects
Harry B. Friedman, contractor
1932

In 1926, Fort Worth's Masonic lodges and orders agreed to pool their resources to build an impressive new Masonic temple. Construction was announced in May 1929, but groundbreaking did not take place until late 1930.[51]

Reliefs, **Masonic Temple, Fort Worth**

RIGHT
Entrance, **Masonic Temple, Fort Worth**

The Masonic Temple's doors are of Monel, an alloy of nickel and copper that resists corrosion. Reliefs depict the three ancient Masters of Masonry responsible for the construction of Solomon's Temple in Jerusalem. From left to right are King Hiram of Tyre, who secured the architect, craftsmen, and materials for the temple; King Solomon, who built the temple; and Hiram Abiff, the Phoenician architect who designed the temple.[52]

Masonic Temple, Dallas
507 South Harwood Street, Dallas
Flint & Broad, architects
Hal C. Dyer, contractor
1941

Nine local Masonic organizations came together in late 1939 to finance the forty-three-thousand-square-foot Dallas Masonic Temple, which contained recreation, dining and lodge rooms, offices, a library, and five-hundred-seat auditorium. Thomas Broad of Flint & Broad designed the building with an exterior of Cordova limestone; the entrance is framed in black granite over a staircase of white Missouri limestone. The Masons no longer own the building.[53]

Entrance, **Masonic Temple, Dallas**

Detail, **Masonic Temple, Dallas**

Danville Lodge No. 101
later Iglesia de Dios Pentecostes
919 Broadway Boulevard, Kilgore
Charles T. Freelove (Fort Worth), architect
Shaw & Estes (Fort Worth), contractors
1949

Masonic Temple, Longview
436 North Center Street, Longview
Charles T. Freelove (Fort Worth), architect
Milo J. Choate Construction Co. (Tyler), contractors
1950

When construction contracts were let in June 1949, the *Longview Daily News* noted that architect Charles T. Freelove had designed Masonic temples across the South.

Medical

Mother Frances Hospital
later CHRISTUS Mother Frances Hospital
800 East Dawson Street, Tyler
T. Shirley Simons, architect
Dolph-Bateson Construction Co. (Dallas), contractors
1937

The City of Tyler financed its new $300,000 municipal hospital with a bond issue supplemented by a grant from the federal Public Works Administration. Before the building was completed, local officials approached the Sisters of the Holy Family of Nazareth to operate the facility, which opened as Mother Frances Hospital in honor of Frances Siedliska (1842-1902), the order's founder.

Dedication ceremonies, scheduled for March 19, 1937, never took place. The hospital began accepting patients a day early, when a hundred students injured in the gas explosion that leveled the New London Consolidated School were brought to Tyler for treatment. (See "New London Cenotaph," p. 217.)[54]

The original building is still in service amid several large additions.

Rear entrance, **Mother Frances Hospital**

Harris Clinic
later Fifth Avenue Clinic
demolished
650 Fifth Avenue, Fort Worth
Joseph J. Patterson, architect
1938

Harris Clinic, built by prominent surgeon Dr. Charles H. Harris, was known for a variety of "firsts." It was one of Fort Worth's first specialty clinics, the first to offer all areas of outpatient care, the first to use electrocardiographs and oxygen tents, and the first to promote intravenous therapy.[55]

City-County Hospital, Fort Worth
later John Peter Smith Hospital
1500 South Main Street, Fort Worth
Wiley G. Clarkson & Co., architects
Gurley Construction Co., contractors
1939

The original E-shaped hospital building survives, though it is nearly completely obscured by later additions.

Camp Normal Industrial Hospital
506 West Methvin Street, Longview
Walter Brittain, contractor
1940

When it opened on March 15, 1940, this hospital was the only medical facility dedicated to serving African Americans in Gregg County. The Camps Normal Industrial Institute for Colored Youths was a vocational school located six miles west of Longview in the rural community of Camps. The boarding school opened in 1923 and had closed by 1930. The institute's Board of Directors reincorporated to form the Camp Normal Industrial Hospital and construct this building. No explanation could be found for the change from Camps (plural) Normal for the school to Camp (singular) Normal for the hospital.[56]

Detail, **Camp Normal Industrial Hospital**

Coats-Gafney Clinic
later People Attempting to Help (PATH)
402 West Front Street, Tyler
J. Hobart Plunkett, designer and builder
1941

Hurst Eye, Ear, Nose & Throat Clinic, 1940s
also known as Hurst Hospital
315 North Center Street, Longview
Zimmerman & Morgan, architects
Lawrence Birdsong, contractor
1941

Hurst Eye, Ear, Nose & Throat Clinic, 2016

Lenox Clinic
later Central Avenue Clinic, The Claunch Law Firm
301 West Central Avenue, Fort Worth
Consolidated Architects and Engineers, architects
1946

Architect Charles T. Freelove was the senior partner in Consolidated Architects and Engineers, which operated in the years following World War II. During this period, Freelove also designed buildings under his own name.

Memorial

Graham Memorial Auditorium
628 Third Street, Graham
Voelcker & Dixon (Wichita Falls), architects
H. J. Naylor (Wichita Falls), contractor
1929

Addie M. Graham, widow of one of the town's founding brothers, donated the site for the building. Her son, Malcolm, provided a gift of forty thousand dollars from the Graham Foundation that was matched by local residents to fund construction of the auditorium to honor those who served in World War I.[57]

Detail, **Memorial Auditorium, Graham**

Hillcrest Mausoleum
later Sparkman/Hillcrest Mausoleum
7405 West Northwest Highway, Dallas
Anton F. Korn, architect
Henger Construction Co., contractors
1937

West entrance, **Hillcrest Mausoleum**

New London Cenotaph
700 block of South Main Street
(State Highway 42), New London
Matchett Herring Coe (Beaumont), sculptor
Donald S. Nelson (Dallas), architect
1939

In the spring of 1937, a faulty connection allowed odorless gas to accumulate beneath the New London Consolidated School. At 3:05 p.m. on March 18, a spark triggered an explosion that destroyed the building and killed almost three hundred students and teachers. The disaster resulted in the passage of a state law requiring odorants be mixed in all natural gas for commercial and industrial use.[58]

Detail, **New London Cenotaph**

The sculptural block of Texas pink granite bears twelve life-sized figures of students bringing gifts and handing in homework to two teachers.

Crown Hill Mausoleum
9700 Webb Chapel Road, Dallas
B. Gaylord Noftsger (Oklahoma City), architect
1940

Detail, **Crown Hill Mausoleum**

Ecclesiastical

Riverside Evangelistic Temple
later Fort Worth Harvest Church
620 North Chandler Drive, Fort Worth
Aleck B. Withers, architect
1939

Members of the Riverside congregation donated much of the labor and materials to construct the sanctuary. The adjacent Education Building was completed in 1941.[59]

Detail, **Riverside Evangelistic Temple**

Education Building, **Riverside Evangelistic Temple**

Gaston Avenue Baptist Church Educational Building
later Criswell College
4000 block of Gaston Avenue, Dallas
Mark Lemmon, architect
H. L. McBride, contractor
1940

Detail, **Gaston Avenue Baptist Church Educational Building**

RIGHT
Gaston Avenue Baptist Church Auditorium
Mark Lemmon, architect
1950

When ground was broken in 1939, the $115,000 educational building was intended to be the first project in a four-year, $400,000 construction program culminating in the construction of a new auditorium for Gaston Avenue Baptist Church.[60]

Ground was eventually broken on the two-thousand-seat auditorium in 1947. The estimated cost was $600,000, but the postwar building boom drove up the price of construction materials. By the time the facility was dedicated in 1950, the cost had risen to more than a million dollars. The exterior is sheathed in Austin stone; the interior features Italian marble and an aluminum balustrade.[61]

The property became the campus of Criswell College after the church relocated to suburban Dallas.

Detail, **Gaston Avenue Baptist Church Auditorium**

Calvary Baptist Church
later Iglesia Nueva Vida
104 West Bow Street, Tyler
T. Shirley Simons, architect
1946

Only the ground floor of the church had been completed when the United States entered World War II; construction resumed after the government lifted wartime restrictions on the use of building materials.[62]

The Gospel Lighthouse
later Vision Regeneration
1914 South Ewing Avenue, Dallas
Christensen & Christensen, architects
1950

Jordan Carl Hibbard, founder and pastor of this non-denominational church, told the *Dallas Morning News* he saw the two-thousand-seat sanctuary in a vision and worked with the architects to design a lighthouse "beckoning sinners to safety." The round building is clad in Austin Cordova Cream and shell limestone and is topped by a thirty-foot tower that was originally covered in blue, white, and rose-colored neon.[63]

OPPOSITE

Residence for Mr. & Mrs. Charles M. Davis
2055 Ward Parkway, Fort Worth
Robert P. Woltz Jr. and Phillip G. Willard, architects
Charles M. Davis, contractor
1937

Efficiency Home
1010 West Devitt Street, Fort Worth
Charles M. Davis and Zoe Davis, designers
Charles M. Davis, contractor
1935

CHAPTER 7
RESIDENTIAL

"Your new home should be lovely and livable—safe against the attacks of fire and storm, of termites and decay. And, it can be!"

Advertisement for Worthcrete Structural Wall Tile
in the *Fort Worth Star-Telegram*
March 27, 1938

NO ONE HAD TO SELL CHARLES M. DAVIS on using Worthcrete structural tile to build his new home because the Fort Worth civil engineer was already a proponent of using cement and concrete products to construct comfortable, affordable houses. In fact, Davis and his daughter Zoe had designed and built small homes of tile block and stucco in neighborhoods around Texas Christian University to demonstrate the benefits of masonry residential designs.

Charles Davis gained his expertise in concrete construction through on-the-job training with the Texas and Pacific Railway and the US Reclamation Service and while working on major projects such as the Galveston Seawall and Houston Ship Channel. Zoe Davis earned a fine arts degree and trained as a painter, but she had aspirations to become an architect. Idled during the Great Depression, the Davises experimented with concrete home design and construction. Their work was widely publicized by the Fort Worth Concrete Tile Company (later Chase Building Products, Incorporated), the manufacturer of the materials used in the Davis houses.[1]

Although Charles Davis did pioneering work with poured concrete, his houses were constructed of Worthcrete brand structural tile, a hollow tile block that resembled a small cinder block. Plaster and stucco were applied directly to the scored faces of the tile blocks to provide smooth interior and exterior wall surfaces. Davis insulated the hollow tile walls and promoted the ventilated homes for their year-round comfort, fire safety, and low upkeep.[2]

The father-daughter team's first effort was a small house at 1010 West Devitt Street built as a rental unit in the backyard of an existing home. A rather ungainly building, it nonetheless featured classic Art Moderne elements, including a flat roof, asymmetrical facade, streamlining, casement windows, and horizontal banding. These elements would be repeated and refined in most of the subsequent Davis homes.[3]

The Davises then designed and built houses at 3240 and 3241 Waits Avenue and 2945 Lubbock Avenue, although the Lubbock Avenue

1010

Apartment Home
3241 Waits Avenue, Fort Worth
Charles M. Davis and Zoe Davis, designers
Charles M. Davis, contractor
1935

Apartment Home
3240 Waits Avenue, Fort Worth
Charles M. Davis and Zoe Davis, designers
Charles M. Davis, contractor
1936

Portland Cement House
Fair Park, Dallas
Harold "Bubi" Jessen (Austin), architect
Charles M. Davis (Fort Worth), contractor
1936

house was later significantly altered. These homes were larger than the West Devitt house and stood on their own lots. At some point the houses were dubbed "Aparthomes," although the *Fort Worth Star-Telegram* referred to the West Devitt building as an "efficiency home" and the house at 3241 Waits as an "apartment home." Charles Davis advertised the properties as having an "efficiency arrangement."[4]

The Davis family's nine-room house on Ward Parkway was definitely not an Aparthome. The four-bedroom, two-bath house was built with an artist's studio, two-car garage, and terraces accessible by a freestanding, circular staircase of concrete and steel. As in the other Davis projects, the house was built using Worthcrete structural tile. The architects for the Davis home were employed by Worthcrete's manufacturer to design demonstration houses using the company's products.[5]

The Davises also attracted attention and support from the Portland Cement Association, which actively promoted the use of cement and concrete in residential construction. In 1935, the organization held a contest to design the Portland Cement House as one of four Centennial Model Homes to be built for the 1936 Texas Centennial Exposition in Dallas. The winner, Austin architect Harold "Bubi" Jessen, created a more traditional design than the typically modernistic masonry houses. Charles Davis served as the contractor for the Portland Cement House at Fair Park.[6]

The Contemporary House, another Centennial Model Home, bore a strong resemblance to the larger modernistic homes built in affluent neighborhoods during and after the fair. Designed by prominent Dallas architects DeWitt & Washburn, the air-conditioned home had three bedrooms, each with its own bath. The Contemporary House was the subject of a great deal of publicity and was featured in newspapers across the state. Although it is not possible to prove a definite connection between the

Rendering, **Portland Cement House**

model homes and private development, many of the modernistic masonry houses in Dallas and Fort Worth were constructed in 1937, the year after the Portland Cement House and the Contemporary House opened to the public.[7]

Art Deco and Art Moderne houses were never common in the United States, where traditional residential styles dominated, but both Dallas and Fort Worth possess sizable collections of modernistic homes. The Dallas houses are usually found in such affluent suburbs as Lakewood and the Park Cities. In Fort Worth, Moderne design made its way into middle-class neighborhoods, thanks in large measure to Charles Davis and Zoe Davis.

Two impressive modernistic country houses were also built in the region: the Kennady House on Eagle Mountain Lake outside Fort Worth and the Crim House on the outskirts of Kilgore. The style found its way to smaller cities and towns as well. In Tyler, designer and builder J. Hobart Plunkett created unique Moderne houses in traditional residential neighborhoods, and brothers Everett and Hilton Shepherd built an early modernistic house of their own design in Denton.

Shepherd Residence
demolished
312 Marietta Street, Denton
Everett M. Shepherd and Hilton D. Shepherd, designers and builders
1935

To avoid the cost of financing a home for themselves and their mother, brothers Everett and Hilton Shepherd designed and largely built this two-story, six-room house as well as most of its fixtures and furnishings, even though neither had experience in architecture or construction. This tax-office photo shows the house several years after it was completed.

Bricklayers built the home's shell of hollow tile and a carpenter constructed the floor and ceiling joists, but the brothers did the rest of the work over a two-year period, buying building materials on a pay-as-you-go basis. The Shepherds insulated the ceiling with a two-inch layer of packed cottonseed hulls and made use of salvaged items, including a car seat refashioned as a divan based on one they had seen pictured in a magazine. An estimated crowd of 750 toured the house when it was opened to the public in 1935.[8]

Contemporary House
demolished
Fair Park, Dallas
DeWitt & Washburn, architects
1936

The Contemporary House at Fair Park was promoted as "the ultimate ideal home for the Southwest." Although clearly designed for the affluent, the three-bedroom, three-bath model home included some features that would become standard in post-World War II suburbia: central air conditioning, sliding closet doors, a patio, an attached garage, and "a noticeable absence of moldings and cornices."[9]

The Contemporary House was donated to the Dallas Council of Girl Scouts in 1938 and hosted events and activities as the Girl Scout Little House until 1949. The house was subsequently demolished.[10]

House for the Mayflower Investment Co.
6851 Gaston Avenue, Dallas
Reynolds Fisher, architect
1936

Local tradition holds that this is the Contemporary House built for the 1936 Texas Centennial Exposition and that the house was moved from Fair Park to Gaston Avenue after the Centennial celebration ended. Although the structures look somewhat similar, Mayflower Investment Company built this house on this site the same year the exposition was held; the Contemporary House was never moved from Fair Park and has been demolished.[11]

Mayflower Investment Company was an important developer in Dallas from the firm's incorporation in 1936 through the 1970s. Mayflower was a wholly owned subsidiary of Fidelity Union Life Insurance Company (later Allianz Life Insurance Company of North America), which also owned Fidelity Union Abstract & Title Company.

Residence for
Mr. & Mrs. Marshall H. Kennady
Boat Club Road, Fort Worth
Patterson & Teague, architects
A. C. Luther, contractor
c. 1935

A profile of Marshall H. Kennady (1892-1967) noted that the prominent insurance executive's chief hobby was developing his country estate on Eagle Mountain Lake, a newly completed reservoir northwest of Fort Worth.[12]

When visitors made the twenty-mile drive from the city to the Kennady house, they were confronted with an austere yet impressive entry. The flanking doors with wide portholes made the house much less intimidating by reminding guests of the boating, swimming, and barbecues that took place along the lakefront.

Lakeside facade, **Residence for Mr. & Mrs. Marshall H. Kennady**

Boaters had a more welcoming view of the house, which was built on a bluff above the lake. Each of the home's five bedrooms had its own balcony with water views. The Kennady family moved to the lake house permanently by 1936 and entertained frequently, securing the property a year-round place on the Fort Worth social calendar.

Residence for Mr. & Mrs. Roy Lee
1203 South College Avenue, Tyler
J. Hobart Plunkett, designer and builder
1936

The Lees sold their home soon after it was built, and the property is known locally as the Saleh house after a subsequent owner. Simon Saleh (1872-1948) was born in Baabdat, Lebanon, then a part of Greater Syria within the Ottoman Empire. He owned Simon's Candy Company, a wholesaler of candy, tobacco, and drugs. The original casement windows on this house were removed after this photo was taken.

House for the Fidelity Union Life Insurance Co.
5203 Pershing Street, Dallas
Luther E. Sadler, architect (attributed)
Luther E. Sadler, contractor
1936

Fidelity Union Life Insurance Company was the parent company of the Mayflower Investment Company, an important Dallas development firm that built several houses in the 5100 and 5200 blocks of Pershing Street in Cochran Heights beginning in 1935.

The building permit for 5203 Pershing lists Luther E. Sadler as the general contractor. Sadler often served as contractor for houses he designed. In some cases, Sadler also marketed the homes, as he did for the traditional houses he planned, built, and sold at 5122 and 5202 Pershing Street in 1935.[13]

House for Rodger W. Thompson
5103 Pershing Street, Dallas
Luther E. Sadler, architect (attributed)
Luther E. Sadler, contractor
1936

The building permit and construction contract for 5103 Pershing name Rodger W. Thompson as the owner of the property, but he is not listed in city directories as the home's occupant. The house was advertised in the *Dallas Morning News* as being ultramodern, attractively furnished, and available for rent for $75 a month; by 1951, the rent had increased to $125 per month.[14]

House for the Mayflower Investment Co.
5102 Pershing Street, Dallas
1937

M. M. Herring, an officer of the Mayflower Investment Company, awarded the day labor contract for 5102 Pershing in February 1937.[15]

House at 4593 Belfort Place
Highland Park
Luther E. Sadler, architect
1937

House for the Flippen-Prather Realty Co.
4637 Mockingbird Lane, Highland Park
John Astin Perkins, architect
1937

Flippen-Prather Realty began marketing 4637 Mockingbird Lane at the end of January 1937. The two-story residence was built of steel and concrete and contained three bedrooms and two bathrooms. When the house did not sell, the firm began promoting the property as the "House of Today."[16]

For two years, the home was regularly opened to the public without attracting a buyer. In May 1938, the house was shown for inspection with furniture and interior design by the Sanger Brothers department store. Finally, in March 1939, Mr. & Mrs. C. M. Joiner purchased the furnished home for twenty thousand dollars.[17]

Columbus Marion "Dad" Joiner was the wildcatter who discovered the great East Texas Oil Field when his well, Daisy Bradford No. 3, came in on October 3, 1930. As the "father" of the world's largest oil field to that time, he was nicknamed "Dad."[18]

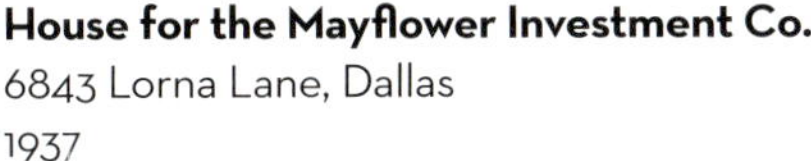

House for the Mayflower Investment Co.
6843 Lorna Lane, Dallas
1937

Residence for Mrs. Nellie Morris
4601 Mockingbird Lane, Highland Park
Mrs. Nellie Morris, contractor
1937

Mrs. Morris (1886-1968), a local author and clubwoman, served as her own contractor when she began construction of this home in November 1936.[19]

House at 3017 Simondale Drive
Bellaire Addition, Fort Worth
Edward L. Wilson, architect
1937

It is not clear whether Edward L. Wilson designed this home for his family or built it as a speculative house and could not sell it. City directories and the *Fort Worth Star-Telegram* indicate that the Wilsons were the first owners and occupants of this house before offering the property for sale in 1941.[20]

House at 3021 Simondale Drive
Bellaire Addition, Fort Worth
Edward L. Wilson, architect
1937

Residence for Mr. & Mrs. Arch R. Shinder
4401 Beverly Drive, Highland Park
Reynolds Fisher, architect
1937

Residence for Mr. & Mrs. Harry Allsman, 1938
1901 South Chilton Avenue, Tyler
J. Hobart Plunkett, designer and builder
1937

This photo of the Allsman House was featured in an advertisement for Insulux Glass Block in the February 1938 issue of *House & Garden* magazine. The home has been significantly altered since then.

Residence for Mr. & Mrs. Harry Allsman, 2016

Residence for Mr. & Mrs. Eugene Sanger
3216 Jacotte Circle, Dallas
Howard R. Meyer, architect
1937

Entry, **Residence for Mr. & Mrs. Eugene Sanger**

The Highlander
later Park Plaza Condominiums
4217 Lomo Alto Drive, Highland Park
Luther E. Sadler, architect
1938

When it opened as residential hotel, this building contained forty-six air-conditioned units, including ten “bachelor apartments” composed of a bedroom and bath. Each family apartment had a living room, dining room, one or two bedrooms, a kitchen, and one or two baths. Residents could have their meals in the main dining room or delivered to their apartments. Other hotel features included a lounge, roof garden, tennis court, and service by bellhops, parking attendants, maids, and janitors. The Highlander was eventually converted into a traditional apartment building, and it later became condominiums.

The building has been significantly altered and expanded; almost none of its original architecture is visible today.[21]

Westinghouse Tomorrow’s Home Today

1302 Cedar Hill Avenue, Dallas
C. D. Havens, designer
1938

C. D. Havens, district sales promotion manager for the Westinghouse Electric Supply Company, is credited with designing this house and was its first owner. The home was built by Westinghouse in cooperation with the Portland Cement Association and was initially open to the public. The home was air conditioned and had a fully electric kitchen, as well as an electric laundry and water heater and a radio-controlled electric garage door opener.[22]

Residence for Mr. & Mrs. Liggett N. Crim
2023 South Henderson Boulevard, Kilgore
Llewellyn W. Pitts (Beaumont), architect (attributed)
1939

The Crims became some of the earliest beneficiaries of the East Texas oil boom when an exploratory well, the Lou Della Crim No. 1, blew in on the family farm outside Kilgore on December 28, 1930. The *New York Times* reported that an unnamed oil company had immediately purchased the lease on the well and the surrounding 1,440 acres for $2.1 million. Liggett N. Crim was one of Lou Della Crim's sons.[23]

Local historians state that this house was designed by a Beaumont architect. At the time the house was built, Llewellyn W. Pitts of Beaumont was designing the Crim Theater in downtown Kilgore (see page 147) for Liggett N. Crim.[24]

Residence for Mr. & Mrs. Liggett N. Crim

Residence for Mr. & Mrs. B. J. Hoopingarner
demolished
4512 Potomac Avenue, University Park
Luther E. Sadler, architect
1939

Luther E. Sadler's design was noted for its use of a breakfast bar with "restaurant-like stools" instead of a breakfast nook. Indirect lighting was installed between the rows of glass brick in the curved corner of the living room, which also featured a curved sectional sofa. A lighted staircase was set into the back wall of the living room to create a shadow-box effect.[25]

Residence for Mr. & Mrs. R. H. McLean
443 Allison Drive, Dallas
Maurice Peterman, architect
1939

Emil A. Fretz Jr. was the home's designer with Peterman. The house has seen some sympathetic additions, including most of its second floor.

CHAPTER 8

CENTENNIAL

Detail, **Trail Drivers Memorial Tower, Will Rogers Memorial Center**

"You'd think Dallas had invented Texas just because they bid higher for the Centennial than any other city. But we're going to put on a show of our own and teach those dudes over there where the West really *begins!"*

Amon G. Carter
in the *March of Time* newsreel
Battle of a Centennial
June 1936

OPPOSITE
Will Rogers Memorial Center
3401 West Lancaster Avenue, Fort Worth
Wyatt C. Hedrick, Inc., and Elmer G. Withers Architectural Co., architects
Butcher & Sweeney Construction Co., R. F. Ball Construction Co., and James T. Taylor Construction Co., contractors
1936

THE TIRADE FROM AMON CARTER, DELIVERED in a newsreel that was released coast to coast days after Dallas opened its Texas Centennial Exposition, was typical of the newspaper publisher and tireless Fort Worth promoter's bravado. Carter had driven plans for a large-scale livestock show in Fort Worth to celebrate the one hundredth anniversary of Texas independence from Mexico, arranging for the city to build a new fairgrounds to host it. And when concerns emerged that the entertainment offered in Fort Worth might pale in comparison to the dance orchestras, lavish historical pageant, and "leg shows" at the Dallas fair, Carter brought in Broadway producer and impresario Billy Rose to take the reins.[1]

Rose, working for the exorbitant salary of a thousand dollars a day, promised Fort Worth a true extravaganza. He envisioned a cavalcade of movie stars, endless chorus lines, a three-ring circus, a swimming pool the size of a city block, and, in his words, "a Texas pageant to be called 'The Fall of the Alamo,' 'The Battle of San Jacinto' or some other Texas name." Most important, Rose vowed to one-up Dallas at every opportunity. "I plan to drive Dallas nuts," he told reporters. "Every time Dallas says something about its exposition, I'll give 'em Shirley Temple." Later, Rose coined the slogan that appeared in some form on eleven thousand billboards across nine states: "For education, go to Dallas; for entertainment, come to Fort Worth." (Dallas itself wasn't immune from the marketing blitz. Directly across from the entrance to Fair Park, where the Texas Centennial Exposition was being held, a three-story neon sign flashed a constant reminder that there was "Wild & Whoo-pee, 45 Minutes West.")[2]

Many of Rose's announcements were simply headline fodder, but he did make a splash in Fort Worth. Rose moved his circus-themed Broadway musical *Jumbo* lock, stock, and barrel to the Frontier Centennial and built a replica frontier city that doubled as a midway, an arena for a rodeo and wild-west show, and a vast dance hall. The centerpiece of the exposition was a 4,500-seat outdoor dinner theater called Casa Mañana, where an elaborate nightly revue presented scenes inspired by past world's fairs on a 130-foot revolving stage. Among the show's

"Whoo-pee" Sign
demolished
First and Parry Avenues, Dallas
Corn Signs, Inc. (Fort Worth), builders
1936

headliners was Sally Rand, who became the toast of the 1933 Century of Progress Exposition in Chicago when she (barely) concealed her nude figure with skillfully deployed ostrich plumes in the "fan dance." Rand also starred in the Frontier Centennial's Nude Ranch, a midway attraction where, according to the *Fort Worth Star-Telegram*, "Sally . . . and a dozen fair damsels clad in little more than lariat ropes or bows and arrows will amuse themselves with sunbathing and outdoor sports."[3]

Billy Rose's portion of the Texas Frontier Centennial, including Casa Mañana, the frontier midway, and the Nude Ranch, no longer exist, but the Will Rogers Memorial Center, the auditorium and coliseum complex that the city built just north of the fairgrounds, does. The complex, another of Fort Worth's centennial projects, was designed by the architectural firms of Wyatt C. Hedrick and Elmer G. Withers and named for the extremely popular actor-cowboy-humorist who died in an airplane crash in August 1935.[4]

The Will Rogers Center was the culmination of a couple of Fort Worth's civic goals. One was construction of a municipal auditorium, which local leaders had been planning since the late 1920s. The other was a push to build new facilities for the annual Southwestern Exposition and Fat Stock Show. The discussion of where to locate those facilities opened a rift between Fort Worthers who wanted to keep the stock show at its traditional site around the Stockyards on the city's North Side and those who wanted to build a completely new complex on bare land in the Arlington Heights area west of downtown. Those who favored the old site pointed to its convenience and tradition, but officials argued that it was in a crowded and rather unsavory neighborhood. The new site, on the other hand, offered room for expansion and a view of Fort Worth's growing skyline. In the end, a compromise was made: a cattle exhibit building would be built at the Stockyards, with the remainder of the complex in Arlington Heights.[5]

The architects designed the Will Rogers coliseum, auditorium, and tower in the restrained PWA Deco style, the kind of architecture typically found on federally funded public buildings of the later 1930s—an appropriate choice considering that the complex was partly financed through the Public Works Administration. Ornamentation was kept to a minimum, a deci-

Trail Drivers Memorial Tower, Will Rogers Memorial Center
later Will Rogers Memorial Tower, Pioneer Tower

The 208-foot Pioneer Tower, variously called the Trail Drivers Memorial Tower and the Will Rogers Memorial Tower in its early days, visually breaks the long, low facades of the flanking auditorium and coliseum and serves as a landmark in Fort Worth's Cultural District. Each side of the structure originally featured six-foot-wide, eighty-foot-high panels of backlit glass block. The lighting continued through at least the 1950s. Later, maintenance concerns led to the glass-block panels being covered with metal louvers.[6]

RIGHT
Rotunda, **Trail Drivers Memorial Tower**

A ground-floor rotunda inside the tower contains Fort Worth sculptor Joseph Eddy Lipe's 1942 bust of Will Rogers and four cast-aluminum plaques bearing quotations from Republic of Texas President Mirabeau B. Lamar, Texas Governor Lawrence Sullivan "Sul" Ross, lawyer and judge Britain R. Webb, and the Texas Constitution. The rotunda is the only public space in the tower.[7]

Grille detail, **Trail Drivers Memorial Tower**

Coliseum, Will Rogers Memorial Center

The Will Rogers coliseum and auditorium share identically composed facades, but the structures behind them are drastically different. The coliseum, the larger of the two, centers on a 125-by-250-foot arena and was designed with a seating capacity of 6,161.[8]

The coliseum is most notable for its innovative domed roof, the work of self-educated engineer Herbert McDonald Hinckley (1897-1938). Hinckley remembered being frustrated by an obstructed view at a boxing match, so he determined to design the Will Rogers coliseum with no interior columns. Massive arched steel trusses spanned most of the space, but there was concern about the expansion and contraction of parts of the roof in the North Texas heat, particularly the curved sections at either end of the building. Hinckley's revolutionary solution involved pinned flexible joints that allowed different segments of the roof to move independently as they heated and cooled. Architect Wyatt Hedrick thought the design was too risky, and several experts agreed, but Hinckley persuaded Hedrick to move ahead with construction. In the end, the roof functioned exactly as Hinckley had said it would. "When the design was completed, Herbert had overlooked nothing, from the smallest rivet to the huge curved steel beam," his son later wrote.[9]

Hinckley only designed one other domed roof, for a coliseum at Louisiana State University in Baton Rouge, before he died of a heart attack in 1938 (his family said the attack was brought on by the stress of working on the Will Rogers design). However, the techniques Hinckley developed for the Will Rogers roof were the basis for all other large domed steel roofs that followed, including those on the Astrodome in Houston and the Superdome in New Orleans.[10]

sion that was partly stylistic and partly financial. Rather than defining itself with intricate details, the complex, which stretches eleven hundred feet along West Lancaster Avenue, makes an impact with simple lines and sheer size.

Although the Texas Centennial Exposition grounds in Dallas were far more extensive and costly, simplicity was the byword there as well, largely because sixty percent of the exposition's buildings were intended to be used for years to come by the State Fair of Texas. "For this reason, we have held down the experimental aspect of things more than we would have done if the structures were to be used but a season," George Dahl, the exposition's chief architect, explained.[11]

Dahl and his team of architects laid out Fair Park's principal buildings along expansive esplanades, designing the massive exhibit halls with blank, buff-colored walls and very little ornamentation. The buildings tended to serve as backdrops for monumental reliefs, murals, and sculptures executed by an array of artists who were experienced in decorating world's fairs. Certain privately constructed buildings, such as Albert Kahn's exhibit hall for the Ford Motor Company and the William Lescaze-designed Magnolia Lounge, made their own architectural statements, but even they had to be approved by Dahl's group—a rare level of control in exposition design. "From the largest towering building to the smallest hot dog or peanut stand . . . all physical details have been subject to the approval or rejection of the architect in charge," the *Dallas Morning News* noted.[12]

North Texas is fortunate to have its two large-scale centennial complexes extant and in use. The Will Rogers Memorial complex is a vital part of Fort Worth, hosting what has come to be known as the Fort Worth Stock Show and Rodeo and countless other events. And in Dallas, Fair Park's modernistic buildings, the largest surviving collection of 1930s Exposition architecture, are

Auditorium, Will Rogers Memorial Center

Construction of a new municipal auditorium and convention facility was among the goals Fort Worth's business leaders included in their Five-Year Work Program, a blueprint for the city's development drawn up in the late 1920s. The Will Rogers Memorial Auditorium, which seated 2,994 and included exhibit and meeting rooms, finally fulfilled that objective nearly a decade later. In her book *Cowtown Moderne*, Judith Singer Cohen attributes the auditorium's restrained Moderne interiors to Donald S. Nelson, who worked as chief designer for the Elmer G. Withers Architectural Company at the same time he was assisting George Dahl with the design of the Texas Centennial Exposition grounds at Fair Park in Dallas.[13]

The auditorium was the last part of the Will Rogers complex to open to the public in late 1936. The buildings were officially declared complete after the architects conducted a final inspection in January 1937.[14]

Detail, **Auditorium**

Detail, **Auditorium**

Details, tile murals,
Will Rogers Memorial Center

A pair of tile murals, each ten feet high and two hundred feet long, adorns the facades of the coliseum and auditorium. The murals depict historical and cultural scenes from Texas and the Southwest, including Spanish settlement, railroad expansion, and the building of modern cities, all formed from glazed nine-inch-square tiles.[15]

According to the *Dallas Morning News*, subjects for the murals were suggested by William J. Hammond, a Texas Christian University history professor who later served as Fort Worth mayor, assisted by TCU art professor Samuel Ziegler and Fort Worth artists. The murals were designed by Kenneth Gale, director of design at the Mosaic Tile Company of Zanesville, Ohio, working with an assistant, Byron Shrider. Workers at Mosaic Tile used full-sized patterns to paint each tile by hand.[16]

Ticket pavilion,
Will Rogers Memorial Center

A pair of ticket pavilions using the same materials and decorative elements as the coliseum and auditorium were built as part of the initial construction of the Will Rogers complex. The pavilions anchor each end of a run of modernistic steel fencing that encloses an expansive forecourt. Large gates at the center of the forecourt, which originally admitted throngs of visitors as well as horses, have been replaced with a ticket office and visitor center building.[17]

the home of the Texas state fair as well as a year-round collection of museums and event spaces.

Although both sites attract those who appreciate Art Deco and classic fairs, the events and buildings of the Texas Centennial remain largely unknown outside the Lone Star State—and it seems that has long been the case. In 1940, *Dallas Morning News* writer John Rosenfield had a strong sense of déjà vu as he strolled the modernistic grounds of the Golden Gate International Exposition in San Francisco, which he thought bore a strong resemblance to Fair Park. "We told more than one San Franciscan of this fact, and how could we help it?" he wrote. "But again we were confronted by a sheerness of indifference and incredulity. As if a dot on the map called Dallas could have staged a world's fair."

Rosenfield even encountered Sally Rand staging a Nude Ranch in San Francisco, four years after the attraction made its debut in Fort Worth. "We knew what this was like in 1936, [but] we didn't bother to explain about the Fort Worth fair," he sighed. "This time, we just saved our breath."[18]

The modernistic buildings of the Will Rogers center are covered in this chapter, as are certain structures and artworks from the Texas Centennial Exposition. For more on Fair Park's buildings and art, see Willis Cecil Winters's 2010 book *Fair Park* and our own *Fair Park Deco: Art and Architecture of the Texas Centennial Exposition*, published in 2012.

Ticket office and visitor center, Will Rogers Memorial Center
Hahnfeld Hoffer Stanford, architects
1999

Fort Worth architects Hahnfeld Hoffer Stanford designed a new ticket office and visitor center using a style and materials that complement the 1936 structures. The horse-and-rider figure inlaid in the pavement in front of the ticket office is based on an unexecuted terrazzo pattern that Wyatt Hedrick's chief designer, Herman P. Koeppe, prepared for the lobby of the coliseum.[19]

Cattle Exhibit Building
later Globe Aircraft Corp., Billy Bob's Texas
2520 Rodeo Plaza, Fort Worth
Wyatt C. Hedrick, Inc., and Elmer G. Withers Architectural Co., architects
Thomas S. Byrne, Inc., contractors
1936

The Cattle Exhibit Building was the only centennial livestock project built in the Stockyards area on Fort Worth's North Side. The structure, with a facade that stretched 570 feet, housed cattle pens, an arena and auction room, and 1,257 animal stalls in more than three acres of floor space. Newspaper accounts indicate that a section of the building was demolished in the late 1940s.[20]

The Southwestern Exposition and Fat Stock Show announced plans to move to the Will Rogers Memorial Center in 1943. Shortly afterward, this building was occupied by the Globe Aircraft Corporation, which had expanded its operations to produce twin-engine Beechcraft AT-10 training planes for the world war. A department store moved in later, and then the building sat vacant for some time before reopening in 1981 as Billy Bob's Texas, which bills itself as "the world's largest honky tonk."[21]

Fair Park

ABOVE
Aerial view of **Fair Park**, 1936

Fort Worth's Frontier Centennial was sensational, but the main celebration of Texas's one hundredth birthday was organized by, in Amon Carter's words, the "dudes" in Dallas.

State officials had developed the idea for the Texas Centennial Exposition as part of their plans for a statewide centennial commemoration. Projects were to be carried out in all of Texas's 254 counties, with a large-scale central exposition going to the city that could provide the largest financial pledge and commit at least two hundred acres of land for the exposition grounds. Dallas, Houston, and San Antonio submitted bids, and Dallas came out on top with a pledge of $7.8 million, which included the use of the city-owned state fairgrounds at Fair Park. (The eventual price tag for the exposition, including state and federal allocations and private investment, was around $25 million.)[22]

The selection galled residents of San Antonio and Houston, which felt that their historical pedigrees should count for something. San Antonio was home to the Alamo, and Houston was a short drive from the San Jacinto Battleground, where Texas won its independence, whereas Dallas had not even existed at the time of the Texas Revolution. Dallasites came up with a rather convoluted response, suggesting that theirs was the kind of city the freedom fighters of a hundred years before had *wanted* to establish. "Dallas, a community

Esplanade of State, Fair Park

Fair Park's principal esplanade, stretching a thousand feet from the entrance court to the State of Texas Building, was one of the most dramatic spaces of the Centennial Exposition. Flanked by the fair's two largest exhibit halls, with the State of Texas Building as a visual terminus, the esplanade drew comparisons to an ancient Egyptian or Babylonian temple approach. Its scale, symmetry, and color were designed to draw visitors into the exposition grounds, creating a sense of awe and wonder as they went.

As splendid as it was during the day, the esplanade was truly magical by night, when concealed lighting turned it into a riot of color. Floodlights trained on the exhibit halls cycled through the spectrum, while the reflecting basin running along the esplanade's center was lit in gold and green. Behind the State of Texas Building, a group of twenty-four colored searchlights shot into the skies over Dallas, creating a dramatic effect visible for miles. "It is the nearest approach man ever has made to a gorgeous Texas sunset," one exposition visitor said. Unfortunately, no color photographs of the esplanade at night are known to exist.[23]

The esplanade light show, and lighting across the exposition grounds, were the work of General Electric Corporation lighting engineer C. M. Cutler.[24]

OPPOSITE
Esplanade of State, 1936

of typically Texanic Texans, is representative of the Texas that the fathers had thought to build," the *Dallas Morning News*'s Harry Benge Crozier wrote.[25]

Once Dallas secured the exposition, the task of creating a setting for it fell to architect George Dahl and his group of designers and engineers, known as the Exposition Technical Staff. Their job was to completely overhaul Fair Park's 183 acres, demolishing some existing buildings, totally remodeling others, and building more than fifty from the ground up. In addition, Dahl's team was responsible for laying streets and sidewalks within the exposition grounds, running new utility lines, and installing landscaping, all in the amazingly tight timeframe of nine and a half months.[26]

The finished product, dubbed the "Magic City," wowed Texans when its gates swung open on June 6, 1936. Masses of visitors poured into Fair Park that day, strolling the landscaped esplanades, crowding the Midway and marveling at the displays in the vast exhibit halls, which ran the gamut from bug zappers to television. That night, an airplane trailing a four-hundred-foot tail of fire made a power dive toward the heart of Fair Park, triggering a wave of light that washed over the exposition grounds and turned the Magic City into a fairyland. As popular as other aspects of the fair were, most visitors said the nightly light show was their favorite attraction. "As the Chicago Exposition will be best remembered for its modern architecture and San Diego for the luxuriance of its landscaping, so the Centennial Exposition at Dallas will live long in the memory of its visitors for the sheer beauty of its illumination," architect Ralph Bryan predicted.[27]

Since the lights were extinguished for the last time in late November 1936, the exposition has proven to have a more enduring impact than even its most ardent promoters would have predicted. In the gloom of the Depression, it

Portico of Texas, Esplanade of State

Six porticoes break up the long facades of the Hall of Transportation (later the Centennial Building) and the Hall of Varied Industries, Communications, and Electricity (later the Automobile Building)—the exhibit halls that flank the Esplanade of State. Each portico features a twenty-foot cast-stone statue representing one of the six nations whose flags have flown over Texas. Lawrence Tenney Stevens sculpted three of the figures, including Texas, pictured here; Raoul Josset was responsible for the other three.[28]

The Centennial Exposition's signature architectural style, which stressed simplicity and geometry, is evident in the porticoes. George Dahl said the design was meant to suggest the Spanish Colonial style as well as that of other countries with climates similar to the Lone Star State's. "The hundred years of Texas that we are celebrating has an individuality that developed from many threads of tradition," he noted.[29]

The exposition's main exhibit buildings were painted a uniform buff color that Dahl said was selected to best complement the Texas sunlight. Bright color was used in painted frieze bands, polychrome reliefs, murals, and richly tinted architectural features including building entrances and the ceilings of porticoes and loggias—"where it counts," Dahl said.[30]

established Dallas's image as a busy, modern, forward-looking city—an impression local leaders happily cultivated in the years that followed. And decades later, Fair Park's surviving centennial buildings and artwork have taken on national and international significance as prime examples of 1930s exposition design. "The Centennial still ranks as the greatest public relations coup in a city that has routinely equated self-promotion with salvation," architecture critic David Dillon wrote. "It is also Dallas's finest example of monumental civic planning."[31]

In the end, the Texas Centennial Exposition lost money. Most expositions did. But as banker R. L. Thornton, the fair's chief backer and promoter, told his investors: "It's the best loss you ever made."[32]

Unless otherwise noted, the Fair Park buildings in this chapter were designed by the Exposition Technical Staff, the team of architects and engineers supervised by George Dahl, and were built by a group of Dallas contractors.

Mural, **Esplanade of State**
Photographic Process
Pierre Bourdelle, artist

Pierre Bourdelle's murals at the Hall of Varied Industries, Communications, and Electricity deal with various aspects of industry, labor, science, and technology, including X-rays, hydroelectric power, construction, and electricity. Their strikingly modern style is a sharp contrast to the more classical work of muralist Carlo Ciampaglia on the Hall of Transportation across the esplanade.

The original Bourdelle murals were destroyed when the Varied Industries building burned in 1942. In 1999 EverGreene Painting Studios of New York used historic photographs and the artist's drawings to recreate the murals on what is now called the Automobile Building. The project was funded with proceeds from the State Fair of Texas.[33]

Administration Building, Fair Park
later The Women's Museum

Conversion of the Fair Park Coliseum (1910, C. D. Hill & Company) into offices for more than 250 members of the Centennial Exposition's staff was one of the first steps in the rebuilding of Fair Park. The former arena was floored over at the balcony level, creating a full second story, and a clean modernistic facade was built to conceal the original classically inspired exterior. Although very little of the exposition-era interiors survived through the years, a portion of the 1936 lobby was restored when architect Wendy Evans Joseph converted the building into The Women's Museum in 2000. The museum closed in 2011.[34]

Spirit of the Centennial, Administration Building
Raoul Josset, designer
Jose Martin, sculptor

Raoul Josset's *Spirit of the Centennial* is a Texan homage to Botticelli's *The Birth of Venus*, although the artist's decision to set his figure atop a saguaro cactus, which does not grow in Texas, is somewhat puzzling. Muralist Carlo Ciampaglia painted the niche in which the statue stands.

The model for the *Spirit* was sixteen-year-old Georgia Carroll, who caught Josset's attention when she appeared in a beauty pageant that he judged. (Carroll said she would not pose nude, so she was only the inspiration for the figure's head and neck.) Carroll went on to become a successful fashion model and actress; she married bandleader Kay Kyser in 1944.[35]

State of Texas Building, Fair Park
later Hall of State
Texas Centennial Architects, Associated, and Donald Barthelme Sr. (Houston), architects
Adams & Adams (San Antonio), interiors
P. O'B. Montgomery, contractor

A structure dedicated to the history of Texas was included in plans for the Centennial Exposition from the very beginning. Even so, the State of Texas Building's opening in September 1936—halfway through the exposition's run—came only after a fraught planning process that pitted local architects against George Dahl's staff and resulted in an eleventh-hour design that is now considered an Art Deco classic.

The controversy began shortly after the Texas legislature appropriated $1.2 million to build, decorate, and furnish the state hall, which was to be the centerpiece of the fairgrounds. The Exposition Technical Staff began designing the building, with Donald S. Nelson taking the lead. Elevations and plans had been prepared by the summer of 1935 when the group received word that officials in Austin were abruptly reassigning the job to a consortium of Dallas architects led by the San Antonio firm Adams & Adams. The locals had petitioned state officials for the commission motivated, Dahl said, by jealousy; Nelson implied that Carleton Adams of Adams & Adams, whom he called "the wisest of the politician-architects," set it all up. Carleton Adams Jr. denied that, contending that the Dallas architects sought the job on their own and the state put his father's firm in charge because of its prior experience with public projects.[36]

Whatever the truth was, it soon became apparent that the Dallas group could not agree on a design for the building, and time was running out. Mark Lemmon, one of the locals, contacted Houston architect Donald Barthelme and offered him the opportunity to design the building if he could come to Dallas and start work immediately.

Barthelme came, and in a few days he produced the basic plan for the State of Texas Building as it was built: a T-shaped structure with a semicircular gallery linking four exhibit rooms and a large central hall. Barthelme's plan also called for two wings projecting from the front of the building. Although their foundations were laid, the wings were never erected.[37]

It seems Barthelme's design was influenced by the work of Philadelphia architect Paul Philippe Cret, with whom he had formerly worked. Cret was a proponent of New Classicism, a style of architecture that blended the proportion and symmetry of ancient Greece with the modern detailing of Art Deco. The State of Texas Building, with its monumental limestone colonnades balancing a grand entry pavilion, is an excellent example of what Donald Nelson called "Paul Cret Modern."[38]

Barthelme's imposing exterior and the building's handsome interiors, the work of Adams & Adams, make the State of Texas Building—commonly called the Hall of State from its opening—one of America's best examples of 1930s Deco. Architecture critic David Dillon called it "an exemplary period building that summarizes visually what public design in the mid-1930s was all about," adding that the combination of architecture and exquisite interior detailing represents "one of the finest, and last, architect-artisan collaborations in the country."[39]

In addition to exhibit rooms and offices, the State of Texas Building houses an auditorium in its basement. The Dallas Historical Society has operated the building as a Texas history museum since 1938.[40]

***Tejas Warrior*, State of Texas Building**
Allie Tennant, sculptor

Dallas sculptor Allie Tennant created the focal point of the State of Texas Building's entrance niche, a heroic figure of a Native American drawing his bow. The title of the piece is a reference to the group alternately known as the Tejas or Hasinai Indians, which was made up of eight tribes that occupied part of what is now East Texas. "The treatment [of the figure] is stylized rather than realistic . . . because no particular Indian or tribe should be featured, as the Tejas were a nation rather than a tribe of Indians," Tennant explained.

The word *tejas* originated as a Native American word meaning "friend" or "ally." Historians do not believe the Hasinais actually referred to themselves as Tejas, but rather used the term as a greeting. The Spanish later used the variant *Texas* in connection with the region as a whole.[41]

Murals, **Hall of State**
Texas of History
Texas of Today
Eugene Savage (New York), artist

Eugene Savage's Hall of State murals deal with the history and culture of Texas. Savage wove a number of prominent themes, including Texas independence, statehood, the establishment of a public education system, and the development of the state's livestock, cotton, oil, and lumber industries, into the epic panoramas. At ninety by thirty feet each, the paintings were said to be the largest oil murals in the world when they were completed.[42]

The selection of an easterner to paint the showpieces of the exposition's central building rankled some locals. Members of the "Dallas Nine," a group of prominent Dallas artists, had spent months preparing unsolicited sketches for the murals in the hope that they could persuade state officials to give them the commission. However, the artists never had the chance to submit their proposals. Jerry Bywaters, a member of the Dallas Nine, later conceded that Savage's murals fit the exposition in a way, but he maintained that the state had missed "an opportunity . . . to use the talent of the area to better advantage and for a longer staying quality."[43]

Dallas artists Reveau Bassett and James Buchanan "Buck" Winn assisted Savage in painting the murals, along with students Lonnie Lyon and William Smith.[44]

LEFT
Hall of State, State of Texas Building

The ninety-four-by-sixty-eight-foot Hall of State, with limestone columns rising four stories to a richly decorated ceiling, is the centerpiece of the State of Texas Building. The space reminded early visitors of the Parthenon and great European cathedrals. One wrote that "there is perhaps no room in America more impressive, and its splendor expresses completely the majestic march of four centuries of the building of an empire." Decades later, it remains one of the outstanding Art Deco rooms in the United States.

Whereas other rooms in the State of Texas Building housed exhibits during the Centennial Exposition, the Hall of State was always meant as a sort of shrine to Texas. It contains four of the building's largest works of art: Eugene Savage's pair of murals on the side walls, the ceiling stencils by George Davidson, and Joseph Renier's *Great Medallion of Texas* at the room's east end. The *Medallion*, twenty-five feet in diameter and covered in three shades of gold leaf, depicts figures representing the six flags of Texas grouped around a lone star.[45]

East Texas Room, State of Texas Building

The State of Texas Building's four "regional rooms" were designed to reflect the culture and history of North, South, East, and West Texas. Each room uses materials that refer to the region to which it is dedicated—for example, gumwood paneling on the walls of the East Texas Room—and each contains at least one large-scale work by a local or Texas artist. The four regional rooms were filled with historical exhibits during the Centennial Exposition. In modern times, the rooms have principally been used as event and meeting spaces, though they still house occasional exhibits.[46]

South Texas Room, State of Texas Building

Federal Building, Fair Park
later Tower Building

The building that housed the offices of federal exposition officials and the federal government's exhibits was the work of Donald S. Nelson, a member of the exposition's architectural staff. Its concave facade centers on a 175-foot tower capped by a stylized, gilded eagle, a landmark at Fair Park. At ground level, California artist Julian Garnsey created a 175-foot-long sculptural frieze representing significant scenes and figures from Texas history.[47]

In the Federal Building's exhibit hall, government departments presented exhibits worth an estimated twenty-five million dollars. The US Post Office Department laid out ten million dollars' worth of rare stamps; the National Capital Park and Planning Commission showed a fifteen-foot-long scale model of Washington, DC, and representatives of the Smithsonian Institution spent the entire run of the exposition assembling a dinosaur skeleton that had been unearthed in Utah. One of the most popular features was the Department of Labor's "mechanical man," a robot that gave a speech on the advantages of mechanization every fifteen minutes.[48]

Detail, **Federal Building**

Reception Room, **Federal Building**

The Reception Room, used for conferences and to entertain visiting dignitaries, is one of the Federal Building's most striking interior spaces. The room has changed little since 1936; even the original Herman Miller-designed conference set, armchairs, and couches remain in place.

George Dahl's office did not allow exposed light bulbs or tube lighting in any building or structure designed by the Exposition Technical Staff, so variations on the indirect lighting seen here were found throughout the exposition grounds.[49]

Texas Woofus, Fair Park
Lawrence Tenney Stevens (New York), sculptor

Lawrence Tenney Stevens's *Texas Woofus* is one of the best-known artworks at Fair Park. The fantastical figure is a composite of six animals: the head of a sheep, the neck and mane of a horse, the body and legs of a pig, the wings of a duck, a turkey's tail, and a pair of longhorns. Stevens apparently had fun with the work, even taking the time to write an origin story for what he called the "Great Australian Woofus." It began with an Australian ewe "of uncertain virtue and careless habits" who visited America and became enamored of a variety of animals. "The ewe flitted lightly from amour to amour and from beast to beast, to bird and back to beast, taking her pleasure where she found it—and often, too," Stevens wrote. "When she came to her accouchment it was difficult, indeed, to fix the parentage upon anyone . . . so, bravely enough, she decided to start a new species. Thus was born the great Australian Woofus."[50]

Workers placing beams for a new livestock arena in 1941 broke the *Woofus*'s nose, at which point the statue was removed and apparently destroyed. Fifty-six years later, the nonprofit Friends of Fair Park began raising funds to have the statue recreated. Sculptor David Newton used historic photos and Stevens's original model to create molds for a new *Woofus* of bronze, designed to be more durable than the original concrete sculpture. However, the molds were lost in a fire before casting could begin. Newton created a second set of molds that were used to cast the new *Woofus*, which was dedicated in 2002.[51]

Interior, **Livestock Building No. 2, Fair Park**
later Swine Building

Livestock Building No. 2, part of an expansive agricultural and livestock complex on the north side of the Centennial Exposition grounds, is notable in that it is the only exhibit hall at Fair Park that has remained largely untouched since 1936. Many of the fixtures in the building appear to date from the time of the exposition, as does the interior paint, which has faded from its original rich tones.

The building was divided into pens for swine, sheep, and goats, a judging arena, and an exhibition room that contained a goat-milking demonstration and displays from the mohair industry. Although the exhibition room no longer exists, most of the structure's 1936 layout remains intact.[52]

***Christian Science Monitor* pavilion, Fair Park**
later Dallas Aquarium Education Center
Luther E. Sadler, architect

The streamlined design of the *Christian Science Monitor*'s building is typical of the modernistic work of its architect, Luther Sadler, who was known for the homes he planned and built in Dallas. Displays inside the building dramatized the editorial, advertising, and circulation aspects of the national daily newspaper.[53]

Magnolia Lounge, Fair Park
later Theatre '47, Friends of Fair Park
William Lescaze (New York), architect

Retailer Stanley Marcus recommended the Swiss-American William Lescaze, whom Marcus had considered as a possible architect for his own home, to design the Magnolia Petroleum Company's hospitality building at the Centennial Exposition. The result is often called the first true European Modern building in Texas. Lescaze's design was rather austere compared to some of the other exposition buildings, leading fair officials to wonder whether it might be too modernistic for local tastes. Lescaze responded, "What they mistook for 'modernistic' is really simply good modern architecture."

During the exposition, visitors to the Magnolia Lounge could relax in an air-conditioned lounge room furnished by Neiman Marcus or take advantage of outdoor seating that overlooked a cactus garden. In 1947, the building became the home of Margo Jones's Theatre '47, the first professional arena theater and the first modern nonprofit professional regional theater in the United States.[54]

Ford Motor Company Building, Fair Park
demolished
Albert Kahn (Detroit), architect

At fifty-five thousand square feet, Ford's building was the largest private exhibit hall at the Centennial Exposition. Its imposing main entrance faced the Court of Honor, a major cross-axis of the exposition grounds; from there, a long, low wing wrapped around an intensively landscaped courtyard. Detroit architect Albert Kahn's office, working with famed industrial designer Walter Dorwin Teague, chose to forgo the style George Dahl's team was using elsewhere on the exposition grounds. Instead of taking its cues from the Southwest, the Ford Building aligned stylistically with the European modernism William Lescaze used at the Magnolia Lounge.

Inside, exhibits designed by Teague followed the theme "From the Soil to Finished Car Parts." Visitors could watch as latex became tire rubber, soybeans were pressed and processed to make plastic, and cotton was turned into upholstery by the "multipleater," a giant sewing machine that could make four hundred stitches per second. All the Ford exhibits—475 linear feet of them—were air conditioned, which proved to be an attraction in itself. "[People] all but wilt when the first blast of heat strikes them in the face," an employee working the Ford entrance noted. "Many come right back for another trip through the building."[55]

As impressive as it was, the Ford Building was meant to be temporary. It was used for general exhibits during the 1937 Greater Texas and Pan-American Exposition, then was demolished before the opening of the 1938 state fair. The Women's Building, later called Grand Place, was built on the site in 1954.[56]

Hall of Negro Life, Fair Park
demolished

The Hall of Negro Life was one of the most significant structures at the Texas Centennial Exposition: it was the first exhibit building at a major American fair dedicated to the history and culture of African Americans. Although the structure was modest compared to some of the exposition's other buildings, it was located steps from the fair's main entrance and was landscaped and floodlit in the same manner as the largest exhibit halls.

Getting the hall built was not easy. Dallas's black leaders had asked city and state officials to fund an African American facility at the exposition to no avail. Later, they found an ally in white oilman and exposition official Walter D. Cline. Local African Americans sold fifty thousand dollars in exposition bonds as a "show of good faith," and Cline paved the way for a federal allocation of one hundred thousand dollars. Half that amount was to be used to construct the building, and the other half was intended for exhibits and operating costs.[57]

The Hall of Negro Life contained exhibits from thirty-two states and the District of Columbia related to African American contributions to American education, fine arts, health, agriculture, mechanical arts, and business. Perhaps the best-known feature of the building was a set of four murals in the main lobby by the New York painter Aaron Douglas, one of the leading artists of the Harlem Renaissance. Two of Douglas's panels are known to survive, one held by the de Young Museum in San Francisco and the other by the National Gallery of Art in Washington.[58]

Although the Hall of Negro life was always intended to be a temporary building, it was expected to reopen when Fair Park hosted the Greater Texas and Pan-American Exposition in 1937. Instead, the building was demolished soon after the Centennial Exposition over the objections of a number of prominent Dallasites, including Mayor George Sergeant. "Some strange things happened, and with all amounts of investigation we are not yet absolutely sure who was primarily responsible for the discontinuing of Negro participation or the basic cause therefor," Jesse O. Thomas, who managed the building during the centennial, later wrote.[59]

Band Shell and Amphitheater, Fair Park
W. Scott Dunne with
Christensen & Christensen, architects
1936
Christensen & Christensen, architects
1941, ticket and restroom building

W. Scott Dunne, one of Texas's premier theater architects, studied amphitheaters across the country before designing the Band Shell at Fair Park, and it seems Dallas was pleased with the result. "Roll the Hollywood Bowl and all other well-known band shells and pavilions into a bundle, take out only the good parts and you will get an idea of the work done to bring Dallas one of the finest structures of this kind," the *Dallas Morning News* crowed.

The stage, set in a series of concentric arches highlighted at night by concealed lighting, could accommodate a 160-member orchestra; early reports boasted that all 5,500 seats had unobstructed views of the entire stage. A streamlined building behind the shell housed dressing rooms, a music library, offices, and storage space.[60]

RIGHT
Detail, **Band Shell and Amphitheater**

OPPOSITE PAGE
Ticket and restroom building, Band Shell and Amphitheater

Although the Band Shell's ticket and restroom structure was included in original plans, it was not built until 1941.[61]

WOMEN

ARCHITECTS, DESIGNERS, AND ARTISTS

Architects

ADAMS & ADAMS was the well-known San Antonio architectural partnership established in 1909 by **Carl C. Adams (1881-1918)** and his nephew **Carleton W. Adams (1885-1964).** Carl Adams died in 1918, after which **Max C. Friedrich (1891-1949)** became an associate member of the firm. Adams & Adams built its reputation through a number of significant commissions statewide, including the Main House of the King Ranch (1917) and San Antonio's widely publicized Thomas Jefferson High School (1932). During the Depression, the firm produced modernistic designs for prominent public projects such as the State Highway Building (1931) inAustin and the Alamo Cenotaph (1939) on Alamo Plaza in San Antonio.[1]

ALFRED S. ALSCHULER (1876-1940) was a native of Chicago and one of the city's most prolific architects. A graduate of the Armour Institute of Technology and the School of the Art Institute of Chicago, he began his architectural career in 1900 as a draftsman in the office of famed architect Dankmar Adler. After five years of study under Adler, Alschuler was with Samuel Treat's firm for two years, then opened his own office in 1907. Alschuler's versatile designs included warehouses, department stores, industrial buildings, and synagogues. He planned many stores for the W. T. Grant chain of 5¢-to-$1 stores, including major modernistic outlets in Buffalo (1939, demolished) and Chicago (1939, demolished), created in partnership with celebrated industrial designer Raymond Loewy.[2]

JAMES P. BAUGH (1898-1973) was born in Waco. In 1923, the *Waco News-Tribune* noted that Baugh had established an office in the city after working with architect Birch D. Easterwood; Baugh also had an office in Tyler. He maintained practices in both cities until 1939, when the *Dallas Morning News* announced that Baugh's firm had relocated to Dallas, where he designed residences and small business buildings. By 1947, Baugh was again practicing in Waco, designing banks, hotels, and stores.[3]

ALBERT H. BOREN (1900-1936) was born in Chicago. His family moved to Dallas in 1918, and Boren started working as a draftsman for the Clem Lumber Company. In the early 1920s, Boren was employed by the Russell Brown Company, which designed and built custom homes, and by architect J. W. Westbrook. Boren then started his own architectural practice, and the *Dallas Morning News* featured his designs for houses in Oak Cliff in 1924 and 1934. The architect died on January 25, 1936, in the crash of a small plane he had chartered to fly to Victoria, Texas, where contracts were being awarded for a hospital he designed. Department of Commerce investigators blamed heavy fog for the crash, which happened shortly after the plane took off from Curtiss-Wright Airport in Grand Prairie. Boren was killed one month before his only child, Albert H. Boren Jr., was born. The architect's last projects, Hotel Kilgore in Kilgore, Bobo Hospital and Clinic in Arlington, and DeTar Memorial Hospital in Victoria, were completed in 1936.[4]

THOMAS D. BROAD, see FLINT & BROAD.

BRYAN & SHARP was the professional partnership of Ralph Bryan and Walter C. Sharp from 1925 to 1933. In addition to the firm's later modernistic designs, its Dallas projects included the roof garden atop the Adolphus Hotel (1929, demolished), the Moorland Branch YMCA (1930, demolished) and Roger Q. Mills School (1931).

Ralph Bryan (1892-1965) earned a bachelor of science degree in architecture from Washington University in St. Louis, his hometown. After graduating in 1913, he worked as a draftsman and designer in St. Louis and Hannibal, Missouri, and served as a lieutenant in a construction battalion in the US Army Signal Corps during World War I. In 1921, Bryan received a bronze medal from the Beaux-Arts Institute for Design of New York. After his practice with Sharp ended, Bryan operated his own office from 1933 to 1942, then served as commanding officer of the Seabee Depot Battalion, New Hebrides, South Pacific, during World War II. He was employed as regional hospital architect for the US Public Health Service from 1947 until his retirement in 1963.[5]

Walter C. Sharp (1885-1949) was born in Nashville and graduated from the University of Pennsylvania School of Architecture. He worked in his hometown and in New York City before relocating to Dallas in 1919. While in independent practice, he was known for his elegant residential designs and for supervising repairs to the Hall of State (originally the State of Texas Building) at Fair Park after the Greater Texas and Pan American Exposition of 1937. Beginning in 1944, Sharp was senior partner in the firm Sharp & Richter, designing homes and schools with Will Scott Richter. Sharp was found shot to death in his country home outside Garland, Texas, in 1949.[6]

CARSEY & LINSKIE was the relatively short-lived partnership of Dallas architects Jon D. Carsey and Robert H. Linskie. Newspaper coverage indicates they were collaborating on residential projects as early as 1929, but the firm name Carsey & Linskie did not appear until 1930 and was not mentioned in newspapers or city directories after 1933.[7]

Jon D. Carsey (1900-1962) was born in Tennessee and was practicing in Dallas by 1929. He typically designed large traditional homes in revival styles, although he occasionally produced modernistic buildings. After his partnership with Linskie ended, Carsey worked with R. Lovell Edgeworth on residential projects as early as 1936; the firm name Carsey & Edgeworth first appeared in newspapers in 1938. The practice lasted until 1940, when Edgeworth was killed in a traffic accident. Carsey made news later in life as founder of the Texas Soaring Association and president of the Soaring Society of America.[8]

Less is known about **Robert H. Linskie** (1904-1966). A Dallas native, Linskie was collaborating with architect Fonzie E. Robertson designing houses in Highland Park in 1928; their work together appears to have ended that same year. Linskie's involvement with Carsey began in 1929.[9]

CHRISTENSEN & CHRISTENSEN was the architectural firm of two Dallas brothers, **William O. Christensen** (1903-1953) and **George E. Christensen** (1905-1979). Both brothers graduated from the Agricultural & Mechanical College of Texas (later Texas A&M University), and each worked for other architectural firms before they established their practice together in Dallas in 1933. The Christensens were known for designing houses in the city's Lakewood section, and they collaborated with W. Scott Dunne on the Fair Park Band Shell for the 1936 Texas Centennial Exposition. William Christensen left the firm in 1952 and moved to San Augustine, Texas; he died the following year. George Christensen continued in practice and designed several facilities for the Dallas Zoo.[10]

WILEY G. CLARKSON (1885-1952) attended the University of Texas at Austin before studying engineering at the Armour Institute of Technology and architecture at the School of the Art Institute of Chicago. He opened a practice in his hometown of Corsicana, Texas, in 1908 before moving to Fort Worth in 1912. Seven years later, he formed a partnership with A. W. Gaines, which lasted until Gaines's death in 1921. Although Clarkson's early work was typically in historical revival styles, in the 1920s and 1930s he became Fort Worth's most prominent exponent of what came to be known as Art Deco and Art Moderne design.[11]

MARTIN T. CLEMENTS (1883-1955) was raised on a farm near Kildare, Texas, until his father moved the family to Hamblin, Texas, and established a construction business. The younger Clements worked as an independent contractor until 1916, when he joined David S. Castle Company, Architects & Engineers, in nearby Abilene. In 1925, he began working for architects Voelcker and Dixon in Wichita Falls. Clements supervised sixteen courthouse projects for the firm, including the modernistic Gregg County Courthouse in Longview. He also worked on independent commercial projects. Clements remained with Voelcker & Dixon until 1943, when he established his own practice in Wichita Falls. Clements retired in 1952.[12]

CONSOLIDATED ARCHITECTS AND ENGINEERS, see CHARLES T. FREELOVE.

JACK M. CORGAN, see CORGAN & MOORE.

CORGAN & MOORE was the partnership between Dallas architects Jack M. Corgan and W. J. "Bill" Moore, which lasted from 1938 to 1940. The practice specialized in movie theaters.

Jack M. Corgan (1911-2000) was born in Hugo, Oklahoma, and earned a bachelor of architecture degree from Oklahoma A&M College (later Oklahoma State University) in 1935. As a young architect and licensed pilot, Corgan built his practice by flying to small cities and towns in Texas and surrounding states to design movie theaters. After serving as a flight instructor during World War II, he reorganized his firm as Jack Corgan & Associates. Aviation projects became an important part of the company's work. With Flint & Broad, Corgan designed a new terminal for Dallas's Love Field; when the building opened in 1958, it featured the first moving sidewalks for airline passengers. Other significant works include the Braniff International Airlines Terminal (1969) and the American Airlines Terminal (1969) at Dallas-Fort Worth International Airport. His architecture practice continues as the Dallas-based firm Corgan.[13]

W.J. "Bill" Moore (1913-1982) was born in Lane City, Texas, and raised in Oklahoma. He graduated from Oklahoma A&M College (later Oklahoma State University) with a degree in architecture. After his partnership with Corgan ended, Moore and his wealthy uncle, R. E. Griffith, planned to build a resort in New Mexico. During a side trip to Las Vegas, the pair was so impressed with the desert city's business potential they bought thirty-five acres on US Highway 91. Moore repartnered with Corgan to design the Hotel Last Frontier, which opened in 1942 as the second hotel-casino on the Las Vegas Strip. Moore sold the Last Frontier in 1951, and with other associates developed the El Cortez and Showboat hotel-casinos. Later, Nevada's governor appointed Moore to the Tax Commission. In 1955, Moore was the principal witness in the Kefauver Crime Commission hearings in Las Vegas.[14]

HUBERT HAMMOND CRANE (1893-1959) attended the University of Louisville in his Kentucky hometown before serving as a lieutenant in the field artillery during World War I and receiving a major's commission in the Red Cross as chief of motor operations for Europe. In 1920, he moved to Dallas to work as a draftsman for innovative residential architect David R. Williams. Crane established his own practice in 1922; like Williams, he designed historically inspired homes for prosperous clients. Crane moved his firm to Fort Worth just before the stock market crash of 1929 and used his background in European architecture to build his practice creating traditional houses in affluent neighborhoods.[15]

PAUL PHILIPPE CRET (1876-1945) was a prolific Philadelphia-based architect whose influence was felt across the country. He was born in Lyon, France, and studied architecture at the École des Beaux-Arts in both Lyon and Paris. After winning many architectural awards, the twenty-seven-year-old Cret was recruited to serve as Professor of Design at the University of Pennsylvania. He joined the French army at the outbreak of World War I and did not return to the United States until he was discharged at the end of the war. In addition to teaching, Cret operated a busy firm that specialized in the design of public buildings. His best-known works include the Detroit Institute of Arts (1927) and the Folger Shakespeare Library (1932) in Washington, DC. He also served as an adviser on the monumental Art Deco Union Terminal (1933) in Cincinnati. In 1930, Cret was hired as supervising architect for the University of Texas at Austin and was commissioned to create a development plan for the campus. He drew up the master plan and designed the Main Building with its 307-foot tower (1937), the focal point of the campus.[16]

GEORGE L. DAHL, see HERBERT M. GREENE, LAROCHE & DAHL.

JOHN B. DANNA, see DANNA & WELCH.

DANNA & WELCH was the periodic partnership of Dallas architects John B. Danna and Everett V. Welch during the construction boom that followed World War II. Danna & Welch won several commissions from the Dallas Independent School District between 1947 and 1953.

John B. Danna (1903-1973) was born and spent his entire career in Dallas. He attended Southern Methodist University in his hometown before transferring to the Agricultural & Mechanical College of Texas (later Texas A&M University) and earning a bachelor of science degree in architecture. He studied at the École des Beaux-Arts in Fontainebleau, France, in 1926 and returned to Dallas to work as a draftsman and designer for architect C. H. Griesenbeck. After nine years, Danna became a partner in Griesenbeck & Danna. In 1941, he established his own firm, John B. Danna, Architect.[17]

Everett V. Welch (1897-1953), a native of Parsons, Kansas, studied at the Armour Institute of Technology in Chicago, the School of the Art Institute of Chicago, and the University of Illinois School of Architecture. He briefly worked as a draftsman in Chicago before relocating to Dallas, where he was employed as a draftsman by several architectural firms. In 1932, Welch established his own practice and designed a number of private homes. During World War II, he was a partner in Thomas, Sharp & Welch (later Thomas, Sharp, Welch & Goodwin), which received significant contracts designing housing complexes for the employees of wartime industries. Welch maintained his own practice after the war, but entered periodic partnerships with other architects on special projects, particularly schools and churches.[18]

JAMES B. DAVIES (1891-1966) practiced as an architect

in Texas and Louisiana, but his training was largely in engineering. Davies was born in Austin and raised in Fort Worth. He graduated from the University of Texas at Austin in 1916 with a bachelor of science degree in electrical engineering and a bachelor of arts degree; he then studied physics at the University of Chicago and education at Southern Methodist University in Dallas. Davies worked as an assistant engineer for the Alabama Power Company for a year before serving two years in the US Navy. After his discharge, Davies moved around Texas and was employed by David S. Castle Company, Architects and Engineers, of Abilene; Walsh & Burney, construction contractors of San Antonio; and R. O. Jameson, consulting engineer of Dallas. In 1922, he established James B. Davies & Company in Fort Worth and advertised himself as an architect and structural engineer. Davies left Texas in 1938 to work as a structural engineer for the US Department of Agriculture (USDA) in Washington, DC, before moving to New Orleans to serve as construction engineer for the USDA's Southern Regional Research Laboratory (1941, altered), a massive Art Deco building. Davies established an architectural practice in New Orleans and remained there through World War II.[19]

DeFEE & WHITE was the partnership of architects Marvin E. DeFee and Emory S. White during the East Texas oil boom of the early 1930s. From their office in Henderson, they designed the Gaston Public School Complex (1932), a Recorded Texas Historic Landmark in Joinerville; the National Register-listed Rusk County Jail (1933) in Henderson; and Kilgore Junior-Senior High School (1933). DeFee & White were also the architects of the New London Consolidated School (1932), which was destroyed in an explosion caused by an undetected gas leak that killed almost three hundred students and teachers on March 18, 1937. A subsequent investigation determined that the architects were not at fault.[20]

Marvin E. DeFee (1896-1984) was born and raised in Madison County, Texas. According to the 1920 US Census, DeFee was employed as a draftsman in an Amarillo architect's office. By 1922, he was working in Austin as a draftsman for prominent architect Roy L. Thomas. DeFee later served as a draftsman for Giesecke & Harris, an Austin partnership known for its school designs; DeFee represented the firm during construction of the Eagle Lake School (1924). After leaving DeFee & White, he worked as an engineer examiner for the Public Works Administration in Fort Worth and for the Federal Works Agency in San Antonio during World War II.[21]

Emory S. White (1904-1972) was born in Henderson, Texas, and spent most of his career in Houston. He arrived in Houston in the early 1920s and worked as a draftsman for architect John McLelland before returning to Henderson. In the late 1930s and early 1940s, White operated his practice from Livingston in East Texas. By 1947, he had moved back to Houston, where he specialized in designing school buildings, gymnasiums, and auditoriums.[22]

DeWITT & WASHBURN was the successful Depression-era partnership of Dallas architects Roscoe P. DeWitt and G. H. Thomas Washburn. The firm was first mentioned in local newspapers in 1929 and continued to receive recognition through 1940.

Roscoe P. DeWitt (1894-1975) graduated from Dartmouth College and earned a master's degree in architecture from Harvard University in 1917. After serving in World War I, DeWitt returned to his hometown of Dallas and established his practice, R. P. DeWitt, Architect. He worked with architect Mark Lemmon through much of the 1920s; by 1929, DeWitt and G. H. Thomas Washburn had formed their partnership. In 1937, DeWitt worked as the local agent for Frank Lloyd Wright, who was designing a home for Neiman Marcus department store owner Stanley Marcus. When Marcus and Wright had a falling out, DeWitt received the commission for the Marcus house (1937). During World War II, DeWitt served as a lieutenant colonel in the US Army's Monuments, Fine Arts, and Archives Division and was sent to France to inspect and secure historic buildings. After the war, he formed a successful partnership with Arch B. Swank. DeWitt later worked on the restoration of the original Senate and Supreme Court chambers in the United States Capitol and the extension of the Capitol's East Portico.[23]

G. H. Thomas Washburn (1890-1972) was born in Ottawa, Kansas; his father, George P. Washburn, was the state's most prominent architect in the early twentieth century. Thomas Washburn earned his architecture degree from the Massachusetts Institute of Technology and served in the US Navy during World War I, working on the construction of bases around the Great Lakes. He returned to Kansas to work with his older brother Clarence, who was also an architect. He moved to Dallas by 1928 and was in partnership with Roscoe P. DeWitt by 1929. In 1941, the US Navy sent Washburn to Trinidad to consult on the construction of a base to protect the Panama Canal. He eventually joined architect Wyatt C. Hedrick's firm in Fort Worth. At the time of his death in Houston, Washburn's obituary listed his occupation as landscape architect.[24]

CHARLES STEVENS DILBECK (1907-1990) was born in Fort Smith, Arkansas, and raised in Tulsa, Oklahoma, where his father built churches and apartment buildings. Dilbeck learned drafting from his father and studied architecture at Oklahoma A&M College (later Oklahoma State University). He left school after two years to start his own firm in Tulsa. Dilbeck moved to Dallas in 1932 and developed an affluent clientele. He was known for his French-inspired farmhouses and his development of the Texas Ranch-style house. Dilbeck designed hundreds of houses during his long career, particularly in the Preston Hollow neighborhood and the Park Cities.[25]

JAMES L. DOWNING (1891-1954) was born in Tyler, Texas, and spent much of his career in the region. The 1900 US Census indicates that his father was an architectural draftsman; when the younger Downing registered with the military in 1917, he stated he was employed as a draftsman for the Texas and Pacific Railway in Dallas. By 1920 he was an associate in the office of architect John Tulloch in Sherman; Downing then moved to Houston, where he worked as a draftsman for Endress & Cato, Architects. He settled in Henderson in 1934 and opened his architectural practice. In 1937, Downing was questioned during the official inquiry into the cause of the explosion that destroyed the New London Consolidated School and killed almost three hundred students and teachers. Downing had assisted the architects, DeFee & White, in drawing up the school plans; the investigation determined that the architects were not at fault.[26]

W. SCOTT DUNNE (1886-1937) earned his architecture degree from Washington University in St. Louis, his hometown. In 1917, the Agricultural & Mechanical College of Texas (later Texas A&M University) hired Dunne as an instructor in the Architecture Department with joint duties as a draftsman in the office of the college architect. He briefly partnered with architect Alfred C. Finn in Houston, then opened his own office in Dallas by 1924. Dunne specialized in movie theater design. His works can be found across Oklahoma and Texas, where he created theaters for the region's largest film exhibitors: Interstate Theaters, Jefferson Amusement Company, Robb & Rowley Theaters, and Saenger Amusement Company. In the 1930s, Dunne began designing most of his theaters in the modernistic style and gave many older theaters modernistic updates.[27]

ELMER G. WITHERS ARCHITECTURAL COMPANY, see WITHERS & THOMPSON.

ALFRED C. FINN (1883-1964) is most often associated with Houston, but also designed significant buildings in Fort Worth and East Texas. Born in Bellville, Texas, Finn moved to Houston in 1900 and worked for the Southern Pacific Railroad as a carpenter and a draftsman. In 1903, the architectural firm Sanguinet & Staats hired Finn; he worked in the Dallas and Fort Worth offices before being sent to the Houston branch. In 1913, he started his own practice in Houston and received a job supervising construction of the Rice Hotel for Mauran, Russell & Crowell of St. Louis. The project began Finn's lifelong association with Jesse H. Jones, the developer, banker, publisher, and philanthropist who dominated Houston's business and political spheres through the first half of the twentieth century. By the 1920s, Finn was Houston's most prominent commercial architect, designing office buildings, hotels, and movie palaces, usually for Jones. During this time, Finn also collaborated with Wyatt C. Hedrick on projects Jones developed in Fort Worth. After President Franklin D. Roosevelt appointed Jones head of the Reconstruction Finance Corporation during the Great Depression, Finn received many commissions for publicly financed projects, culminating in the 567-foot San Jacinto Monument outside Houston.[28]

REYNOLDS FISHER (1907-1977) appears to have had a busy architectural practice in the mid-to-late 1930s, based on the number of his projects mentioned in Dallas newspapers. In December 1936, the *Texas General Contractors Association Bulletin* noted that Fisher was designing twenty-five one- and two-story houses for the Mayflower Investment Company, a major real estate developer. For the most part, Fisher designed traditional suburban homes; many are located in Cedar Crest Heights south of downtown Dallas. According to the 1940 US Census, Fisher was born in Texas and had lived in Dallas since at least 1935.

FLINT & BROAD was the Dallas architecture firm of Lester N. Flint and Thomas D. Broad; the partnership lasted from 1923 until Flint's death in 1938. In addition to its work in North Texas, Flint and Broad designed the Medical Arts Building (1928) in Shreveport, Louisiana, and the Hotel Black (1930, demolished) in Oklahoma City.

Lester N. Flint (1886-1938) was born in Carlisle, Arkansas, and attended school in Pine Bluff. By 1910, he was working as a draftsman in Little Rock and became associated with architect C. G. Curtis in Paris, Texas, just before the fire that destroyed the city's business district and adjacent residential areas in 1916. By 1920, Flint had moved to Dallas and established his own practice. He designed the Trinity Heights School (1922, now Harrell Budd Elementary) and Cannon's Village (1922) in Oak Cliff before going into partnership with Thomas D. Broad.[29]

Thomas D. Broad (1893-1985) earned a bachelor of science degree in architecture from the University of Texas in 1915 and had begun graduate studies in architecture at Harvard University when a devastating fire razed large sections of Paris, Texas, his hometown. The young architect returned to Paris as a partner in Curtis, Broad & Lightfoot. He and Lester Flint established their own firm in Dallas in the early 1920s. Beginning in 1933, Broad took a five-year leave of absence from the firm to work for federal relief agencies in Texas and Oklahoma. After Flint's death in 1938, Broad continued his independent practice and designed the modernistic air terminal at Love Field (1940, demolished). Broad & Nelson, Broad's subsequent partnership with Donald S. Nelson, received a Texas Society of Architects Honor Award for Waco's Memorial Masonic Grand Lodge Temple (1949). With Jack M. Corgan, Broad & Nelson designed the airline terminal (1958) that replaced Broad's earlier building at Love Field.[30]

FOOSHEE & CHEEK was the partnership of two of Dallas's best-known residential architects: **Marion F. Fooshee** (1888-1956) and **James B. Cheek** (1895-1970). Fooshee was born in Weatherford, Texas, but grew up in Dallas. Rather than attend college, he apprenticed with Hal Thomson, an architect whose commissions included many eclectic mansions along Dallas's Swiss Avenue. Cheek, a native of Hillsboro, Texas, studied architecture at the University of Texas at Austin before beginning an apprenticeship with Thomson in 1918. He and Fooshee established their own firm in Wichita Falls around 1920, but had moved back to Dallas by 1925. In addition to eclectic houses, Fooshee & Cheek's most celebrated project was Highland Park Village (1931), the country's first self-contained, auto-oriented shopping center. Like most of the firm's designs, Highland Park Village took its inspiration from the architecture of Spain, Mexico, and southern California. Cheek remained in practice after Fooshee's death and retired in 1966.[31]

CHARLES T. FREELOVE (1905-1968) was born on Christmas Day 1905 in Thurber, Texas. He learned to fly as a lieutenant in the US Army Air Corps during World War I; reporters later dubbed him "the flying architect" for piloting a private plane to his firm's various construction projects across Texas and surrounding states. Around 1945, Freelove became the senior partner and architect for Consolidated Architects and Engineers. The company designed and built a wide variety of projects, including churches, shopping centers, auto showrooms, hospitals, schools, and industrial facilities. During his time with Consolidated, Freelove also designed buildings under his own name.[32]

PRESTON M. GEREN (1891-1969) was born in Sherman in North Texas and graduated from the Agricultural & Mechanical College of Texas (later Texas A&M University) with a degree in architectural engineering in 1912. He was the supervising architect for buildings on the A&M campus for two years, then spent two years in private practice. After serving with distinction in France during World War I, he returned to Texas as chief engineer for an Austin contractor. In 1921, Geren was hired to head the Department of Architecture and Engineering at Oklahoma A&M College (later Oklahoma State University). Two years later, Geren joined the Fort Worth architectural firm of Sanguinet, Staats & Hedrick as chief engineer. He stayed with the company after it became Wyatt C. Hedrick, Incorporated, and worked on several of Fort Worth's modernistic landmarks. Geren established his own architectural practice in 1934 and remained active in his firm until his death.[33]

GRAYSON GILL (1893-1990) was born in Port Clinton, Ohio, and studied at Ohio State University, but did not receive a degree. He entered the US Army in 1916 and served until 1919, when he enrolled at the University of Michigan. Gill earned a bachelor of science degree in architectural engineering in 1921 and joined the faculty of the Agricultural & Mechanical College of Texas (later Texas A&M University) as an associate professor of architecture. In 1926, Gill was hired as an engineer for architect Herbert M. Greene's Dallas firm, and he remained with Greene for eight years. Gill established his own office in 1934, and five years later he formed Gill & Bennett with architect J. Murrell Bennett. In 1942, prominent architect Otto H. Lang retired and removed his influential firm, Lang & Witchell, from active practice. In a published announcement, Lang stated he was transferring his firm's principal plan files and its goodwill to Grayson Gill. At the same time, Gill announced the end of his partnership with Bennett and the resumption of the firm Grayson Gill, Architect and Engineer.[34]

HERBERT M. GREENE, LaROCHE & DAHL was the successful partnership of three Dallas architects: Herbert M. Greene, E. B. LaRoche, and George L. Dahl. The firm was established in 1928, when LaRoche and Dahl were made partners in the Herbert M. Greene Company. After Greene's death, the firm continued to advertise as Herbert M. Greene, LaRoche & Dahl until 1938, when the name was shortened to LaRoche & Dahl. The partnership ended in 1943.[35]

Herbert M. Greene (1871-1932) was raised in Peoria, Illinois, and earned a bachelor of science degree from the University of Illinois. He briefly practiced in Peoria and moved to Dallas in 1897. He operated his own firm until 1900, when he joined James P. Hubbell to form Hubbell & Greene. The firm received significant commissions, including the Scottish Rite Cathedral (1913) in Dallas. Greene went out on his own again in 1918, establishing Herbert M. Greene Company. In 1922, the Board of Regents of the University of Texas appointed Greene to succeed Cass Gilbert as university architect. Greene designed several major buildings for the Austin campus.[36]

E. B. LaRoche (1871-1944) was born in Charleston, South Carolina, and studied at the University of the South in Sewanee, Tennessee, and Cornell University before completing graduate work at the Massachusetts Institute of Technology. Following World War I, he was hired as college architect and professor of architecture for the Agricultural & Mechanical College of Texas (later Texas A&M University). He was the head of A&M's architecture department when he left to join Herbert M. Greene Company in 1925; LaRoche was made a partner in the firm in 1928. At the time of his death, LaRoche was architectural adviser to the Texas Memorial Committee, which was responsible for planning and constructing monuments commemorating World War II. His son, E. B. LaRoche Jr., had died in the crash of a training flight earlier in the war.[37]

George L. Dahl (1894-1987) received a bachelor's degree in architecture from the University of Minnesota in his native Minneapolis. He was in the air service during World War I and entered Harvard University after the war to earn a master's degree. A university fellowship enabled Dahl to study in Europe for two years, including time at the American Academy in Rome. Before moving to Texas, Dahl was employed as a designer for architectural firms in New York and Los Angeles. He arrived in Dallas in 1926 to work for the Herbert M. Greene Company; two years later, Dahl became a partner in Herbert M. Greene, LaRoche & Dahl. In 1934, Dahl produced a series of imaginative renderings that helped Dallas win the bid for what became the Texas Centennial Exposition of 1936. Dahl was hired as the centennial architect and technical director of the exposition in 1935 and was either directly involved or gave approval for every aspect of the fair's design. He established his own firm in 1943 and maintained a nationwide practice. Among Dahl's notable designs was Hillcrest State Bank (1938) in University Park, Texas, the first drive-in bank in the country.[38]

C. H. GRIESENBECK (1892-1970) was a San Antonio native who studied architecture at the Agricultural & Mechanical College of Texas (later Texas A&M University), graduating with a bachelor of science degree in 1912. After working for a short time in San Antonio and Corpus Christi, Griesenbeck was put in charge of architectural design for the Missouri-Kansas-Texas Railroad; among his projects were the depots at Temple, Taylor, Sealy, and Lockhart, Texas. In 1919, he joined Fonzie E. Robertson in Robertson & Griesenbeck, Architects. The partnership specialized in school buildings. By 1923, Griesenbeck was on his own in a varied practice that designed schools, industrial plants, hotels, and auto showrooms, as well as homes in affluent neighborhoods.[39]

HARE & HARE was an influential landscape architecture firm founded in 1910 in Kansas City, Missouri. Through the 1920s, the father-son partnership earned a national reputation designing college campuses, subdivisions, parks, and cemeteries. Its best-known project is probably Country Club Plaza (1923), a landmark shopping center in Kansas City. Hare & Hare also planned the 183-acre site of the 1936 Texas Centennial Exposition in Dallas. **Sidney J. Hare** (1860-1938) was largely self-taught, gaining early experience as superintendent of Forest Hill Cemetery in Kansas City. He was a proponent of naturalized design and earned a reputation for his innovative ideas in cemetery and park planning. His son **Herbert Hare** (1888-1960) studied landscape architecture under Frederick Law Olmstead at Harvard University before joining the family business in 1910. The firm continues operation as Ochsner Hare & Hare.

HAYNES & KIRBY was the Lubbock partnership established by S. B. Haynes and L. H. Kirby in 1947. The firm created an extensive portfolio of courthouses, schools, and hospitals in West Texas and occasionally worked outside the region.

S. B. Haynes (1893-1970) was born in Livingston, Texas, and graduated from the Agricultural & Mechanical College of Texas (later Texas A&M University) in 1916 with a bachelor of science degree. He worked as a draftsman for C. L. Wignall in Port Arthur, Texas, and for various other architects until 1922, when he established the first in a series of offices in Lubbock. Haynes retired in 1964; he died in Methodist Hospital in Lubbock, which Haynes & Kirby had designed.[40]

L. H. Kirby (1912-1972) spent his entire career with S. B. Haynes in Lubbock, first as a draftsman for S. B. Haynes, Architect, from 1934 to 1936, and then as a designer for Haynes & Strange, Architects, for ten years. In 1945, the Sherman, Texas, native earned a bachelor of science degree from Texas Technological College (later Texas Tech University); the following year, he was named a partner in Haynes, Strange & Kirby, Architects-Engineers. In 1947, the firm became Haynes & Kirby, Architects-Engineers.[41]

WYATT C. HEDRICK (1888-1964) was born into a tobacco-farming family in Chatham, Virginia. He earned a bachelor of arts degree from Roanoke College in 1909 and an engineering degree from Washington and Lee University in 1910. He worked as an engineer in Virginia until the Stone & Webster Engineering Corporation of Boston hired him as a construction engineer for the firm's Dallas office. In 1914, Hedrick established his own construction company in Fort Worth; he worked as an independent contractor until 1921, when he joined the prominent Fort Worth architectural firm Sanguinet & Staats. Hedrick opened his own practice in 1925 with offices in Fort Worth, Dallas, and Houston. Hedrick was an engineer by training; when it came to architecture, he depended on his talented chief designer, Herman P. Koeppe, whom he had hired away from Sanguinet & Staats. When both Marshall R. Sanguinet and Carl G. Staats retired in 1926, Hedrick bought the remaining interest in their firm. From the 1920s through the 1950s, Hedrick maintained a national presence and developed what became the third-largest architectural firm in the country.[42]

P. R. L. HOGNER (1884-1966) devoted most of his architectural career to two major corporations: the Aluminum Company of America, or Alcoa, and the Gulf Oil Corporation. Hogner was a Swedish immigrant who majored in civil engineering and architecture at the Massachusetts Institute of Technology. In 1908, he transferred to Harvard University for his final year to receive his bachelor of science degree in architecture from Harvard. Hogner spent one year at the Atelier Trélat, École Speciale d'Architecture, Paris, and then returned to Harvard for another year to earn a certificate in structural engineering. He worked as a draftsman for prominent architectural firms in Boston and Seattle before forming a partnership with A. E. Harvey in Portland, Oregon. Hogner later moved to Illinois and worked as a designer for the city of Chicago before enlisting in the US Army and serving as assistant quartermaster of a construction division. By 1920, Hogner was an architect for Alcoa in Pittsburgh, a position he held until 1932. One year later, he became chief architect for the Gulf Oil Corporation, also headquartered in Pittsburgh. He was responsible for the design of all of Gulf's service stations, and in 1934 he designed Gulf's standard Automotive Garage. Hogner retired from Gulf Oil in 1955 and set up his own practice in Fort Lauderdale, Florida.[43]

ALBERT KAHN (1869-1942) was born in Rhaunen, Germany, and moved to Detroit with his family at age eleven. When he was fifteen, he went to work as an office boy in the architectural firm of Mason & Rice, where he learned drafting from partner George D. Mason. By nineteen, Kahn was supervising the firm's residential work; three years later he won a scholarship to study architecture in Europe. On his return to Detroit, he opened his own firm, Albert Kahn Associates. Kahn attracted worldwide attention in 1905 when he designed a section of the Packard Motor Car Company plant using a reinforced concrete structural system; among his admirers was Henry Ford, who hired Kahn to design Ford Motor Company assembly plants. Kahn also designed many of Detroit's landmarks, including the General Motors headquarters (1923) and the stunning Art Deco Fisher Building (1928). His firm remains in business as Kahn.[44]

ANTON F. KORN (1886-1942) was born in New York City and graduated from DeWitt Clinton High School in 1903. He spent the next five years working in architects' offices learning the fundamentals of his profession before entering Cornell University in 1908 to study architecture. In 1914, he moved to Galveston, Texas, and served as associate architect on the remodeling and expansion of the original John Sealy Hospital (1890, demolished). He established his practice in Dallas in 1917 and developed an outstanding reputation for designing imposing homes in affluent areas such as Swiss Avenue and Highland Park. Korn was later employed as the architect for Hilton Hotels of Texas. He was working at the Bluebonnet Ordnance Plant near Waco when he died of a heart attack. Korn was interred in the Hillcrest Mausoleum (1937, later Sparkman/Hillcrest Mausoleum) in Dallas, which he designed.[45]

LANG & WITCHELL was the dominant architectural firm in Dallas in the decades before World War II. The partnership was responsible for some of the city's most significant buildings and influenced design across Texas.

Otto H. Lang (1864-1947) had traveled from his native Frieburg, Germany, to the United States for a wedding in 1888 when he decided to remain in Dallas. He worked for local architects for two years before being put in charge of architecture and design for the Texas and Pacific Railway. In 1905, Lang formed a partnership with Frank O. Witchell. The firm began receiving important commissions in Dallas, including office buildings, hotels, and department stores, and designed several county courthouses in other parts of Texas. On his retirement in 1942, Lang also retired Lang & Witchell from active practice and transferred the firm's principal plan files to architect-engineer Grayson Gill.[46]

Frank O. Witchell (1879-1958) emigrated with his family from Wales to San Antonio when he was two years old. He was educated in the city's public schools until the fifth grade, when he entered the office of a local architect. Witchell was later employed as a designer and draftsman by the prominent Fort Worth firm Sanguinet & Staats, after which he entered into partnership with Otto H. Lang. Although Lang was thirty-three years older than his partner, Witchell retired in 1938, four years before Lang's retirement.[47]

C. H. LEINBACH (1881-1970) was a native of Nickerson, Kansas, who trained in architecture through private study and by working in the building trades. He started his architectural practice in Mineral Wells, Texas, in 1908 and moved to Dallas seven years later. He was particularly known for his school buildings and was estimated to have planned more than one hundred educational facilities in Texas. Among the buildings he designed outside Dallas are the Avenue D School (1923) in Killeen and the Wood County Courthouse (1925) in Quitman; both are Recorded Texas Historic Landmarks.[48]

MARK LEMMON (1889-1975) was born in Gainesville, Texas, and raised in Sherman. He earned a degree in geology from the University of Texas at Austin and degrees in architecture and engineering from the Massachusetts Institute of Technology before enlisting in the US Army during World War I; he spent a year building roads and bridges with an engineering division in France. He moved to Dallas in 1919 and worked for architect Hal Thomson until 1921, when Lemmon partnered with Roscoe P. DeWitt. Lemmon established his own practice in 1927. Three years later, he designed the original Cotton Bowl Stadium at Fair Park in Dallas. Although best known for his use of architectural revival styles in his designs for schools and churches, Lemmon also produced significant modernistic designs.[49]

WILLIAM LESCAZE (1896-1969) was born near Geneva, Switzerland, and studied at the Eidgenössische Technische Hoschscule in Zurich. He moved to the United States in 1920 to work for the Cleveland architecture firm of Hubbell & Benes before opening his own office in New York in 1923. Lescaze established himself as one of America's early modernist architects. He was said to be the only American at the first International Congress of Modern Architecture in 1928 and was one of the few Americans whose works were included in the Museum of Modern Art's landmark 1932 *Modern Architecture: An International Exhibition.* He attracted worldwide attention for his design, with partner George Howe, of the PSFS Building (1932) in Philadelphia; shortly after that project was completed, Dallas retailer Stanley Marcus interviewed and rejected Lescaze for the job of designing his home. Marcus then recommended Lescaze as architect of the Magnolia Lounge (1936) at the Texas Centennial Exposition. Though Lescaze continued his career well into the 1960s, he was somewhat overshadowed after noted modernists including Walter Gropius and Ludwig Mies van der Rohe immigrated to the United States from Germany in the late 1930s.[50]

WILL H. LIGHTFOOT (1892-1979) was a native of Paris, Texas, and spent most of his career there. He received his bachelor of science degree in architecture from the University of Texas at Austin in 1914; the following year, he took postgraduate studies at Harvard University. He briefly worked in Austin before returning to Paris in the aftermath of the 1916 fire that destroyed most of the city's business district and many residential areas. During that time, he was associated with two local firms, Curtis, Broad & Lightfoot and Curtis & Lightfoot. After serving in World War I, Lightfoot spent the latter part of the 1920s as part of the Amarillo firm Townes, Lightfoot & Funk, where he worked on the Potter County Courthouse (1932), one of the state's Art Deco landmarks. Lightfoot then returned to Paris and established an independent practice.[51]

THEO. S. MAFFITT (1895-1958) was born in Palestine, Texas, where he spent most of his career. He attended the University of Texas School of Architecture from 1913 to 1916 and studied navigation at the University of California before entering the US Navy's Officers Material School during World War I. He worked briefly as a draftsman for Neff & Thompson of Norfolk, Virginia, before returning to Palestine and establishing his practice, concentrating on projects in his hometown and the surrounding region. Theodore (Ted) S. Maffitt Jr. joined his father's firm in 1948.[52]

MAURAN, RUSSELL & CROWELL was the influential St. Louis partnership of **John Lawrence Mauran** (1866-1933), **Ernest J. Russell** (1870-1956), and **William DeForrest Crowell** (1879-1967). The firm was established in 1900 by Mauran and Russell and soon gained prominence designing everything from massive commercial exchanges, department stores, and skyscrapers to revival-style homes and churches in affluent neighborhoods. By the time Crowell was brought on as a partner in 1911, the practice had a national reputation for its tall buildings. In the 1920s, Crowell employed his fascination with aviation and marine design in the creation of many significant examples of Art Deco and Art Moderne architecture.[53]

HOWARD R. MEYER (1903-1988) was one of Dallas's most accomplished modern architects. While still a student at Columbia University, the native New Yorker worked in the office of architect William Lescaze, a leading proponent of modernist design. After graduating with a bachelor of architecture degree in 1928, Meyer embarked on a yearlong tour of Europe, where he met the architect Le Corbusier and became a convert to what came to be known as the International Style. Meyer returned to New York and worked for other architects before entering a partnership with Morris B. Saunders, but the Depression limited the firm's success. The prospect of work brought Meyer to Dallas in 1935. He designed a series of modern homes, though his best-known work is probably Temple Emanu-El (1957) in Dallas.[54]

NEILD-SOMDAL-NEILD was a prominent Louisiana-based architectural firm that achieved national influence through its association with President Harry S. Truman. Although the practice was rechristened Neild-Somdal-Neild in 1936, the firm was usually advertised by its original name: the Office of Edward F. Neild, Architect.

Edward F. Neild (1884-1955) created outstanding Art Deco and Art Moderne designs for his hometown of Shreveport, Louisiana, and the surrounding region. After graduating from Tulane University's School of Engineering, Neild spent two years in Europe studying architecture and the applied arts. He returned to Shreveport and set up his practice in 1908. In 1932, Harry S. Truman, then a county judge from Missouri, visited Shreveport looking for a building that could serve as a model for a new courthouse; the future president was impressed with Neild's design for the Caddo Parish Courthouse (1928) and hired the architect as a consultant for the modernistic Jackson County Courthouse (1934) in Kansas City. Neild would later be one of the architects selected for President Truman's restoration and rebuilding of the White House (1948-1952). Neild died in Kansas City while working as lead architect for the Harry S. Truman Library and Museum (1957).[55]

Dewey A. Somdal (1898-1973), of Mansfield, Illinois, attended the University of Illinois for two years. Edward F. Neild hired Somdal as a draftsman-designer in 1922 and made him a partner in the renamed Neild-Somdal Associates in 1935. **Edward F. Neild Jr.** (1908-1958) graduated from Tulane University with a degree in architecture and joined the firm by 1936, the first documented appearance of the Neild-Somdal-Neild name. He served as associate architect for many buildings on the campus of the Louisiana Polytechnic Institute (later Louisiana Tech University) in Ruston.[56]

DONALD S. NELSON (1907-1992) was a Chicago native who earned his architecture degree from the Massachusetts Institute of Technology in 1927 and won the Prix de Paris scholarship to study at the École normale supérieure des Beaux-arts, where he remained until 1930. Nelson returned to Chicago and joined the architectural firm of Bennett, Parsons & Frost, where he played a significant role in planning the 1933 Century of Progress International Exposition. He moved to Dallas to work as the assistant to Centennial Architect George L. Dahl for the 1936 Texas Centennial Exposition; he also helped design the Will Rogers Memorial Center, Fort Worth's Centennial complex. Nelson opened a private practice in Dallas after the fair.[57]

B. GAYLORD NOFTSGER (1897-1979) was one of Oklahoma's first licensed architects. A native Iowan, he attended the University of Oklahoma, but left without earning a degree. During the 1920s he was superintendent of construction for John J. Harden, Incorporated, a prominent Oklahoma real estate development company. In the 1930s, Noftsger maintained his own practice, but Harden remained a major client. The architect designed some of Oklahoma's best Art Deco buildings for Harden, including Rose Hill Mausoleum (1937) in Oklahoma City, where Noftsger is interred, and the Warehouse Market Building (1938) in Tulsa, which resembles Noftsger's Fort Worth Public Market (1930).[58]

JOSEPH J. PATTERSON, see PATTERSON & TEAGUE.

PATTERSON & TEAGUE was the four-year partnership (1935-1939) of Fort Worth architects Joseph J. Patterson and James Teague.

Joseph J. Patterson (1894-1976) was born in Danville, Illinois, and earned a bachelor of science degree in architecture from the University of Illinois before enrolling in graduate studies at Oklahoma A&M College (later Oklahoma State University). Patterson served as an associate professor at Oklahoma A&M and worked as a designer-draftsman in Chicago before joining Wyatt C. Hedrick's Fort Worth architectural firm as a designer in 1925. After a decade in Hedrick's office, Patterson joined James Teague to establish their firm. After his partnership with Teague ended, Patterson and Edward L. Wilson, another former Hedrick associate, formed Wilson & Patterson (later Wilson, Patterson & Associates) in 1939.[59]

James Teague (1863-1947) was born and educated in Tennessee. He began his peripatetic career in Norfolk, Virginia, in 1891, where he was associated with designing several large residences and the Prince William County Courthouse (1892) in Manassas. He established a successful practice in Sault Sainte Marie, Michigan, in 1898, but left in 1907 to work in Seattle. By 1911, he had moved his office to Calgary, Alberta, Canada, where he designed the nine-story Lancaster Block (1919), one of the city's tallest commercial buildings at the time. In 1913, Teague applied for membership in the American Institute of Architects, noting that he was an American citizen practicing in Canada. It does not appear he was granted AIA membership. Teague returned to Seattle in 1914, but moved to Butte, Montana, within a year. In 1923, he relocated once again, this time to Dallas, before moving to Fort Worth and entering into partnership with Joseph J. Patterson.[60]

JOSEPH R. PELICH (1894-1968) was five years old when his family emigrated from Prague (then part of Austria-Hungary) and settled in Cleveland, Ohio. Pelich earned a bachelor's degree in architecture from Cornell University in 1916. While at Cornell, he was awarded several medals for his academic and design work, and he received a graduate scholarship that allowed him to study at the Sorbonne in Paris. Pelich served in the US Army Air Corps from 1917 to 1919 and became the chief flying instructor for Fort Worth's three army airfields. After his discharge, he stayed in Fort Worth and established his architectural practice. In addition to designing private homes for prominent residents, Pelich received commissions for major public buildings, several projects on the Texas Christian University campus, and showman Billy Rose's original Casa Mañana outdoor dinner theater (1936, demolished). Pelich's masterwork was likely the passenger terminal at Greater Fort Worth International Airport (1953, demolished).[61]

JOHN ASTIN PERKINS (1907-1999) was born in McKinney, Texas, and educated at Yale University, where he earned a bachelor of arts degree in 1929. Perkins graduated from the University of Texas at Austin with a bachelor of architecture degree in 1931. He worked as a draftsman for the prominent Dallas firm of Lang & Witchell and in the Architecture Department at the Agricultural & Mechanical College of Texas (later Texas A&M University). Perkins established his own practice in Dallas in 1935 and began designing homes and clubhouses for affluent clients. After studying at the New York School of Fine and Applied Arts (later Parsons School of Design), Perkins also became an in-demand interior designer.[62]

MAURICE PETERMAN (1896-1971) was a Dallas-born architect who spent his entire career in his hometown. After serving in World War I, Peterman worked as a draftsman for architect H. A. Overbeck in the early 1920s and for his brothers' firm, Fred F. & C. F. Peterman, Architects and Structural Engineers, from the late 1920s through the early '30s. Peterman established his own practice in the late 1930s; his works included private homes and small churches. After World War II, Peterman received significant commissions from Dallas County and became an architectural inspector.[63]

NOAH L. PETERS, see ZIMMERMAN, PETERS & STRANGE.

PETERS, STRANGE & COMPANY,
see ZIMMERMAN, PETERS & STRANGE.

H.F. PETTIGREW, see PETTIGREW, WORLEY & COMPANY.

PETTIGREW, WORLEY & COMPANY was a Dallas firm established by architects H. F. Pettigrew and John A. Worley in 1939. It specialized in movie theater design.

H. F. Pettigrew (1906-1976) was born in Chisholm, Texas, and began his independent design and construction career in 1925 after working with some of the state's leading architectural firms and builders.

John A. Worley (1913-1982), a Dallas native, received engineering, architectural, and military training at the Agricultural & Mechanical College of Texas (later Texas A&M University) and graduated in 1935. He worked with several Dallas firms before forming his partnership with Pettigrew.

With the unexpected death of W. Scott Dunne, the primary architect for Interstate Theaters, Pettigrew and Worley became the de facto designers for the largest motion picture chain in Texas. In addition to their work in North Texas, the partners created modernistic theaters in other parts of the state, including the Queen (1939) in Bryan, the Broadway (1939) in San Antonio, the River Oaks (1939) in Houston, and the Pershing (1940) in El Paso.

When theater construction was halted during World War II, Worley enlisted in the armed forces, and Pettigrew organized the Texas Prefabricated House and Tent Company, which manufactured sixteen-by-sixteen-foot plywood "Victory Huts" that the military used in place of canvas tents. The firm shipped more than 200,000 units during the course of the war. It was later revealed that Pettigrew's firm had also produced the prefabricated "Homettes" provided for workers at Oak Ridge, Tennessee, the top-secret facility where materials were developed for constructing the atomic bomb. Meanwhile, Worley was serving as an engineering battalion commander in North Africa and Italy; he received the Bronze Star for housing sixty thousand troops in record time. After fifty-five months of active duty, Worley returned to Dallas and rejoined the firm in 1946.[64]

In the 1950s, when television's impact slowed theater construction, the company began building and selling houses in the suburbs surrounding Dallas and Fort Worth as Pettigrew-Worley & Reynolds, Builders. Worley eventually became a major homebuilder and apartment developer in his own right, and Pettigrew established Pettigrew and Company, Designers and Builders.[65]

PHELPS & DEWEES (later **PHELPS & DEWEES & SIMMONS**) was a San Antonio architectural firm established in 1919. The partnership was best known for designing educational facilities and such public projects as the Gonzales Memorial Museum (1937) for the Texas Centennial.

Raymond P. Phelps (1890-1958) was a native of San Antonio who established his architectural practice in the city in 1908. His obituary states that he "attended school in Austin," but it is not clear if that refers to the years his family lived in the state capital when his father served as Texas's assistant adjutant general or means that he studied architecture at the University of Texas. Phelps served as a field artillery captain in France during World War I and formed his partnership with Dahl Dewees after he returned to San Antonio.[66]

Dahl Dewees (1888-1965) was born in Bexar County, Texas. He received his training while traveling through Europe with the San Antonio architect Carl von Seutter and by serving as a draftsman for architects J. Flood Walker and Henry T. Phelps, the brother of his future business partner.[67]

C. C. Simmons (1901-1981) joined Phelps & Dewees as a designer, draftsman, and office manager in 1925 after graduating from the University of Texas at Austin with a bachelor of science degree in architecture. The Bartonville, Texas, native was made a partner in the firm in 1937.[68]

LLEWELLYN W. PITTS (1906-1967) grew up in Uniontown, Alabama, and attended the Georgia School of Technology (later the Georgia Institute of Technology). In 1927, Pitts earned a bachelor of science degree in architecture and received the American Institute of Architects Student Medal for excellence in architecture. He moved to Beaumont, Texas, soon after graduation. In 1929, he began working as a draftsman for architect Fred C. Stone on major commissions including the Jefferson County Courthouse (1931), one of Texas's most significant Art Deco buildings. In 1934, Stone made Pitts a partner in the firm Stone & Pitts. Their office excelled at modernistic design and specialized in planning bottling facilities for the Coca-Cola Company.[69]

PITZINGER-LANE ASSOCIATES was the Dallas partnership of Joseph A. Pitzinger and Roy E. Lane from 1938 to 1940; the firm specialized in commercial and industrial buildings. The partners' most significant projects, the Packard-Dallas showroom (1940) on Ross Avenue and a modernistic factory for the Haggar pants company (1941) at Lemmon Avenue and Mockingbird Lane, have been demolished.

Joseph A. Pitzinger (1891-1972) was an Austrian immigrant who held degrees from the University of Vienna. He arrived in the United States in 1912 and settled in Detroit. Pitzinger moved to Dallas as the architectural superintendent for United Motors, a division of General Motors, but left the company in 1920 to establish his own architectural and structural engineering practice. Although Pitzinger designed some private homes, the majority of his commissions were for manufacturing, warehouse, and garage buildings. Most of Pitzinger's buildings have been demolished, including several large facilities in the former wholesale district developed by the Missouri-Kansas-Texas Railroad. His surviving works in Dallas include the Sanger Brothers department store garage (1925) at 711 Elm Street and the John E. Mitchell Company Building (1928, later The Mitchell Lofts) at 3800 Commerce Street. Pitzinger was very active in civil defense planning after World War II and remained in practice well into his seventies.[70]

Roy E. Lane (1884-1956) was born in Kansas City, Missouri, and earned degrees in architecture and civil engineering from the University of Minnesota. He opened a practice in his hometown but moved to Waco, Texas, in 1907. His best-known work is Waco's twenty-two-story Amicable Life Insurance Company (ALICO) Building, which he designed in association with Sanguinet & Staats of Fort Worth. On its completion in 1911, the skyscraper was known as the tallest building west of the Mississippi and south of the Mason-Dixon line; it survived the devastating 1953 tornado that leveled parts of downtown Waco. Lane moved to Dallas in 1936 to work for the Housing Division of the Public Works Administration before entering into partnership with Joseph A. Pitzinger.[71]

WILLIAM R. RAGSDALE (1881-1963) was born in Greenville, Texas. He began practicing architecture in his hometown as early as 1915, designing schools in nearby communities such as Humphrey (its townsite was inundated by Lake Tawakoni in 1959) and Emory. His later work included remodeling Greenville's Rita Theater (1933, demolished) and designing the Texan Theater (1934, remodeled in 1951 by L. C. Kyburz). Ragsdale also designed the Greenville Chamber of Commerce Building (1954, with Jimmy Smith) and the Greenville Public Library (1954, with Roy Kilmer, demolished). He spent the last years of his life in Beaumont, Texas.[72]

S. W. RAY (1878-1964) was born in Philadelphia, Mississippi, and described his architectural training as "Scranton Correspondence School and continuous home study." He worked in his own practice in Palestine, Texas, from 1905 to 1906 before briefly moving to Amarillo. He returned to East Texas and established an office in Jacksonville, where he designed churches, schools, and commercial buildings along with facilities for Lon Morris College in Jacksonville and Texas College in Tyler. He later relocated to Tyler and was still in practice at the age of eighty.[73]

LUTHER E. SADLER (1885-1965) was a native of Hickory, Mississippi, who moved to Dallas in 1910. Sadler's 1918 draft registration card listed his occupation as "arch'tl draughtsman" for the Clem Lumber Company; the 1920 US Census also listed his occupation as "draughtsman," but a 1927 newspaper ad for the Republic Building & Loan Association, of which Sadler was a director, described him as "an architect of 14 years' experience" as well as an appraiser. During the 1930s, Sadler was recognized for his distinctive modernistic houses along with his more traditional home designs. He also created the Art Moderne-style *Christian Science Monitor* pavilion for the 1936 Texas Centennial Exposition at Fair Park in Dallas. In 1946, he and John W. Armstrong formed Sadler & Armstrong, Architects-Builders, to design, build, and market homes in Dallas and Highland Park.[74]

JESSE M. SHELTON (1895-1976) was an Atlanta-based architect who frequently received commissions to design bottling plants and other facilities around the country for the Coca-Cola Company. Shelton attended the Georgia School of Technology (later Georgia Institute of Technology); although Georgia Tech listed him as an alumnus, Shelton's response to the 1940 US Census indicated that he had only completed two years of college. Shelton later served as president of Robert & Company Associates, a prominent Atlanta architectural and engineering firm that was one of three companies selected in 1954 to design, plan, and construct the new US Air Force Academy in Colorado Springs. In 1955, Shelton formed a partnership with Roscoe P. DeWitt of Dallas and Alfred Easton Poor of New York to design the extension of the US Capitol's East Portico.[75]

EDWARD F. SIBBERT (1899-1982) left his mark on business districts across the United States as the chief architect for S. H. Kress & Company. Sibbert was born in New York City in 1899 and earned a structural engineering degree from the Pratt Institute in 1920 and an architecture degree from Cornell University in 1922. He formed a short-lived partnership, Pancoast & Sibbert, with a Cornell classmate, then joined the New York firm of E. H. Faile & Company. In 1929, Samuel H. Kress (1863-1955), founder of the S. H. Kress variety store chain, hired Sibbert as the corporation's chief architect. Sibbert was responsible for designing stores from New York to Hawaii and served as the company's vice president of buildings until 1954. He went into private practice after leaving Kress.[76]

T. SHIRLEY SIMONS (1897-1963) was born in Taylor in Central Texas and raised in Fort Worth. He served in the field artillery during World War I before earning a bachelor of science degree in architecture from Houston's Rice Institute (later Rice University). Simons remained in Houston after graduation to work for architect William Ward Watkin, who had been one of Simons's professors at Rice. Simons established his own practice in Lufkin in 1922 and would remain in East Texas for the rest of his life. He moved to Tyler in 1928 and became a founding director of the Texas Society of Architects in 1939. Simons's three sons, T. Shirley Simons Jr., Edwin Simons, and Watson Townes Simons, eventually joined his architectural practice in Tyler.[77]

HOKE SMITH (1896-1943) was a self-trained architect who designed public buildings across North Texas, usually under the Works Progress Administration (WPA). Raised on a farm in Duncanville, Texas, Smith attended East Texas State Teachers College (now Texas A&M University-Commerce). After college, he farmed for a time before joining the Dallas County school system's maintenance department. He was promoted to engineer and developed his talents as an architect while assisting the school system in planning and completing numerous projects with WPA support. In 1936, he became a licensed architect and went into private practice. Smith designed many small-town school buildings, frequently in the Art Moderne style, and was also architect of the Tomato Bowl (1940), the landmark high school football stadium in Jacksonville, Texas.[78]

RAYMOND F. SMITH (1901-1978) was born in Allentown, Illinois, and earned a bachelor of science degree in architectural engineering from the University of Illinois. Smith opened his practice in Dallas in 1937 and designed movie theaters in cities and towns around North Texas and outside the region, including the Grenada (1948) in Houston and its twin, the Capitan (1949, altered), in the Houston suburb of Pasadena. He later worked as an architect at US Air Force headquarters in Washington, DC.[79]

JOHN F. STAUB (1892-1981) was an influential Houston architect best known for designing large homes in romantic and revival styles for affluent clients. Born in Knoxville, Tennessee, Staub studied at the University of Tennessee, earned a master's degree in architecture from the Massachusetts Institute of Technology, and served as a US Navy aviator during World War I. He worked in New York with prominent architect Harrie T. Lindeberg, who specialized in country houses. Lindeberg sent Staub to Houston in 1921 to supervise the construction of three private homes. Two years later, Staub established his own practice in Houston and became one of the city's most celebrated residential architects. Somewhat surprisingly, his designs also included the 1929 prototype for the Humble Oil & Refining Company's service stations.[80]

THEODORE H. STUEBER (1899-1983) was from Parsons, Kansas, and earned his architecture degree at Kansas State Agricultural College (later Kansas State University). Stueber was the corporate architect for Wyatt Food Stores of Dallas from the grocery chain's founding in 1931 through 1961, when the Kroger Company acquired Wyatt. In addition to designing Wyatt grocery stores, supermarkets, and warehouse/distribution centers, Stueber also planned the restaurants in the Wyatt's Cafeteria chain, which were originally located inside Wyatt Food Stores. Stueber continued to work in architectural consulting and planning after he left Wyatt.[81]

ARTHUR E. THOMAS, see THOMAS, JAMESON & MERRILL.

THOMAS, JAMESON & MERRILL was the partnership of architects Arthur E. Thomas and W. Ralph Merrill and structural engineer Robert O. Jameson. The firm was active in Dallas from 1945 to 1963 and was responsible for several major commissions, including expansions of the Titche-Goettinger department store (1954, altered) and the Southwestern Bell headquarters (1959), both in downtown Dallas, and the Smith County Courthouse (1955) in Tyler. The firm also designed several facilities in the Baylor University Medical Center at Dallas.[82]

Arthur E. Thomas (1893-1973) was born near Crockett, Texas, and studied at the University of Texas at Austin from 1913 to 1916 without earning a degree. According to his World War I draft registration card, he was working as a draftsman for the Mosher Manufacturing Company in Dallas in 1917. Thomas established his architectural practice in Dallas in 1925 and gained attention the following year for designing one of the *Dallas Times Herald*'s "Pasadena Perfect Homes" as part of an early suburban development in the Lakewood area. He partnered with Corneil G. Curtis on two Texas courthouses: the Rusk County Courthouse (1928) in Henderson and the Art Deco Liberty County Courthouse (1931) in Liberty. Thomas later designed the Art Moderne-style Falls County Courthouse (1939) in Marlin, Texas.[83]

Robert O. Jameson (1890-1978) was born in Aubrey, Texas, but spent most of his life in Dallas. He graduated from Dallas High School in 1908 and began an apprenticeship at the Mosher Manufacturing Company before entering the University of Texas at Austin, where he earned a degree in structural engineering. Jameson returned to Mosher Manufacturing as chief draftsman around the time his future partner Arthur E. Thomas was employed as a draftsman for the company. After briefly working for architect Wyatt C. Hedrick, Jameson established his own office. In 1922, he advertised in the *Dallas Morning News* as a consulting engineer specializing in reinforced concrete and structural steel designs. He served as a civilian engineer during World War II before becoming a partner in Thomas, Jameson & Merrill. Robert O. Jameson was posthumously inducted into the Texas Structural Engineering Hall of Honor in 2012.[84]

W. Ralph Merrill (1906-1991) was a native of Harvey, Illinois. He attended the University of Illinois, Chicago Technical College, and the School of the Art Institute of Chicago, and traveled extensively in Europe studying architecture. In the late 1930s, Merrill worked as a designer for Dallas architect Mark Lemmon before establishing his own practice in Oklahoma City. Merrill returned to Dallas in 1945 when Thomas, Jameson & Merrill was organized.[85]

IRVIN R. TIMLIN (1880-1955) spent his entire career with the Southwestern Bell Telephone Company. Timlin was born in Cleveland, Ohio, and was educated in the public schools of Kansas City, Missouri. He attended Washington University in St. Louis for two years before completing correspondence courses in architectural, structural, mechanical, and electrical engineering while working in the offices of architects Van Brunt & Howe and W. R. Chesney. Timlin joined Southwestern Bell in 1904 as a draftsman in Kansas City. He was made assistant equipment engineer in 1907 and appointed architect in 1911. He was promoted to chief architect for the company and moved to St. Louis in 1917, the same year he was accepted into the American Institute of Architects. Timlin designed approximately 140 buildings for Southwestern Bell throughout the company's service area before retiring in 1945.[86]

VOELCKER & DIXON was the architectural firm established by Herbert Voelcker and Jesse G. Dixon in Wichita Falls, Texas, in 1918. For more than a quarter century, Voelcker & Dixon designed private homes, schools, colleges, post offices, and county and federal courthouses.

Herbert Voelcker (1888-1971) was born in New Braunfels, Texas. He attended the Agricultural & Mechanical College of Texas (later Texas A&M University) and graduated in 1909 with a degree in architecture and engineering. He worked as a draftsman with C. H. Page & Brother in Austin and with Sanguinet & Staats in Fort Worth before spending three years with Lewis & Kitchen in Kansas City, followed by six months in the firm's Chicago office. Voelcker was then an associate of Albert Kahn's in Detroit for six months before moving to Wichita Falls in 1916, when the city was experiencing a construction boom in the aftermath of several major oil discoveries. Voelcker worked with E. S. Fields before establishing his long-standing partnership with Jesse G. Dixon in 1918. After his association with Dixon ended in 1945, Voelcker moved to Houston, his wife's hometown, and established the firm Herbert Voelcker & Associates.[87]

Jesse G. Dixon (1889-1962) was a native of Paducah, Kentucky. According to the US Census, he moved to Texas by 1910. Dixon's World War I draft registration states he was an architectural draftsman in the Dallas office of the Russell Brown Company, which was known for designing and building homes throughout the state. After the war, he moved to Wichita Falls and began his association with Herbert Voelcker. When their partnership ended, Dixon began an independent practice, Jesse G. Dixon, AIA. He retired in 1958.[88]

EMILE WEIL (1878-1945) was one of Louisiana's most prominent architects in the first decades of the twentieth century. A New Orleans native, Weil graduated from Tulane University and worked as a draftsman for several architects before starting his own practice in 1899. He designed significant homes in a variety of revival styles along affluent St. Charles Avenue and created classically inspired banks and commercial buildings for New Orleans's business district. Weil's office prospered and he expanded his firm into a large, modern practice called Emile Weil, Incorporated. By the 1920s, Weil was well regarded throughout the South; his commissions can be found in all the states surrounding Louisiana. His firm was especially known for its ornate movie palaces. Weil's Texas theaters include Texarkana's Saenger (1924, later the Perot), Beaumont's Jefferson (1927), and Marshall's Paramount (1930, partially demolished). Weil closed his office in 1933.[89]

WEISS, DREYFOUS & SEIFERTH was an influential architectural firm founded in New Orleans by three Louisiana natives: **Leon C. Weiss** (1882-1953), **F. Julius Dreyfous** (1896-1975) and **Solis Seiferth** (1895-1984). The young architects gained prominence in the 1920s designing luxury hotels and became well known for their early embrace of Art Deco design and European modernism.

Leon Weiss established the firm as his private practice after graduating from Tulane University with an engineering degree in 1912. He hired Solis Seiferth as his chief draftsman in 1915, the same year Seiferth received his bachelor of architecture degree from Tulane. In 1919, Weiss formed a partnership with Julius Dreyfous, who held a bachelor of science degree in architecture from the University of Pennsylvania. Seiferth remained with the new partnership and was made a partner in 1923. When controversial Louisiana governor Huey Long came to power in the late 1920s, he selected the firm to design several of his monumental public projects, including the Art Deco Louisiana State Capitol (1934) in Baton Rouge, a National Historic Landmark. The three architects worked together until 1939; Dreyfous and Seiferth continued the practice until 1960.[90]

WILEY G. CLARKSON & COMPANY, see WILEY G. CLARKSON.

PHILLIP G. WILLARD (1913-1993) was a Texas-born architect who became a proponent of masonry residential construction. Willard was in practice in Fort Worth by 1937 and frequently worked in association with architect Robert P. Woltz Jr. designing masonry houses for Chase Building Products, Incorporated, using the company's Worthcrete brand tile. Willard later designed homes as an architectural consultant for the Acme Brick Company. He moved his practice to Houston by 1944 and continued his interest in masonry houses, selling a now-demolished house of "brick, tile and structural steel" in the Houston suburb of Bellaire in 1947. During the early 1950s, Willard worked in association with architect Lucian T. Hood Jr. to create several houses under the auspices of the Ceramic Construction Company. Willard also designed homes in Lake Jackson, Texas.[91]

EDWARD L. WILSON (1899-1964) graduated from the Armour Institute of Technology in his native Chicago in 1919. He worked as a draftsman in Tulsa from 1920 to 1925, when he was hired as a draftsman-designer for Wyatt C. Hedrick in Fort Worth. After serving as Hedrick's chief designer, Wilson established his own practice. In 1939, Wilson and J. J. Patterson formed Wilson & Patterson (later Wilson, Patterson & Associates). Wilson retired on New Year's Day, 1964, and died on New Year's Eve that same year.[92]

ALECK B. WITHERS (1890-1982) was the younger brother of prominent Fort Worth architect Elmer G. Withers. Like his brother, Aleck Withers appears to have been self-trained. He spent the 1920s and 1930s in practice in Mineral Wells, Texas. One of his more significant commissions from this period, the Bevans Hotel (1928), still stands in Menard, Texas. Aleck Withers moved to Fort Worth in the late 1930s and maintained his own office separate from his brother's firm. During World War II, he began designing educational facilities for the Castleberry and White Settlement school districts outside Fort Worth; school design remained an important facet of Withers's work for the rest of his career.[93]

ELMER G. WITHERS, see WITHERS & THOMPSON.

WITHERS & THOMPSON was the brief partnership of Elmer G. Withers and Jesse C. Thompson. During their short time working together, the architects designed two Texas landmarks: the Menard County Courthouse in Menard and the Young County Courthouse in Graham. Both Art Deco buildings were completed in 1932.

Elmer G. Withers (1881-1938) was born in Caddo Peak, Texas, south of Fort Worth. He appears to have gained his architectural training through apprenticeships and correspondence courses. He established his practice in Fort Worth in 1910 and won commissions for the Jones County Courthouse (1911) in Anson, the Marion County Courthouse (1912) in Jefferson, and the Armstrong County Courthouse (1912) in Claude. In 1928, he formed the Elmer G. Withers Architectural Company in Fort Worth, and the following year he worked with Mauran, Russell & Crowell of St. Louis to design the landmark Blackstone Hotel. Withers collaborated with Wyatt C. Hedrick on major projects including the Will Rogers Memorial Center (1938) and Fort Worth City Hall (1939). Withers was designing a public housing project for the Fort Worth Housing Authority at the time of his death.[94]

Jesse C. Thompson (1876-1942) was born in Ohio and completed one year of college, according to the 1940 US Census. Newspaper advertisements, city directory listings, and public records show that he frequently moved around Texas. He was a partner with Charles J. Pate in the architectural firm Pate & Thompson in Wichita Falls in the late 1920s, followed by his partnership with Withers in Fort Worth. The 1940 census found him in Port Isabel, Texas; a city directory lists Thompson as an architect in Longview the following year. Thompson's death certificate placed him in Texarkana in 1942.

ROBERT P. WOLTZ JR. (1905-1993) was born in Fort Worth and spent his entire career there. Woltz earned a bachelor of architecture degree from the Agricultural & Mechanical College of Texas (later Texas A&M University) in 1930 and did graduate studies at the University of Pennsylvania. He worked as a draftsman for architect Hubert Hammond Crane from 1933 to 1935, then established his own practice in 1936. In the late 1930s, he was associated with architect Phillip G. Willard designing masonry homes for Chase Building Products, Incorporated, using the company's Worthcrete brand tile. Woltz designed the Texas Garden Clubs headquarters building (1959) in the Fort Worth Botanic Gardens. In 2011, the building was designated a Recorded Texas Historic Landmark. Woltz retired in 1970.[95]

PERCY E. ZIMMERMAN, see ZIMMERMAN & MORGAN and ZIMMERMAN, PETERS & STRANGE.

ZIMMERMAN & MORGAN was the partnership of architects Percy E. Zimmerman and William B. Morgan from 1935 to 1941. The firm was in general practice designing large and small commercial buildings as well as private homes and public buildings in Longview. The firm's major commercial projects in the city, including downtown stores for Sears, Roebuck & Company (1940) and the M. E. Moses Company (1940), have been demolished.

Percy E. Zimmerman (1902-1987) was born in Troy, Texas, and graduated from the Agricultural & Mechanical College of Texas (later Texas A&M University) in 1925. Beginning in 1926, he worked as head draftsman for Houston architect James Ruskin Bailey. Later, as Bailey's associate architect, Zimmerman moved to Longview to represent the firm on its projects there. Zimmerman left Bailey and established his own practice in Longview in 1931 before briefly joining Zimmerman, Peters & Strange. From 1935 to 1941, he was a partner in Zimmerman & Morgan with William B. Morgan; Zimmerman returned to Houston in December 1941 to work on defense contracts and later became a partner in Zimmerman & Bible, Architects-Engineers.[96]

William B. Morgan (1906-1962) was born in St. Louis, Missouri, and earned an architecture degree from Houston's Rice Institute (later Rice University) in 1927. After graduation, Morgan worked as a draftsman in the office of Houston architect James Ruskin Bailey, where his future business partner, Percy Zimmerman, was also employed. It is not clear what Morgan did between leaving Bailey's employ around 1930 and the formation of Zimmerman & Morgan in 1935. In December 1941, the *Longview Daily News* reported that Zimmerman had moved to Houston to assist a large architecture firm with its defense contracts, but Morgan would maintain Zimmerman & Morgan's practice in Longview. In January 1942, Morgan was commissioned to design a TNT plant at what would become the Longhorn Army Ammunition Plant (also known as the Longhorn Ordnance Works) in Karnack, Texas. Morgan had relocated to Houston by 1945, when he formed a partnership with fellow Rice graduate Hermon Lloyd. In 1958, Lloyd & Morgan became part of Associated Architects, the joint venture that designed the Harris County Domed Stadium (1965), better known as the Astrodome. Morgan did not live to see the project completed.[97]

ZIMMERMAN, PETERS & STRANGE was the brief Longview-based partnership of three architects who had each earned their degrees from the Agricultural & Mechanical College of Texas (later Texas A&M University). The firm's first major project was built in 1933 and the partnership had ended by 1935. For the biography of **Percy E. Zimmerman**, see the profile of Zimmerman & Morgan.

Noah L. Peters (1893-1969) was born and raised on his family's farm in Medina County, Texas. He practiced architecture for a short time in Las Vegas, New Mexico, before relocating to Lubbock, Texas, in the early 1920s and becoming a partner in Peters & Haynes. The practice was renamed Peters, Haynes & Strange when William T. Strange Jr. joined the firm. As Peters, Strange & Bradshaw, the architects designed Lubbock High School (1931), a Recorded Texas Historic Landmark. Peters and Strange had relocated to Longview by 1933 and entered a brief partnership with Percy E. Zimmerman. After Zimmerman left the practice, the firm operated as Peters, Strange & Company. Peters had returned to individual practice by 1937, when he applied for membership in the American Institute of Architects. He relocated to Edmonton, Alberta, Canada, during World War II and moved to California in the late 1940s.[98]

William T. Strange Jr. (1899-1972) was born in Ardmore, Oklahoma, and grew up in San Antonio. He earned a bachelor of science degree in architecture from the Agricultural & Mechanical College of Texas (later Texas A&M University) in 1922. After traveling the world, Strange settled in Lubbock, where he became a partner in Peters, Haynes & Strange and its successor firm, Peters, Strange & Bradshaw. Strange spent the 1930s in Longview with Zimmerman, Peters & Strange and Peters, Strange & Company. In 1947, he became a partner in the Los Angeles firm Orr, Strange, Inslee & Senefeld. In the 1960s, as Strange, Inslee & Senefeld, the office specialized in school design.[99]

Designers

A. EPSTEIN was the early name of a Chicago-based structural engineering firm that expanded into architectural design and construction. The company was founded by **Abraham Epstein** (1887-1958), an immigrant from Kiev, Ukraine, in tsarist Russia. Epstein received a bachelor of science degree in civil engineering from the University of Illinois in 1911 and worked as a draftsman, designer, and engineer for a number of companies. In 1921, he established his own office in Chicago with the Central Manufacturing District, a privately owned industrial development, as his primary client. A. Epstein grew to become Epstein, an international corporation providing architectural, engineering, and construction services.[100]

CHARLES O. CHROMASTER (1891-1955) was the designer for Wiley G. Clarkson on some of Fort Worth's most significant modernistic buildings. Before moving to Texas, Chromaster was a partner in two short-lived architectural firms in his native Wisconsin. Chromaster & Speer lasted from 1913 to 1914 in Wausau; after the partnership dissolved, Chromaster returned to his hometown of Milwaukee and worked as a draftsman for Fitzhugh Scott, one of the city's leading architects, before joining Marzillier & Chromaster from 1920 to 1922. By 1924, he was in Fort Worth employed as a draftsman by Wiley G. Clarkson & Company; he was later promoted to designer. Chromaster established his own practice in 1942.[101]

CHARLES M. DAVIS (1886-1974) was a largely self-trained civil engineer who learned his profession through home study and firsthand experience. In 1902, the Rockdale, Texas, native was hired as part of a survey party for the Texas and Pacific Railway and worked in Louisiana under the division engineer building a line between Natchitoches and Shreveport. Two years later he passed the exams for the rating of civil engineer and joined the US Reclamation Service working on a series of canals and dams in Wyoming, Nebraska, and South Dakota. Davis came to Fort Worth as the chief engineer for a proposed interurban railway between Fort Worth and Mineral Wells, and he was then hired as a special engineer to explore the possibility of creating Clear Fork Lake to provide surface water for Fort Worth. Neither the railway nor the surface water project was built. Davis spent most of his career as a consulting engineer. He was an innovator in the use of reinforced concrete and pioneered the slip form of concrete construction for bridges and large structures. He later applied his experience with concrete to the construction of private homes.[102]

MARTHA ZOE DAVIS (1911-1996) was the daughter of engineer Charles M. Davis. Zoe Davis had hoped to become an architect, but when that career path was blocked, she enrolled at Sophie Newcomb College in New Orleans and earned a degree in fine arts in 1933. After studying at the Art Students League of New York, she returned to Fort Worth in 1935 and joined her father in designing and constructing concrete houses. Zoe Davis continued painting and later became head of the art department at Edinburg College (later the University of Texas-Pan American) in the Rio Grande Valley before moving to Colorado and returning to engineering.[103]

EVERETT L. FRAZIOR (1912-2009) was born in Dublin, Texas, and was brought to Fort Worth as an infant. He graduated with honors from Polytechnic High School in 1930, but could not afford to attend college. Frazior studied architecture and design through a correspondence course. City directories indicate that he worked as a draftsman through the 1930s; by 1941 he was employed as a draftsman for Preston M. Geren in Marshall. He moved to Fort Worth as a designer with Geren and remained with the firm through at least 1971. Stamp collecting was a hobby of Frazior's; he served as president of the Texas Philatelic Association from 1961 to 1963. His name is frequently misspelled *Frazier*.[104]

EMIL A. FRETZ JR. (1915-1983) was the Dallas-born designer for architect Maurice Peterman; he later became Peterman's business partner. The historical record contains very little information about Fretz, who appears to have spent his life in Dallas. Fretz worked as Peterman's designer in the late 1930s; in 1939 and 1940, Peterman and Fretz advertised themselves as architects in the *Dallas Morning News*. In the 1940 US Census, Fretz indicated that he had three and a half years of college and listed his profession as "Architect." By 1941, Fretz listed himself as an independent architect. He designed the First Seventh-day Adventist Church (1951) in Dallas.

DUDLEY S. GREEN (1883-1948) was born in London, England, and emigrated with his family to the United States before 1900. He worked as a draftsman in Waco for more than a decade, including time with architect M. W. Scott. Green had moved to Dallas by 1918, when his World War I draft registration card listed his occupation as draftsman with the Lang & Witchell architectural firm. Green attended the Paris Exposition of 1925, which helped spread Art Deco design throughout the world; as chief designer for Lang & Witchell, he worked on the firm's major modernistic projects. Green established his own architecture practice in 1940.[105]

A. GEORGE KING (1906-1984), originally from Corsicana, Texas, worked for some of Fort Worth's leading architectural firms. He attended Rice Institute (later Rice University) in Houston and was awarded a bachelor of arts degree in 1927 and a bachelor of science degree in architecture in 1928. After graduating, he accepted a position as draftsman with Wyatt C. Hedrick, Incorporated, in Fort Worth. King won an architectural competition in 1931 that provided a five-month scholarship to study modern architecture in Europe. He was a designer for Preston M. Geren from 1934 to 1943, served in the US Army Corps of Engineers during World War II, and returned to Fort Worth to work as an architect with Wiley G. Clarkson & Company from 1946 to 1952. He established his own firm, A. George King & Associates, in 1952.[106]

HERMAN P. KOEPPE (1876-1941) was born in Leipzig, Germany. His family immigrated to Galveston, Texas, when he was a child. Koeppe developed an interest in architecture and spent a year in the 1890s touring major European cities and attending classes at the Sorbonne, although he did not receive a degree. On returning to Galveston, Koeppe worked for architect D. M. McKinsey and the Santa Fe railroad before joining Sanguinet & Staats, the influential Fort Worth architectural firm, in 1904. In 1925, Wyatt C. Hedrick hired Koeppe as his chief designer. Working with Hedrick, Koeppe would create some of Fort Worth's most significant Art Deco and Art Moderne buildings.[107]

J. HOBART PLUNKETT (1899-1970) was a successful building contractor in Tyler, Texas, who was responsible for some exceptional Streamline Moderne buildings. According to the US Census, Plunkett was raised in rural Prairie Township in the Ozark Mountains of Arkansas. He left high school without graduating and moved to Ada, Oklahoma, in the early 1920s. Plunkett worked as a building contractor in Oklahoma until he moved to Tyler in the early 1930s. Plunkett is credited with building Tyler's first air-conditioned house as well as its first house constructed on a concrete slab.[108]

EVERETT M. SHEPHERD (1903-1983) and **HILTON D. SHEPHERD** (1910-1976) were brothers and educators turned amateur architects and builders who designed and constructed an early modernistic house in Denton for themselves and their mother. At the time, Everett was an administrator with the Texas Department of Education, and Hilton taught business administration at North Texas State Teachers College (later the University of North Texas). Everett held a doctorate in education and had been a professor of history, professor of education, and band director at McMurry College in Abilene, Texas; later, he served as deputy director of the state Department of Education in Austin before joining the faculty at East Texas State Teachers College (later Texas A&M University-Commerce), where he was a professor of education administration and dean of men. Hilton earned a PhD from New York University and served as a captain in the US Air Force during World War II. He later moved to Fort Worth, where he became a respected management consultant and author. Hilton was a business professor at Texas Christian University in Fort Worth and a visiting professor at the Harvard Graduate School of Business.[109]

WALTER DORWIN TEAGUE (1883-1960) is often called the "dean of industrial design" for his many contributions to the field. Born in Decatur, Indiana, Teague moved to New York in 1903 to study at the Art Students League. He worked as a freelance designer and illustrator in New York beginning in 1911, developing a particular interest in product and packaging design after he discovered the work of designer/architect Le Corbusier on a visit to Europe. Teague opened his own industrial design studio in 1926. Among his early jobs was updating the popular Brownie camera line for Eastman Kodak, creating some of the company's most iconic products. Teague would go on to design UPS delivery trucks, streamlined Texaco service stations built from the 1930s to the 1960s, and the interior of the Boeing Stratocruiser passenger plane, a project that led to a decades-long partnership with the aircraft maker. Between 1933 and 1939, Teague also designed pavilions at world's fairs in Chicago, San Diego, Dallas, and New York. He was chairman of the Board of Design for the New York fair, and with Raymond Loewy and Henry Dreyfuss, he launched the Society of Industrial Design (later the Industrial Designers Society of America). Teague is considered a pioneer of professional industrial design; examples of his work are in the collections of museums worldwide. After Teague's death in 1960, his son, Walter Dorwin Teague Jr., continued to operate Walter Dorwin Teague Associates. The firm remains in business as Teague.[110]

Artists

PIERRE BOURDELLE (1901-1966), artist and sculptor, was born in Paris and trained by his father, the celebrated French sculptor Émile Antoine Bourdelle, a contemporary of Auguste Rodin's. Both the elder Bourdelle and Rodin exposed Pierre to architecture and art across Europe; in his late teens, Pierre traveled to Italy, the Netherlands, and across Africa to learn new artistic techniques. He later moved to the United States, where he would create murals, reliefs, and sculptures at the 1933 Chicago world's fair, the 1936 Texas Centennial Exposition in Dallas, and the 1939 New York world's fair. Bourdelle also worked with Raoul Josset on the Mier Expedition and Dawson's Men Memorial, a centennial project in La Grange, Texas, and took on a variety of commissions including murals for SS *America*, the largest ocean liner built in the United States prior to World War II, and NS *Savannah*, the world's first nuclear-powered merchant ship.[111]

WILLIAMSON GERALD "JERRY" BYWATERS (1906-1989), artist, was a native of Paris, Texas, who graduated from Southern Methodist University with a degree in comparative literature. After a lengthy tour of Europe, he studied at the Art Students League of New York before returning to Dallas, where he became a leading figure in the "Dallas Nine," a group of young regionalist artists who found inspiration in Texas landscapes. He assisted in painting murals for the 1936 Texas Centennial Exposition and was commissioned to create several Texas post office murals. Bywaters served as art critic for the *Dallas Morning News* from 1933 to 1939 and as director of the Dallas Museum of Fine Arts from 1943 to 1964, while also teaching art and art history at Southern Methodist University and continuing to create significant original works.[112]

MATCHETT HERRING COE (1907-1999), sculptor, was born in Loeb (later Lumberton), Texas. He majored in electrical engineering at South Park Junior College (later Lamar University) in nearby Beaumont and studied sculpture under Carl Mines at the Cranbrook Academy of Art in Michigan. Among his works are the Art Deco sculptural elements on the Jefferson County Courthouse in Beaumont (1931), First National Bank of Beaumont (1937), and Houston City Hall (1939). Coe's monumental sculptures include the bronze statue of Texas Confederate hero Dick Dowling (1936) at Sabine Pass State Park and the Texas State Memorial (1961) at Vicksburg National Military Park.[113]

KENNETH GALE (1908-1990), artist, spent his entire career in his hometown of Zanesville, Ohio. Little has been published about Gale; newspaper accounts indicate that he joined the staff of the Mosaic Tile Company in Zanesville shortly after finishing high school. Gale later spent time in the company's Chicago office; while there, he studied at the Chicago Academy of Fine Arts and the School of the Art Institute of Chicago. After a ten-month tour of Europe, Gale returned to Zanesville and became director of design and advertising for Mosaic Tile, which once operated the largest tile factory in the world. In addition to creating tile work, Gale was a locally known painter and photographer.[114]

XAVIER GONZALEZ (1898-1999), artist, was born in Spain and raised in Mexico, where he studied at San Carlos Academy. He worked as a draftsman for a railroad company before immigrating to Iowa, where he again worked for a railroad. He moved to Chicago and took a job as a window dresser while attending evening classes at the School of the Art Institute of Chicago. After 1925, Gonzalez held teaching positions with museums and institutions of higher learning across the country, including the Witte Memorial Museum in San Antonio, Sul Ross State Teachers College (later Sul Ross State University) in Alpine, Texas, Sophie Newcomb College and Tulane University in New Orleans, and the Brooklyn Museum of Art. He received a 1947 Guggenheim Fellowship and a 1965 Ford Foundation grant.[115]

WILLIAM ALEXANDRE HOGUE (1898-1994), artist, was born in Memphis, Missouri, and spent his childhood in Denton, Texas. After graduating from high school in Dallas, Hogue spent a year in Minnesota studying at the Minneapolis College of Art and Design, and later worked as a lettering artist for advertising firms in New York. On returning to Dallas in 1925, Hogue established himself as an artist and taught at the Texas State College for Women (later Texas Woman's University) and the Hockaday School. Beginning in 1926, Hogue made long visits to the art colony in Taos, New Mexico, where he forged friendships with several prominent artists; at home, he was also involved with the "Dallas Nine," an influential group of regionalist artists. Hogue's travels through the Southwest exposed him to the effects of the Dust Bowl and led to the creation of the acclaimed *Erosion* series, paintings that documented the effects of poor farming practices on the American landscape. Hogue was head of the art department at the University of Tulsa from 1945 to 1963; he remained a working artist during and after that time, producing well-known landscapes of the Big Bend region of Texas well into the 1980s. Hogue's work is held by museums including the Smithsonian Institution in Washington and the Musée National d'Art Moderne in Paris.[116]

DWIGHT C. HOLMES (1900-1986), sculptor and painter, was born in Oregon, but arrived in Texas early in life when his father was named pastor of a Beaumont congregation. In 1917, his family settled in Fort Worth, where Holmes attended Texas Christian University, earned a bachelor of arts degree, and became a faculty member in the university's art department. He left teaching for a five-year apprenticeship that led to membership in the Modelers & Sculptors of America, a trade union. He then worked as a modeler creating architectural moldings for the C. J. Sutton Company of Fort Worth and the Southern Plastic Relief Company of Dallas. His designs still decorate many post offices and public buildings in Texas and the Gulf South, including the streamlined Houston Municipal Air Terminal (later the 1940 Air Terminal Museum). As a painter, Holmes worked primarily in oils, specializing in landscapes and western scenes. After World War II, he moved to San Angelo, where he taught and maintained his studio.[117]

PETER HURD (1904-1984), artist, was born in Roswell, New Mexico, and spent nearly all his life in the area. Hurd attended the United States Military Academy at West Point, but dropped out to become a painter. He later studied at Haverford College and the Pennsylvania Academy of the Fine Arts in Philadelphia; while there, he met the illustrator N. C. Wyeth and married Wyeth's daughter Henriette, who was also a painter. Hurd returned to New Mexico in the 1930s and began painting landscapes and portraits of subjects around his ranch in San Patricio. His regional realist works included numerous murals, watercolors, lithographs, and an acclaimed series of sketches he executed as a correspondent for *Life* magazine during World War II. Hurd served on the New Mexico Fine Arts Commission and the National Fine Arts Commission, and he continued to paint through the mid-1970s until he developed Alzheimer's disease.[118]

GEORGIA JENSEN, see GEORGIA JENSEN McINTOSH.

RAOUL JOSSET (1899-1957), sculptor, was born in France and studied at the École des Beaux arts and with noted sculptor Émile Antoine Bourdelle. After World War I, Josset received commissions to create fifteen memorials across France; during that time, he also won the Prix de Rome and the Prix de Paris. He immigrated to the United States and worked at the Chicago world's fair of 1933, after which he was recruited to join the sculpture staff at the Texas Centennial Exposition in Dallas. Josset remained in Dallas after the fair and produced several other significant works for the Texas Centennial, including memorials at Goliad, Gonzales, and La Grange.[119]

JOSEPH "JOSE" MARTIN (1891-1985), sculptor, was born in France (his nickname was pronounced "Josie"), where he developed his interest in sculpture studying under his father, a woodcarver. Martin's studies at the École normale sepérieure des Beaux-arts were disrupted by World War I; he enlisted in the French army, was wounded four times, and earned the Croix de Guerre for heroism in combat. Martin briefly returned to school, but left in 1919 to establish his career. After some initial success, he immigrated to the United States, where he found commissions for Marshall Field & Company in Chicago and the Cowan Pottery Company in Ohio. He was hired to create sculptures for the 1933 world's fair in Chicago and was brought to Dallas to do similar work for the 1936 Texas Centennial Exposition. He remained in Dallas for the rest of his career.[120]

ROGER D. McINTOSH and **GEORGIA JENSEN McINTOSH** were husband-and-wife stained-glass designers who met while working in the art glass division of the Pittsburgh Plate Glass Company (PPG) in Dallas. **Roger de Montluzin McIntosh** (1888-1977) was brought to Dallas from Baton Rouge, Louisiana, as an infant; his father died in 1895. McIntosh left school after the fifth grade and took a job with a bookbinder before finding his true calling as an employee of the Dallas Art Glass Company. Around 1910, he worked briefly for the Waco Art Glass Company, but returned to Dallas when his older brother fell ill. The local branch of PPG hired McIntosh, and he remained with the company until he retired; his position was variously described as glassworker, designer, artist, and draftsman. McIntosh developed an outstanding reputation while working with the leading architects of his time. Less is known about his wife, **Georgia Jensen** (1906-1948), who was born in Michigan and had moved to Dallas by the late 1920s. City directories and census records describe her profession as either an artist or designer with PPG. Roger McIntosh and Georgia Jensen worked together on the stained-glass image of the Norse god Thor for the Dallas Power & Light Building. They married in Oklahoma on October 31, 1931, the year their Thor window was first seen by the public.[121]

FRANK ALBERT MECHAU JR. (1904-1946) was a prolific artist despite his relatively short career. Born in WaKeeney, Kansas, Mechau studied at the University of Denver, Denver Academy of Fine Arts, and the School of the Art Institute of Chicago before traveling and studying in Europe. He was awarded three Guggenheim Fellowships and created murals for the federal Public Works of Art Project and the Section of Fine Arts. In addition to his work in Fort Worth's United States Court House, Mechau painted the murals *Horses at Night* (1934) for the Denver Public Library and *Dangers of the Mail* (1937) for the US Post Office Department's headquarters in Washington, DC. In 1940, Mechau became head of Columbia University's Department of Painting and Sculpture, but he took a leave of absence in 1943 to participate in a War Department project that sent selected artists to portray US military activities around the world. Mechau's works are in the collections of the Smithsonian American Art Museum, the National Museum of the United States Army, the Detroit Institute of Arts, and the Denver Art Museum.[122]

EUGENE SAVAGE (1883-1978), artist, took up drawing in connection with his childhood hobby of taxidermy. Around 1899, he moved from his native Indiana to Chicago, where he studied at the Academy of Fine Arts and the School of the Art Institute of Chicago and built a successful career in commercial illustration. His interests later turned to mural painting, for which he won a Prix de Rome scholarship in 1912. In 1925, Savage became a painting professor at Yale University, and during the next decade won a number of significant mural commissions, including works at the Sterling Memorial Library at Yale and the US Post Office Department headquarters in Washington, DC. At the time he painted his murals for the State of Texas Building (later the Hall of State) at Fair Park in Dallas, Savage was serving as commissioner of painting for the United States Commission of Fine Art. He continued teaching at Yale until he was seventy.[123]

EVALINE SELLORS (1903-1995), sculptor, was the Fort Worth-born daughter of Irish immigrants. She began studying art at the age of eight and eventually continued her education at Texas Woman's College Academy (later Texas Wesleyan University). She attended Washington University in St. Louis from 1921 to 1923 and the Pennsylvania Academy of the Fine Arts in Philadelphia from 1925 to 1929. During her time in Philadelphia, Sellors twice received the prestigious William Emlen Cresson Scholarship, allowing her to study in Europe. On her return to Fort Worth, Sellors opened the Texas School of Fine Arts (later the Fort Worth School of Fine Arts). When the United States entered World War II, she closed the school and went to work for North American Aviation as an inspector in the mockup department, which produced plaster models used in the manufacture of airplane parts. After the war, Sellors taught at a variety of institutions across the country and continued to exhibit her work.[124]

THOMAS M. STELL JR. (1898-1981), artist, was a Cuero, Texas, native who had a wide-ranging career. After graduating from high school in 1914, he worked as a draftsman in Hollywood, Dallas, Chicago, and New York. During the 1920s, he attended Rice Institute (later Rice University) in Houston before moving to New York and studying at the Art Students League and the National Academy of Design. Stell also designed sets for Broadway plays and was employed as a technician for silent films. He received a master's degree in art education and art history from Columbia University in 1931, after which he taught at the Dallas Art Institute and assisted in painting murals on the main buildings for the 1936 Texas Centennial Exposition. Stell served as state supervisor for the American Index of Design, a Work Projects Administration program that documented folk art objects, and he was later a member of the art faculties of Trinity University in San Antonio and the University of Texas at Austin. Stell is best known for his work as a portrait artist.[125]

LAWRENCE TENNEY STEVENS (1896-1972), sculptor, was born in Boston. He studied at the School of the Museum of Fine Arts, Boston, took courses in anatomy and dissection at Tufts Medical School in Boston, and studied with Louis Comfort Tiffany at his Long Island foundation before winning a Prix de Rome scholarship in 1922. After returning to the United States, Stevens built a national reputation as a sculptor, painter, and engraver, exhibiting at several prestigious institutions and earning prominent commissions. Stevens's preference for monumental public art was well suited to his work at the Texas Centennial Exposition and the New York world's fair of 1939, though his commissions grew smaller in scale as tastes changed after World War II. He settled in Tempe, Arizona, in the 1950s and remained there for the rest of his life.[127]

ALLIE TENNANT (1892-1971), sculptor, was born in St. Louis and moved to Dallas with her family at an early age. Tennant studied under Hans Kunz-Meyer at the Aunspaugh Art School in Dallas before attending the Art Students League of New York. On returning to Texas, she became associated with the "Dallas Nine" group of regionalist artists. Tennant's portrait sculpture and architectural work was widely exhibited and praised throughout the 1930s, and she was elected a Fellow of the National Sculpture Society in 1934. Her best-known work today is *Tejas Warrior*, which she created for the entrance to the State of Texas Building (later the Hall of State) at Fair Park in Dallas. The statue of a Native American stands eleven feet tall and is sculpted in bronze and covered in gold leaf. In 1943, Tennant was one of the founders of the Texas Sculptors Group. She spent the remainder of her life in Dallas sculpting, writing, and teaching.[127]

JAMES DOUTHITT WILSON (1903-1973), a regionalist artist who worked in several cities in Texas. Little biographical information is available about Wilson, who appears to be best known for the murals he painted under the auspices of the Public Works of Art Project for the Carnegie Library in Tyler, Texas.

Acknowledgments

In a project such as this, there are many people to thank and many contributions to be recognized. *DFW Deco* would not have been possible without their assistance and contributions.

We offer our sincere appreciation to Nancy McCoy of Quimby McCoy Preservation Architecture for graciously contributing the foreword to this book and for championing the preservation of historic buildings in Dallas and across Texas.

Dallas, Fort Worth, and the surrounding region are home to several outstanding research institutions whose collections and staff were of incalculable help in this project. We are grateful for the assistance we received from Misty Maberry of the Dallas Public Library's Dallas History & Archives division; Cathy Spitzenberger of the University of Texas at Arlington Libraries Special Collections; John Slate and Kristi Nedderman of the Dallas Municipal Archives; Tiffany Wright, John Anderson and Jacob Dannenberg of the Smith County Historical Society in Tyler; Susie Brown of the Tyler Public Library; Kelly Green and Lindsay Loy of the Gregg County Historical Museum in Longview; Janet Marley of the Kilgore Public Library; Elizabeth Bradshaw of the Marshall Public Library; the staff of The Longview Room at the Longview Public Library; Kim Cupit of the Denton County Office of History and Culture in Denton; the research staff of the Rusk County Library in Henderson and Overton; and, farther afield, Kevin Williams of the Southeastern Architectural Archive at Tulane University in New Orleans. They graciously guided us through their collections and shared in our excitement over unearthing the most obscure bits of information.

David Preziosi and Donovan Westover of Preservation Dallas and Amber Rojas of the City of Tyler are among the outstanding preservation professionals helping to safeguard the region's architectural and cultural treasures. We very much appreciate their help with this project. Thanks also to Bob Brinkman, Greg Smith, and Leslie Wolfenden-Guidry of the Texas Historical Commission in Austin, who do the same work statewide.

A number of people and groups arranged access to historic buildings, making this book infinitely richer. Young County Judge John C. Bullock in Graham; Marlene Edwards with the Old Post Office Museum & Art Center in Graham; B. Garnett Brookshire with the People's Petroleum Building in Tyler; Kilgore Historical Preservation Foundation and Merlyn Holmes of the East Texas Oil Museum in Kilgore; Priscilla McAnnally with the Paris Public Library; Ashley Farha of Hamilton Properties Corporation in Dallas; Jed Wagenknecht of the Courtyard Fort Worth Downtown/Blackstone in Fort Worth; Jay Chapa and Steve Cooke of the City of Fort Worth; Ruben Salas of the Fort Worth Transportation Authority; and Jackie Gates of American Aero FTW were all generous with their time and hospitality. We also want to thank Rita and Andy Singleton and Pat Crowley for welcoming us into their lovely historic homes.

We appreciate the assistance of those who provided us with hard-to-find information or photos: William Knous of CHRISTUS Trinity Mother Frances Health System in Tyler, Dawn Parnell of the Tyler Independent School District, Guy R. Griesch and Michelle Hancock of the City of McKinney, John Faubion of the Lawrence Tenney Stevens Trust, and photographer Steve Clicque of Dallas.

Special recognition is due Willis Winters of the Dallas Park & Recreation Department; Steve Kline, now retired from the US General Services Administration Greater Southwest Region in Fort Worth; and his wife, Susan Allen Kline; and Tiffany Wright of the Smith County Historical Society. They consistently went the extra mile in sharing their knowledge, answering questions, and arranging access to important sites, and we are indebted to them for it.

Don Baynham suggested buildings for inclusion in the book, opening our eyes to locations that we might otherwise have missed.

A number of other people supported our work in a variety of ways that were of great value even though they may be too complicated to fully describe here. They include Dealey Campbell of the Dallas Historical Society, Mary Doty of the City of Dallas, Ellen Buie Niewyk of the Hamon Arts Library at Southern Methodist University, Gigi Westerman of The S&G Group, Judy Alter, Margaret Culbertson, Mark Birnbaum, Scott Fitzgerald, Catherine Horsey, Lovita Irby, Bob Jaeger, Ben Koush, Alan Loudermilk, Virginia Savage McAlester, Sims McCutchan, James Nader, and Bob Thaggard. Thanks to you all.

Finally, our deepest appreciation goes to Dan Williams and the board of TCU Press for their continuing support, and to Melinda Esco, Kathy Walton, Molly Spain, and Rebecca Allen of TCU Press, and to Bill Brammer of fusion29 for helping make this book a reality.

— Jim Parsons and David Bush

Notes

The three most frequently cited newspapers, the *Dallas Morning News*, the *Fort Worth Star-Telegram*, and the *Longview Daily News*, are abbreviated *DMN*, *FWST*, and *LDN*, respectively.

Chapter 1: Introduction

1. "A 3D CBD: How the 1916 Zoning Law Shaped Manhattan's Central Business Districts," the Skyscraper Museum, accessed January 22, 2017, http://www.skyscraper.org/zoning; "The First Tribune Competition Still Influences Architects," *Chicago Tribune*, February 21, 1993.
2. Alfred C. Bossom, *Building to the Skies: the Romance of the Skyscraper* (London: Studio, 1934), 15.
3. Alfred C. Bossom, "The World of Art: Two Views of the Paris Exposition of Decorative Arts," *New York Times Magazine*, August 16, 1925; Jared Goss, "Heilbrunn Timeline of Art History: French Art Deco," the Metropolitan Museum of Art, accessed January 1, 2017, http://www.metmuseum.org/toah/hd/frdc/hd_frdc.htm.
4. "Public Works Administration (PWA), 1933-1943."
5. "Works Progress Administration (WPA), 1935-1943," the Living New Deal, accessed January 24, 2017, https://livingnewdeal.org/programs-created-or-enhanced-by-the-new-deal.
6. "A Year of Progress" (advertisement), *FWST*, December 30, 1928.
7. Jackie McElhaney and Michael V. Hazel, "Dallas, TX," Handbook of Texas Online, accessed January 2, 2017, http://www.tshaonline.org/handbook/online/articles/hdd01.
8. Kilgore, Texas, City Directory for 1936 (Springfield, Missouri: Interstate Directory Co.), 5.

Chapter 2: Commercial

1. "Western Union Is in New Home," *FWST*, August 30, 1931.
2. Ibid.; "Western Union Radio Service" (advertisement), *FWST*, December 7, 1930.
3. "Tonight at Midnight" (advertisement), *FWST*, March 1, 1931, Society & Clubs section; "New Telephone Exchanges," *FWST*, May 1, 1932.
4. "New Telephone Building Here," *LDN*, November 17, 1935.
5. "Commission Clears Way for Building Phone Exchange Second Only to New York," *DMN*, March 19, 1929.
6. "Phone Company to Begin $2,000,000 Building Program," *DMN*, March 21, 1937; "Dallas Hits New Record in Building," *DMN*, January 1, 1949; "$1,000,000 Work Set to Begin on Phone Building," *DMN*, September 7, 1952; "Mosher Steel Awarded Job for SW Bell," *DMN*, August 23, 1962; "Bell to Add 13 Stories to Long-Distance Unit," *DMN*, October 22, 1967.
7. "Contract Let on Rebuilding Pope Building," *McKinney (TX) Daily Courier-Gazette* (*MDCG*), February 13, 1929.
8. "New Pope Building Is about Completed," *MDCG*, August 28, 1935.
9. "A. Harris & Co. Expands" (advertisement), *DMN*, June 22, 1930.
10. Ivert E. Mayhugh, "Hall Furniture Building," National Register of Historic Places Registration Form (December 14, 2001).
11. "Methodist Book Store Building $300,000 Plant," *DMN*, June 21, 1926, sec. 3; "Cokesbury Store Building to Begin for Use in April," *DMN*, August 16, 1936.
12. "Methodist Book Store Building $300,000 Plant," op. cit.; "Cokesbury Store Building to Begin for Use in April," op. cit.; "Cokesbury Book Talk" (advertisement), *DMN*, March 19, 1944, sec. 4; "Boston's Bans," *DMN*, March 31, 1944, sec. 2; Baptist Book Store advertisement, *DMN*, April 9, 1944, sec. 4.
13. Howard J. Cox, "Dallas Diaries," *Legacies: a History Journal for Dallas and North Central Texas* Vol. 21, No. 2 (Fall 2009): 24.
14. "Shelton Building," Texas Historical Commission marker No. 4670 (1981), located at 901 Houston Street, Fort Worth; "McCrory's Thanks You!" (advertisement), *FWST*, April 3, 1938.
15. "New Oak Cliff Tenpin Alleys Open Saturday," *DMN*, June 9, 1939, sec. 2; Don Morrissey, "Strikes-Spares-Splits: Along Timber Lane," *DMN*, August 31, 1947, sec. 2.
16. "Chicagoans Lunch in New Store Cafeteria," *DMN*, June 24, 1938.
17. "Chain Store Will Open House Here," *FWST*, April 6, 1922; "Building Permits," *FWST*, August 6, 1939; W.T. Grant advertisement, *FWST*, November 19, 1939.
18. "Here 'n' There," *LDN*, May 6, 1947, and January 18, 1948.
19. "Bank Buys Part of Site Needed to Build Annex," *DMN*, February 22, 1931.
20. Ann Hudson, "Jacksonville, TX (Cherokee County)," Handbook of Texas Online, accessed January 16, 2017, http://www.tshaonline.org/handbook/online/articles/hej01.
21. "Plano National Bank/I.O.O.F. Lodge Building," Texas Historical Commission marker No. 6194 (1993), located at 1001 East Fifteenth Street, Plano; "Consolidated Plano Bank Opens Friday," *DMN*, January 3, 1931.
22. "Curved Neon Sign Here Only One in Southwest, Is Belief," *FWST*, November 22, 1937.
23. "Bank in Kilgore Forced to Move by Oil Drilling," *DMN*, October 31, 1937.
24. "Announce Plans for Rembert Bank Home," *LDN*, December 4, 1939; "Bank Starts Building Monday," *LDN*, January 21, 1940.
25. "Watched from Kilgore," *DMN*, May 7, 1931.
26. "World's Richest Acre," Texas Historical Commission marker No. 10007 (1966), located at Main and Commerce streets, Kilgore.
27. "Headquarters at Henderson," *DMN*, September 5, 1931; "Complete Shutdown in East Texas Fields: Four Counties Placed under Martial Law," *DMN Extra*, August 17, 1931.
28. "Crude Oil Prices Decline, Now Lowest in 40 Years," *New York Times* (*NYT*), April 26, 1931; "Reopen 1,800 Wells in Texas Oil Fields," *NYT*, September 6, 1931; "Higher Crude Oil Prices Spreading over Midcontinent," *DMN*, October 12, 1932.
29. "Great Edition of Longview Daily News," *San Antonio Express*, June 6, 1936; "Front Window Popular Spot as Many Watch Press Run," *LDN*, May 31, 1936.
30. "Mrs. Elliott Roosevelt Purchases Fort Worth Broadcasting Station," *DMN*, June 12, 1937; "KFJZ Planning Improvements," *FWST*, May 19,

1938.

31. "Public Officials, Sponsors Salute KRLD's Power Hike," *DMN*, July 17, 1939.
32. "Local Firms Employed to Build New WFAA," *DMN*, May 12, 1930, sec. 2; "Today's the Day – Take It Away, KGKO!" *FWST*, May 1, 1938.
33. Michael A. Bernstein, *The Great Depression: Delayed Recovery and Economic Change in America, 1929-1939* (New York: Cambridge University Press, 1989), 124-126.
34. "New Coca Cola Plant Is One of Finest, Most Modern in State," *LDN*, March 26, 1935.
35. "Dr. Pepper Plans Opening of Improved Plant," *Greenville (TX) Evening Banner*, May 25, 1939.
36. "Bonuses Boost Yule Buying," *FWST*, December 23, 1939; "10:50-2:50-4:50: Clock Takes Pause That Confuses," *FWST*, October 3, 1945; "Dr. Pepper Success in Its Formula," *DMN*, March 3, 1947, sec. 5.
37. "Dr. Pepper to Show Public Headquarters Plant Sunday," *DMN*, April 24, 1949.
38. "Gaston Estate Will Remodel Old Structure," *DMN*, August 10, 1934.
39. Lorch Manufacturing Co. advertisement, *DMN*, January 27, 1935, sec. 5.
40. "Firm Makes Dishwashers' Dream Come True Every 2½ Seconds," *FWST*, July 19, 1956.
41. "New Nocona Boot Plant to Be Opened Wednesday," *FWST*, June 6, 1948; "WTCC President Speaks at Nocona Boot Celebration," *FWST*, June 11, 1948; Richard L. Himmel, "Nocona Boot Company," Handbook of Texas Online, accessed November 1, 2016, http://www.tshaonline.org/handbook/online/articles/dln01.

Chapter 3: Skyscrapers

1. Ralph Bryan, "Skyscraper Race in Dallas Offers Esthetic Studies," *DMN*, February 1, 1931.
2. Ralph Bryan, "Mark Milestone in Architecture with Buildings," *DMN*, November 26, 1931.
3. Jay C. Henry, *Architecture in Texas 1895-1945* (Austin: University of Texas Press, 1993), 223; "Colors Mark New Shaft of Progress," *DMN*, November 27, 1931; "Mobile Color Lighting," Ward Leonard Electric Co. Bulletin 74 (1928), accessed January 13, 2017, https://archive.org/details/MobileColorLighting1928.
4. Lawrence E. Hamilton, "Dallas Power & Light Historic Overlay District," Dallas Landmark Commission Landmark Nomination Form (April 28, 2003).
5. "Light Building Unique in Service Ideas," *DMN*, October 11, 1931, sec. 7.
6. Ibid.
7. Ibid.
8. "Beyond the Horizon, an Editorial," *LDN*, May 7, 1935; "Here and There," *LDN*, June 21, 1935.
9. "New Telephone Building Will Be Unique in Its Provision of Facilities for Operation," *DMN*, October 9, 1927; "Enlarge Phone Building Plans," *DMN*, September 25, 1926; "New Telephone Building One of Country's Most Efficient Office and Plant Structures," *DMN*, October 7, 1928; "Phone Office Allows for Growth, Says Hull," *DMN*, November 27, 1928.
10. "Bell Lets Contract on Addition," *DMN*, March 17, 1961; "Dallas' 'Telephone City'" (advertisement), *DMN*, January 20, 1963.
11. "M&W Tower Building Dedication Arranged," *DMN*, April 10, 1949; "Bell Telephone Shows New, Old Office Building," *DMN*, September 30, 1977.
12. "Blackstone Offers Many Late Features; Interior Decorations Elaborate," *FWST*, October 6, 1929; "R.C.A. Radio in Every Room New Blackstone Hotel," *FWST*, October 6, 1929.
13. "Hilton Interests Closing Blackstone Hotel Deal," *FWST*, February 1, 1952; "Improvements Planned for Hilton (Blackstone)," *FWST*, February 3, 1952; "Fort Worth Will Open the New Blackstone Hotel," *FWST*, October 6, 1929; "Luxurious Lobby" (photo), *FWST*, November 12, 1954; "Construction of Hilton Annex to Start Soon," *FWST*, August 23, 1953; "Hilton to Get Back Blackstone Name," *FWST*, January 7, 1962; "Blackstone Future Tied to the Past," *FWST*, September 26, 1982; "Blackstone – Courtyard by Marriott," HRI Properties, accessed January 13, 2017, http://www.hriproperties.com/blackstone-hotel.
14. "Blackstone Offers Many Late Features," op. cit.
15. Amy Sorter, "Art Deco Grandeur Lives on at Restored Blackstone," *Dallas Business Journal*, April 4, 1999, accessed January 13, 2017, http://www.bizjournals.com/dallas/stories/1999/04/05/focus4.html.
16. "Gas Company in New Home Tuesday," *FWST*, September 1, 1929, Gas Company Home section; "An Invitation to Call" (advertisement), *FWST*, September 1, 1929, Gas Company Home section; "$4,657,000 Construction Plan for 1956 Revealed by Lone Star Gas Company," *FWST*, February 5, 1956.
17. "Lone Star Buys Gas Company," *FWST*, May 17, 1931; "Fort Worth Votes for City to Own Gas Distribution," *DMN*, July 22, 1931.
18. "Gas Company in New Home Tuesday," *DMN*, July 22, 1931.
19. "Aviation Building at Fort Worth Planned," *DMN*, August 24, 1929; "Ultra Modern Architecture for Aviation Structure," *FWST*, September 24, 1929; "Biography of C.R. Smith," C.R. Smith Museum, accessed January 22, 2017, http://crsmithmuseum.org/about/c-r-smith.
20. "Ultra Modern Architecture for Aviation Structure," op. cit.; "Modernistic Designs on 16 Stories Found," *FWST*, August 3, 1930; Judith Singer Cohen, *Cowtown Moderne: Art Deco Architecture of Fort Worth, Texas* (College Station, Texas: Texas A&M University Press, 1988), 53-57; "Princes to Survive Attack on 'Palace,'" *FWST*, June 5, 1978; "Record Progress by Texas Fabricators" (advertisement), *FWST*, April 27, 1930; "Golfer Sanders Sells Office Building Here," *FWST*, April 22, 1967.
21. "Princes to Survive Attack on 'Palace,'" op. cit.; Cohen, op. cit., 58-59.
22. "New $1,000,000 Building Plans are Announced," *FWST*, July 14, 1929; "Sinclair Will Open Fort Worth Offices," *DMN*, July 12, 1930; "$1,000,000 Structure Declared 'Perfect,'" *FWST*, November 16, 1930, sec. 2.
23. Cohen, op. cit., 63; Barbara Rose, "Sinclair Renovation Aims for Opulence, Occupants," *FWST*, December 1, 1988, sec. 2; Lisa Hart and Mark LaMay, "Sinclair Building," National Register of Historic Places Registration Form (Austin: Texas Historical Commission, July 10, 1989; November 13, 1991).
24. Hart and LaMay, op. cit.; Sandra Baker, "Sinclair Building Opens Doors up Wide," *FWST*, August 10, 1990, sec. 2.
25. Ralph Bryan, "Gas Company Adds New Silhouette to Skyline of Dallas," *DMN*, September 13, 1931.
26. Bryan, op. cit.; "Skyline Celebrates 20th Sparkling Birthday" (advertisement), *DMN*, April 29, 1930.
27. "City Was Gas-Lit 75 Years Ago," *DMN*, October 2, 1960.
28. "Gas Company Offices Put in New Home," *DMN*, September 6, 1931; Bryan, op. cit.
29. "Tower Petroleum Contract Awarded," *DMN*, April 5, 1930, sec. 2; Ralph Bryan, "Dallas Towers Break out in Rash of Color," *DMN*, June 14, 1931, sec. 3; Charles Cullum, "Casts and Forecasts: Theater Row Goes Modern," *DMN*, January 12, 1937.
30. "New Y.M.C.A. Home, Opening Monday, One

of the Best in Country," *DMN*, September 27, 1931.

31. "City Population History from 1850-2000," *Texas Almanac*, accessed January 22, 2017, https://texasalmanac.com/sites/default/files/images/CityPopHist%20web.pdf; Diane Elizabeth Williams, "People's National Bank Building," National Register of Historic Places Registration Form (Tyler, Texas: City of Tyler/Historic Tyler, Inc., June 20, 2001); "Bids Opened," *Texas General Contractors Association Monthly Bulletin* (*TGCA*) (January 1936): 10; *TGCA* (March 1936): 18.
32. Kelly Gooch, "Building Big: Peoples Petroleum Building Restored and Renovated," *Tyler Morning Telegraph*, September 8, 2014.
33. Ibid.
34. Christopher Long, "Tyler, TX," Handbook of Texas Online, accessed January 22, 2017, http://www.tshaonline.org/handbook/online/articles/hdt04.
35. "Glover-Crim Building Adds Greatly to Looks of Downtown Area," *LDN*, October 4, 1933; "New Building One of the Most Modern, Comfortable in Texas," *LDN*, September 4, 1935.
36. "Contracts for New $125,000 Downtown Office Building to Be Awarded This Month," *LDN*, February 3, 1935, "Contract for New McWilliams Building Here Let to Dallas Firm," *LDN*, April 19, 1935, "New Building Is Filling up Fast," *LDN*, June 18, 1935.
37. Diane Elizabeth Williams, "Blackstone Building," National Register of Historic Places Registration Form (Tyler, Texas: City of Tyler/Historic Tyler, Inc., June 20, 2001).
38. "Fire in Drug House," *DMN*, September 1, 1904; "Building Will Get Another Story," *DMN*, April 10, 1935; "Serves Dallas Oil Industry, Supply Firms," *DMN*, October 1, 1939; Ray Bonta, "Business Notes," *DMN*, October 6, 1940; Hamilton, op. cit.

Chapter 4: Travel and Transportation

1. "Lancaster Tells Banqueters 'Now Get Million People,'" *FWST*, November 4, 1931; "Population of the 100 Largest Urban Places: 1930," United States Census Bureau, accessed January 9, 2017, https://www.census.gov/population/www/documentation/twps0027/tab16.txt;
"$20,000,000 For Building in 2 Years," *FWST*, November 1, 1931, sec. 7; "Projects in View Total $11,000,000," *FWST*, November 1, 1931, sec. 7.
2. "Texas and Pacific Road Is Ready to Rush Big Program," *FWST*, April 29, 1929.
3. "Passenger and Office Building Is Unsurpassed in America," *FWST*, November 1, 1931, sec. 7; "'Nothing so Fine in United States,' Architects Told," *FWST*, November 1, 1931, sec. 7; "A Long-Cherished Ambition Realized to the Fullest," *FWST*, November 1, 1931.
4. "Passenger and Office Building Is Unsurpassed in America," op. cit.
5. "Public Address System, Radio, Takes Guess Out of Train Calling," *FWST*, November 1, 1931, sec. 5.
6. "Passenger and Office Building Is Unsurpassed in America," op. cit.
7. "$1,750,000 T. & P. Warehouse Is One of Largest in Southwest," *FWST*, November 1, 1931, sec. 6; "$8,000,000 Pointing the Way" (American Bank & Trust Company advertisement), *FWST*, November 1, 1931, sec. 7.
8. "Fort Worth Celebrates," *DMN*, November 4, 1931.
9. Fort Worth City Directories for 1933, 1936, 1941, and 1949 (Dallas: Morrison & Fourmy Directory Co.).
10. "Baggage Rides on 2 Elevators," *FWST*, November 1, 1931, sec. 6.
11. "$1,750,000 T. & P. Warehouse," op. cit.
12. "Whistle of T&P No. 26 Becomes Echo in Time," *FWST*, March 23, 1967; Oscar Slotboom, *Dallas-Fort Worth Freeways: Texas Sized Ambition* (self-published, 2014), 495; Judith Singer Cohen, *Cowtown Moderne: Art Deco Architecture of Fort Worth, Texas* (College Station, Texas: Texas A&M University Press, 1988), 82-83; Kelli Rodda, "T&P Station Returned to Former Opulence," *Fort Worth Business Press*, October 29, 1999.
13. Diane Elizabeth Williams, "Jenkins-Harvey Super Service Station and Garage," National Register of Historic Places Registration Form (Tyler, Texas: City of Tyler/Historic Tyler, Inc., June 20, 2001).
14. Stephen Fox, *The Country Houses of John F. Staub* (College Station: Texas A&M University Press, 2007), 227.
15. "Packard Dallas Plans Luxurious Showroom," *DMN*, August 27, 1939; "New Packard Dealer Building Opening Set," *DMN*, December 10, 1939, sec. 4; "War School Building to Be Bought," *DMN*, August 15, 1941.
16. Jack Rhodes, "Busing Industry," Handbook of Texas Online, accessed October 31, 2016, http://www.tshaonline.org/handbook/online/articles/erb01.
17. *Kilgore Daily News*, "Bus Terminal Edition," March 3, 1939.
18. Don Brown, "Longtime Tyler Business Undergoing Remodeling," *Tyler Courier-Times*, December 12, 1975.
19. "Bus Terminal Will Replace Old Landmark," *DMN*, March 24, 1946, sec. 2.
20. "Thousands Join in Underpass Celebration Ceremonies," "Bonehead Christens Underpass and Goes to Jail," both in *DMN*, May 2, 1936.
21. "Underpass Park Will Be Decided by City Tuesday," *DMN*, April 21, 1934, sec. 2; "Underpass Park Is Named Dealey Plaza by Board," *DMN*, September 20, 1935; "Concrete Pylons Will Be Erected in Dealey Plaza," *DMN*, May 16, 1937; "Beautification of Entrance to City Ordered," *DMN*, October 18, 1939, sec. 2; "$92,298 Asked to Beautify Dealey Plaza," *DMN*, February 3, 1940.
22. "Impressive Park for Dealey Plaza Promised Dallas," *DMN*, February 18, 1937; "How Dealey Plaza Will Look in Future," *DMN*, February 21, 1937; "Monument to G.B. Dealey Is Dedicated in Ceremonies," *DMN*, November 15, 1949.
23. "Kilgore, Tex. Hotel Built by James Co.," *Ruston* (Louisiana) *Daily Leader,* March 10, 1936, sec. 3.
24. The Gladewater Museum has receipts from Presley's stays at Res-Mor Courts in its collection.
25. "California-Style Motor Hotel to Open on Oak Cliff Hilltop," *DMN*, September 8, 1946, sec. 5.
26. "Final Plans for New $150,000 American Airways Quarters," *FWST*, March 3, 1933, sec. 2.
27. "Tales from an Era When Airlines Knew Good Design," *Wired* (May 15, 2015), accessed January 21, 2017, https://www.wired.com/2015/05/tales-era-airlines-knew-good-design; "New American Airlines Logo Triggers Ire and a Sense of Déjà Vu," *Adweek* (January 18, 2013), accessed January 21, 2017, http://www.adweek.com/news/advertising-branding/new-american-airlines-logo-triggers-ire-and-sense-d-j-vu-146659.
28. "Through Sleepers Soon for American Airlines," *FWST*, April 6, 1936.
29. "Air Terminal Is Dedicated," *FWST*, June 21, 1937.
30. "Air Minded Throng Dedicates New Administration Building," *DMN*, October 7, 1940, sec. 2.
31. "City Thrills to Aviation Glory in Love Field Ceremony," *DMN*, October 6, 1940, sec. 5.

Chapter 5: Entertainment

1. "New $125,000 Warner Bros. Building," *Daily Times-Herald* (Dallas), January 9, 1930, sec. 2.
2. "Many States Get Films from Here," *DMN*, October 14, 1923.
3. "Minor Changes in Ordinance," *DMN*, May 19, 1915; "New Film House Will Be Built near Union Terminal by Fox Co.," *DMN*, August 1, 1922.
4. "Big Fire in Heart of City," *DMN*, December 11, 1921.
5. "Film Exchanges Check up Loss," *DMN*, December 12, 1921; "Fire Prevention Measures Planned," *DMN*, December 16, 1921.
6. "Specifications for a Three Story, Reinforced Concrete Film Exchange Building to Be Erected on Park Avenue, near Young Street, Dallas, Texas," Box 3, Job No. 760, Weiss, Dreyfous, and Seiferth Office Records, Southeastern Architectural Archive Collection 53, Howard-Tilton Memorial Library, Tulane University.
7. Marcel Quimby and Kate Singleton, "Downtown Dallas Historic District (Boundary Increase)," National Register of Historic Places Registration Form (City of Dallas, October 29, 2007).
8. "Dallas Film Mart of Southwest Says Tradespaper," *DMN*, December 7, 1946, sec. 2.
9. John Rosenfield Jr., "The Passing Show: Elm St. Sports Latest Thing in Movie Houses," *DMN*, February 20, 1937.
10. Karen Kingsley, "Emile Weil," KnowLA Encyclopedia of Louisiana, accessed September 22, 2016, http://www.knowla.org/entry/795.
11. "Marshal Seeking Cause of Burning of Theater," *DMN*, September 23, 1933, sec. 2.
12. "Palace Draws Large Crowds," *FWST*, September 27, 1936; "Palace to Equip for Todd-A-O," *FWST*, August 4, 1959.
13. "Final Curtain to Descend at Palace Theater," *FWST*, May 8, 1977.
14. "Interstate's New Circle Theatre" (advertisement), *DMN*, October 30, 1947, sec. 2.
15. "Exterior of New Forest Theater," "New Forest Features Modern Architectural Innovations," both in *DMN*, July 28, 1949, sec. 2.
16. "Forest to Enter New Film Era as Negro Theater," *DMN*, February 21, 1956.

Chapter 6: Institutional

1. "Practical Public Buildings," *Kokomo (IN) Tribune*, August 6, 1934; "Slashes Building Plans," *New York Times* (*NYT*), August 3, 1934.
2. "New Fort Worth Federal Building to Face Burnett Park," *FWST*, July 8, 1931; Judith Singer Cohen, *Cowtown Moderne: Art Deco Architecture of Fort Worth, Texas* (College Station, Texas: Texas A&M University Press, 1988), 113; "Federal Bldg. Plans Rushed," *FWST*, August 17, 1931; Clarkson's quote from the February 2, 1932, issue of *FWST* is included in Cohen, op. cit., 114.
3. "Fort Worth News Briefs," *FWST*, December 12, 1930; "Views of New Post Office Nearing Completion," *FWST*, February 3, 1933.
4. "Eldon B. Mahon U.S. Courthouse, Fort Worth, TX," General Services Administration, accessed January 20, 2017, https://www.gsa.gov/portal/ext/html/site/hb/category/25431/actionParameter/exploreByBuilding/buildingId/872.
5. Clarkson's quote from the February 9, 1933, issue of *FWST* is included in Cohen, op. cit., 116.
6. James H. Brun, *Great American Post Offices* (New York: John Wiley & Sons, Inc., 1998), 113, 172.
7. "Allege Relief for Building Lags," *NYT*, November 23, 1930; "Architects Press Bill," *NYT*, December 30, 1931; "Federal Architects," *NYT*, March 2, 1936.
8. "Architects to Plan Public Buildings," *NYT*, April 28, 1934; Antoinette J. Lee, *Architects to the Nation: the Rise and Decline of the Supervising Architect's Office* (New York: Oxford University Press, 2000), 290-291.
9. "Texas in Washington: Murals for Dallas Post Office," *DMN*, January 27, 1938; "Full Details for Mural Competition," *DMN*, January 24, 1938; "Assignments for Murals in Texas Given to Sixteen," *DMN*, June 22, 1938; Victoria Green Clow, Marsha Prior and Terri Gilbert, "Fort Worth U.S. Courthouse," National Register of Historic Places Registration Form (Plano, Texas: Geo-Marine, Inc., July 11, 2000).
10. Wayne Gard, "Bass, Sam," Handbook of Texas Online, accessed January 20, 2017, https://tshaonline.org/handbook/online/articles/fbaab.
11. "New Fort Worth Federal Building to Face Burnett Park," op. cit.; Cohen op. cit., 116.
12. Ann Chandler, "Jacksonville Post Office," National Register of Historic Places Registration Form (Cherokee County Historical Commission, July 2003).
13. "Section of Painting and Sculpture," Legal Title to Art Work Produced Under the 1930s and 1940s New Deal Administration, US General Services Administration, accessed January 18, 2017, https://www.gsa.gov/graphics/pbs/legal_fact_sheet_l.pdf.
14. "Mail Shed to Cost $20,000 Being Built," *DMN*, January 12, 1938, sec. 2.
15. "Texas in Washington," op.cit. "Terminal Mail Artist Arrives for Inspection," *DMN*, July 6, 1938; "Peter Hurd Here to Execute Terminal Murals," January 21, 1940, sec. 4.
16. Louise Gossett, "Art and Artists: Thomas Stell Wins Mural Competition," *DMN*, June 24, 1941; Gossett, "Art and Artists: Dallas Artist Commissioned to Do Mural," *DMN*, July 18, 1941.
17. "Young Courthouse Bids Are Held Up," *FWST*, December 13, 1930; "Young Courthouse Work Is Resumed," *DMN*, October 11, 1932.
18. "Gilmer Will Celebrate Completion of New Courthouse," *DMN*, July 4, 1937.
19. "Van Zandt's 50-Year Dream Realized in New Courthouse," *DMN*, June 6, 1937, sec. 2.
20. J. Frank Dobie, "While Traveling over the Country," *DMN*, August 25, 1940, sec. 4.
21. "Longview's Modern New Community Center Is Complete," *LDN*, May 12, 1940.
22. Ibid.
23. "Razing of Rockwall Courthouse Set to Start Monday," *DMN*, March 15, 1941; "New Rockwall Courthouse Dedicated," *DMN*, June 18, 1942.
24. "Central Fire Fighters May Move on Monday," *FWST*, December 27, 1930; "Fire Hall Formal Opening on April 8," *FWST*, March 20, 1931.
25. "Market Contract May Be Let Next Week," *FWST*, October 10, 1929, sec. 2; Public Market advertisement, *FWST*, June 15, 1930; Hugh Cowdin, "110 Dogs on Display at Show Here Today," *FWST*, October 11, 1936, sec. 2; "An Open Letter from the Trade Unions of Fort Worth," *FWST*, May 17, 1941.
26. "Municipally Controlled Water Department Spends Vast Sums in Increasing the City's Supply," *DMN Supplement*, October 1, 1910; "Says Lake Must Be Fished," *DMN*, June 19, 1915; "Plan Zoning at White Rock," *DMN*, June 4, 1927.
27. "Design All Its Own for Library for Negroes," *DMN*, August 15, 1930.
28. Philip Parisi, *The Texas Post Office Murals: Art for the People* (College Station: Texas A&M University Press, 2004), 4-5.
29. James Andy Lambert, "Paris Public Library Murals," East Texas History: A Project by Sam Houston State University, accessed September 24, 2016, http://easttexashistory.org/items/show/86; "Public Works of Art Project (PWAP)," *Encyclopaedia Britannica*, accessed September 24, 2016, https://www.britannica.com/topic/Public-Works-of-Art-Project.
30. "Second Floor Murals in City Hall Will Trace

Development of Dallas," *DMN*, December 24, 1933; "Artists to Finish Murals in Several Weeks Although Pay Checks Cease Thursday," *DMN*, February 14, 1934.
31. "History of Dallas City Hall Buildings," City of Dallas City Secretary's Office, accessed January 21, 2017, http://citysecretary.dallascityhall.com/exhibits/archives_CityHallBlds.html; "Historical Murals Doomed," *DMN*, June 27, 1956; "Cabin Has No Picture Window," *DMN*, July 8, 1956.
32. Jerome Weeks, "The Lost Murals of Dallas' Old Municipal Building," KERA Art & Seek, June 22, 2015, accessed January 21, 2017, http://artandseek.org/2015/06/22/the-lost-murals-of-dallas-old-municipal-building; "Public Art," accessed January 24, 2017, http://www.philiplamb.com/Public.html.
33. Steven R. Butler, "Henry 'Dad' Garrett: the Wizard of Dallas, Texas," *Legacies: a History Journal for Dallas and North Central Texas* Vol. 22, No. 1 (Spring 2010): 24, 26.
34. "New City Hall for Fort Worth," *DMN*, January 4, 1929; "Fort Worth City Jail Is Scored," *DMN*, March 31, 1929.
35. "Cornerstone Laid as Casually as Egg," *FWST*, May 6, 1938; "Fort Worth Occupies New City Hall," *DMN*, January 5, 1939; "City Sports a New Hall," *FWST*, January 8, 1939.
36. "New Library, Civic Center at Fort Worth," *DMN*, February 5, 1939.
37. "Permanent Collection Will Be Hung Today," *FWST*, June 24, 1939.
38. Frank Perkins, "Old Library Meets Wrecking Ball Today," *FWST*, September 16, 1990.
39. "Texas Projects Get OK for WPA Cash," *DMN*, September 24, 1940.
40. "Peacock Military Academy to Move from San Antonio to Campus East of Dallas," *DMN*, October 6, 1929; "Peacock Opens New Quarters," *DMN*, September 15, 1930; "Military School Changes Owners," *DMN*, December 19, 1933; "Peacock Site Sold for New County School," *DMN*, December 15, 1938, sec. 10.
41. "Lee School Will Embody New Type of Architecture," *DMN*, March 22, 1931.
42. Cohen, op. cit., 151.
43. Susan Allen Kline, *Eight Decades of School Construction: Historic Resources of the Fort Worth Independent School District* (Fort Worth: City of Fort Worth, 2003), 33.
44. Cohen, op. cit., 177.
45. "Monster Football Party Opens New Stadium Wednesday Night; 10,000 Expected to Attend," *DMN*, October 1, 1939.
46. "Those Cobbs and Stadiums," *DMN*, December 31, 1957.
47. "In East Dallas, the City's Graveyard for Dead Buildings," *DMN*, May 18, 2012.
48. "Board Selects Architects for School Plans," *DMN*, June 8, 1938; "New Northeast Dallas School Named Jackson," *DMN*, February 1, 1939.
49. "Spence Junior High School Dedicated; Patrons Express Enthusiasm over Building," *DMN*, February 2, 1940.
50. Ibid.
51. "$26,320,000 in Construction for 1929 Is Planned," *FWST*, May 6, 1929; "Mosiah Shrine Program Fall Ceremonial," *FWST*, November 14, 1930.
52. Cohen, op. cit., 112.
53. "Masonic Temple Job Starts Soon," *DMN* August 4, 1940, sec. 2; "New Masonic Temple Well Under Way," *DMN*, February 23, 1941, sec. 2.
54. "Tyler's Hospital to Be Dedicated; Cost Is $350,000," *DMN*, March 14, 1937; "Hospital's Opening Moved up One Day to Succor Injured," *DMN*, March 19, 1937.
55. Carolyn Poirot, "Pioneer FW Clinic Falling to Progress," *FWST*, April 1, 1983.
56. "Camps Normal Inst. Opening Program for Oct. 8 Given," *LDN*, October 5, 1923; "Negro Hospital Opening Friday," *LDN*, March 14, 1940; "Call Hospital at Longview a Modern Unit," *Chicago Defender*, June 21, 1941.
57. "Addie M. Graham," Texas Historical Commission marker No. 85 (1986), located in Fireman's Park, Graham; "Work Is Progressing on Graham Auditorium," *DMN*, April 20, 1929.
58. Irvin M. May Jr., "New London School Explosion," Handbook of Texas Online, accessed September 26, 2016, http://www.tshaonline.org/handbook/online/articles/yqn01; "London School Blast Rites Planned," *DMN*, September 10, 1939.
59. "Unit of $400,000 Baptist Building Program," *DMN*, January 31, 1939, sec. 2.
60. "New Church Fund Raised," *DMN*, October 6, 1947, sec. 2; "New Church Ready: Long Battle Won by Gaston Baptists," *DMN*, April 29, 1950, sec. 3.
61. "1,400 Attend Temple's Dedicatory Services," *FWST*, December 11, 1939.
62. "Calvary Baptist Church," *Chronicles of Smith County Texas* Vol. 22, No. 1 (Tyler, Texas: Smith County Historical Society, 1982).
63. Stewart M. Doss, "Gospel Lighthouse to Dedicate Neon-Topped Dream Church," *DMN*, November 18, 1950.

Chapter 7: Residential

1. E. D. Alexander, "Self-Taught Engineer 'Figured out' Many Things in Career," *FWST*, December 17, 1961, sec. 2; "Charles Davis, Ex-Engineer, Dies at 90; Rites Tuesday," *FWST*, October 28, 1974; "Modernistic and Efficient," *FWST*, July 22, 1935.
2. "Modernistic and Efficient," op. cit.
3. Ibid.
4. "Better Homes" (classified advertisement), *FWST*, November 22, 1936; "Homes under Construction Now in T.C.U. Area," *FWST*, October 20, 1935.
5. "Modern Home Is Built with Tile," *FWST*, October 18, 1937.
6. "Biographical Sketch of Harold Everett 'Bubi' Jessen," Jessen and Jessen Papers, Alexander Architectural Archive, University of Texas Libraries, University of Texas at Austin, accessed November 23, 2016, http://www.lib.utexas.edu/taro/utaaa/00109/aaa-00109.html.
7. "Contemporary House for Use by Southwesterners to Be Dedicated Sunday," *DMN*, July 5, 1936, sec. 9.
8. "Attend Open House, Denton's Most Modernistic Dwelling," *Denton Record-Chronicle* (*DRC*), August 16, 1935; "Modernistic House Draws Large Crowd," *DRC*, August 19, 1935.
9. "Contemporary House for use by Southwesterners to be Dedicated Sunday," op. cit.
10. "Girl Scouts to Get House," *DMN*, May 14, 1938; "New Girl Scout Little House to Be Dedicated," *DMN*, December 9, 1949, sec. 2.
11. "Company Building 39 Homes," *DMN*, December 13, 1936, sec. 4; "Girl Scouts to Get House," op. cit.
12. "Marshall A. Kennady Family Moves to Lake," *FWST*, July 12, 1936, Society and Clubs section; Harrison-Kennady & Company advertisement, *FWST*, May 8, 1938, Oil News section.
13. *Texas General Contractors Association Monthly Bulletin* (*TGCA*) (February 1937): 12; "Building Permits," *DMN*, November 30, 1935, sec. 2.
14. *TGCA* (May 1936): 12.
15. *TGCA* (February 1937): 12; "Building Permits," *DMN*, November 30, 1935, sec. 2.
16. "Highland Park West" (advertisement), *DMN*, April 25, 1937, sec. 4.
17. "Sanger Bros. Cordially Invites You to Visit the House of Today" (advertisement), *DMN*, May 15, 1938, sec. 2; "Joiners Buy New, Furnished

$20,000 Home," *DMN*, March 12, 1939.
18. Dorman H. Winfrey, "Joiner, Columbus Marion [Dad]," Handbook of Texas Online, accessed October 2, 2016, http://www.tshaonline.org/handbook/online/articles/fjo40.
19. *TGCA* (November 1937): 11; "Residential Building Proves Big Factor in Improving Business," *DMN*, November 22, 1936; "Rites Set for Dallas Clubwoman," *DMN*, July 13, 1936.
20. "Mrs. Morley Is Hostess at Luncheon," *FWST*, February 6, 1938, Society and Clubs section.
21. "New Residence Hotel to Open Sunday," "The Highlander" (advertisement), both in *DMN*, March 13, 1938; Phil Stephens, "Plans Finalized for High-Rise Construction," *Park Cities News*, November 2, 1977.
22. "Tomorrow's Home to Be Shown to Public," *DMN*, September 18, 1938, sec. 4.
23. George W. Gray, "East Texas, Poor Many Years, Now Flowing with 'Black Gold,'" *New York Times*, July 5, 1931.
24. Caleb Pirtle III and Terry Stembridge, *Echoes of Forgotten Streets: Memories of Kilgore, Texas, Oil Capital of America* (Berkeley Heights, New Jersey: London Square Media, 2009), 227.
25. "House of Innovations Features Breakfast Bar," *DMN*, August 6, 1939, sec. 4.

Chapter 8: Centennial

1. John Rosenfield Jr., "The Passing Show: 'March of Time' Makes Centennial Observances a Battle of the Leg Shows," *DMN*, June 16, 1936; Jerry Flemmons, "Makin' Whoopee," *D Magazine*, April 1978, accessed January 26, 2017, http://www.dmagazine.com/publications/d-magazine/1978/april/makin-whoopee.
2. "Theatrical Sensation Creator Will Direct Fort Worth's Big 'Texas Frontier Centennial,'" *Corsicana Daily Sun*, March 9, 1936; "Indians and Cowboys and Guess Who Wins," *FWST*, March 11, 1936; Kenneth D. Ragsdale, *Centennial '36: the Year America Discovered Texas* (College Station, Texas: Texas A&M University Press, 1987), 212; Flemmons, op. cit.; "'Whoopee' Sign to Be Smaller," *FWST*, May 23, 1936.
3. Ragsdale, op. cit., 218; Annie O. Cleveland and M. Barrett Cleveland, "Fort Worth for Entertainment: Billy Rose's Casa Mañana," *Theatre Design & Technology* Vol. 44, No. 1 (Winter 2008): 29-31; John Rosenfield Jr., "Fort Worth Show Is Given Colorful Dress Rehearsal," *DMN*, July 18, 1936; "Frontier Show to Be Wonderland of Colors," *FWST*, July 15, 1936.
4. The original Casa Mañana was demolished in 1942 (Bess Stephenson, "Wreckers Coming for Casa Manana and It'll Be Funeral of City's Old Love," *FWST*, May 10, 1942). The present-day building of the same name, an auditorium enclosed by an aluminum geodesic dome, was designed by A. George King and built in 1958.
5. "A Year of Progress" (advertisement), *FWST*, December 30, 1928; Jacob W. Olmstead, "From Old South to Modern West: Fort Worth's Celebration of the Texas State Centennial and the Shaping of an Urban Identity and Image" (doctoral thesis, Texas Christian University, 2011), 88-95; Flemmons, op. cit.; "Show Plans Are Approved," *FWST*, January 21, 1936.
6. Arthur Weinman and Gregory Smith, "Will Rogers Memorial Center," National Register of Historic Places Registration Form (Fort Worth: Arthur Weinman Architects, March 11, 2015).
7. "Ceremony Marks Unveiling of Will Rogers Sculpture," *FWST*, February 17, 1942; Weinman and Smith, op. cit.
8. Judith Singer Cohen, *Cowtown Moderne: Art Deco Architecture of Fort Worth, Texas* (College Station, Texas: Texas A&M University Press, 1988), 126.
9. Weinman and Smith, op. cit.; Richard Panzera, "Engineer Defied Criticism to Build Will Rogers Dome," *FWST*, August 3, 1969. Herbert M. Hinckley Jr.'s quote comes from *Under the Dome* (New York: Carlton Press, 1968), his biography of his father.
10. Panzera, op. cit.; Weinman and Smith, op. cit.
11. John William Rogers, "Innovations in Architecture Get Tryout at Fairs," *Daily Times-Herald* (Dallas), March 8, 1936.
12. "Centennial's Stunning Beauty Due to Unique Style of Architecture," *DMN*, June 7, 1936.
13. "A Year of Progress," op. cit.; Cohen, op. cit., 132-133.
14. Debbie M. Liles, *Will Rogers Coliseum* (Charleston, South Carolina: Arcadia Publishing, 2012), 66.
15. Weinman and Smith, op. cit.
16. "Gigantic 'Jumbo' and Tiny Temple Centennial Stars," *DMN*, April 12, 1936; Clair C. Stebbins, "Local Artists Complete Series of Authentic Murals," *Sunday Times-Signal* (Zanesville, Ohio), May 30, 1937, sec. 2; Liles, op. cit., 117.
17. Weinman and Smith, op. cit.
18. John Rosenfield, "San Francisco's Fair as Ghost of Our Past," *DMN*, August 15, 1940.
19. Weinman and Smith, op. cit.
20. "History," Billy Bob's Texas, accessed January 28, 2017, http://billybobstexas.com/experience/history; "Stock Building Has 3 Acres under One Roof," *FWST*, October 4, 1936; "City Buys Old Stock Show Buildings on North Side," *FWST*, May 20, 1948; "$2,993 Bid Made to Alter Old Cattle Exhibit Building," *FWST*, December 1, 1948.
21. "Globe Aircraft Plant Expands," *FWST*, February 5, 1943; J'Nell L. Pate, *Arsenal of Defense: Fort Worth's Military Legacy* (Denton, Texas: Texas State Historical Association, 2011), 124; "History," Billy Bob's Texas, op. cit.
22. Ragsdale, op. cit., 46-47, 58.
23. "Electrical Features of the Texas Centennial Central Exposition," paper presented during the October 1936 meeting of the American Institute of Electrical Engineers South West District (State Fair of Texas Archive, 1936.0084); "Striking Lighting Effects Achieved at Centennial by Observing Laws of Physics," *DMN*, July 3, 1936; "Esplanade at Night, State Hall, Cavalcade Are Called Most Interesting at Fair," *DMN*, September 13, 1936.
24. "Fair Illumination Declared Foremost Item of Exposition," op. cit.
25. Ragsdale, op. cit., 54; "Dallas Unanimously Chosen for Texas Centennial Site," *DMN*, September 10, 1934; Sarah Hunter, "Fair Park," *Handbook of Texas Online*, accessed February 2, 2017, http://www.tshaonline.org/handbook/online/articles/ggf03.
26. "Texas Centennial Central Exposition," Publicity Department releases, undated, TCE Buildings box, Centennial Collection, Dallas Historical Society; "Speed Proves Amazing Part of Centennial," *DMN*, June 7, 1936.
27. "Centennial Sidelights," *DMN*, June 17, 1936; "Catch Crooks by Television," *DMN*, July 22, 1936; "Official Night Opening of the Texas Centennial Exposition," radio script for NBC network, June 6, 1936; "Fair Illumination Declared Foremost Item of Exposition," *DMN*, June 26, 1936; Ralph Bryan, "Fair Illumination Gives Centennial Individual Class," *DMN*, June 21, 1936.
28. Carol Morris Little, *A Comprehensive Guide to Outdoor Sculpture in Texas* (Austin: University of Texas Press, 1996), 150-151, 163.
29. Rogers, op. cit.
30. Ibid.
31. David Dillon, *Dallas Architecture: 1936-1986* (Austin: Texas Monthly Press, 1985), 11.
32. Ibid., 25.
33. "Vast Blaze Wrecks Fair's Auto Building,"

DMN, February 10, 1942; Louise Elam, "Fair Park Project Summary" (undated report for Dallas Park and Recreation Department).

34. "New Coliseum Is Made Attractive by Lighting," *DMN*, October 2, 1910; "First Centennial Construction to Start in 5 Days," *DMN*, August 13, 1935; "Hall of Administration," Box 14, TCE Buildings File, Texas Centennial Collection, Dallas Historical Society; Ragsdale, op. cit., 94; David Dillon, "The Women's Museum, Dallas," *Architectural Record*, November 2001; Gaile Robinson, "Women's Museum in Dallas to Close Oct. 31," *FWST*, October 6, 2011.
35. "Where Saguaros Grow," Saguaro National Park, accessed January 31, 2017, https://www.nps.gov/sagu/learn/nature/location.htm; Deborah Fleck, "Georgia Carroll Kyser: Inspiration for Fair Park Statue Later Became Actress," *DMN*, January 17, 2011.
36. George Dahl, interview by Sarah Hunter, February 24, 1984, Dallas Historical Society; Ragsdale, op. cit., 179; Carleton W. Adams Jr., interview by Sarah Hunter, March 8, 1985, Dallas Historical Society.
37. Michael V. Hazel, "Building the Westminster Abbey of the New World," *Legacies: a History Journal for Dallas and North Central Texas* Vol. 23, No. 1 (Spring 2011): 20.
38. Ibid.; Anna Irene Del Monaco, "Paul Cret: the American Order," *L'architettura delle città, the Journal of the Scientific Society Ludovico Quaroni* Vol. 4, No. 7 (2015); Donald S. Nelson, interview by Peggy Riddle, Summer 1983, Dallas Historical Society.
39. Dillon, *Dallas Architecture*, 24.
40. Joan Jenkins Perez, "Hall of State," Handbook of Texas Online, accessed February 2, 2017, http://www.tshaonline.org/handbook/online/articles/lch01.
41. Frank Carter Adams, ed., *The State of Texas Building* (Austin: Steck, 1937), 13; Russell M. Magnaghi, "Hasinai Indians," Handbook of Texas Online, accessed January 30, 2017, http://www.tshaonline.org/handbook/online/articles/bmh08; Phillip L. Fry, "Texas, Origin of Name," Handbook of Texas Online, accessed January 30, 2017, http://www.tshaonline.org/handbook/online/articles/pft04.
42. Patricia Peck, "Plenty Room for History, Now and Later, in Hall of State," *DMN*, June 27, 1943.
43. Ragsdale, op. cit., 182-183.
44. Peck, op. cit.
45. Adams, op. cit., 20.
46. Ibid,. 31, 34; Hazel, op. cit., 22-23.
47. Willis Winters, "Planning the Centennial," *Texas Architect*, May/June 1999, 8; "Exhibits in Main Federal Building Valued at $25,000,000," *DMN*, June 7, 1936.
48. "Exhibits in Main Federal Building Valued at $25,000,000," op. cit.
49. Correspondence and exhibit specification files, Centennial Collection, Dallas Historical Society.
50. Lawrence Tenney Stevens, "A Brief History of the Great Australian Woofus" (undated typescript from the archives of the Lawrence Tenney Stevens Trust).
51. "Woofus to Quit His Lofty Post," *DMN*, October 2, 1941; Nicholas McWhirter, "Lost & Found Dallas: the Texas Woofus," *Columns*, Summer 2013, 31; Bill Zeeble, "Oddball Sculpture Returns to 2002 Texas State Fair," KERA News, accessed February 1, 2017, http://keranews.org/post/oddball-sculpture-returns-2002-texas-state-fair.
52. "Livestock Building No. 2," *The Official Guide Book, Texas Centennial Exposition* (Dallas: Texas Centennial Central Exposition, 1936), 61.
53. "Newspaper Opening Exhibit," *DMN*, May 9, 1936.
54. Stanley Marcus, *Minding the Store: a Memoir* (Denton, Texas: University of North Texas Press, 1974), 91; Unidentified newspaper article, January 10, 1936, Texas Centennial Exposition clipping file, Dallas History & Archives division, Dallas Public Library; "King Petroleum Holds Court at Exposition in Permanent Structures Costing $500,000," *DMN*, June 7, 1936; "'Magnolia Lounge' at the Texas Centennial," *LDN*, May 12, 1936; Helen Sheehy, "Jones, Margaret Virginia," Handbook of Texas Online, accessed January 30, 2017, http://www.tshaonline.org/handbook/online/articles/fjo59.
55. "Ford Exhibition Plays Big Part in Opening Fair," *DMN*, June 7, 1936; "'From Soil to Auto' Tells of Processing of Products of Farm," *DMN*, June 7, 1936; "Cooler Inside," *DMN*, June 14, 1936; Willis Winters, "The Ford Motor Company at the Texas Centennial Exposition," *Legacies: a History Journal for Dallas and North Central Texas* Vol. 23, No. 1 (Spring 2011): 13.
56. Winters, op. cit., 17.
57. Jesse O. Thomas, *Negro Participation in the Texas Centennial Exposition* (Boston: the Christopher Publishing House, 1938), 13, 19; Michael Phillips, *White Metropolis: Race, Ethnicity, and Religion in Dallas, 1841-2001* (Austin: University of Texas Press, 2006), 113-114; Ragsdale, op. cit., 107, 177.
58. Thomas, op. cit., 25, 28-29, 34
59. Ibid., 117-124.
60. "Fair Band Shell Declared Acme of Such Structures," *DMN*, May 3, 1936.
61. Susan A. Besser, "Fair Park," Dallas Landmark Commission Landmark Nomination Form (September 18, 2007).

Chapter 9: Architects, Designers, and Artists

1. Christopher Long, "Adams, Carleton W.," Handbook of Texas Online, accessed May 25, 2017, http://www.tshaonline.org/handbook/online/articles/fad25; *San Antonio Architecture: Traditions and Visions*, ed. Julius M. Gribou et al. (San Antonio: AIA San Antonio, 2007), 24, 173.
2. "Grant Store in Loop Will Be Modernized at $175,000 Cost," *Chicago Sunday Tribune*, November 18, 1934; "W.T. Grant's Department Store," PRS Preservation Ready, accessed May 26, 2105, http://preservationready.org/buildings/544MainStreet.
3. "Home Town," *Waco News-Tribune* (*WNT*), March 1, 1923; "Personal Listings/Exclusive: New Architect," *DMN*, July 9, 1939; "Enlargement Work on National City Bank Underway," *WNT*, May 4, 1947; "James P. Baugh (A.I.A.), Architect," advertisement, *WNT*, August 27, 1947.
4. "Three Men en Route Here Killed," *Victoria* (Texas) *Advocate*, January 26, 1936; "Fog Is Blamed as Trio Killed in Plane Crash," *DMN*, January 26, 1936. "Architect for Bobo's Hospital Is Plane Victim," *Arlington* (Texas) *Journal*, January 31, 1936.
5. "Bryan and Sharp Form Architectural Firm," *DMN*, March 29, 1925; "Adolphus to Open New Roof Garden," *DMN*, July 5, 1929; "Dallas Architect, Ralph Bryan, Dies," *DMN*, July 12, 1965.
6. "Burial Rites Pending for W.C. Sharp," *DMN*, October 30, 1949.
7. "English Type Home Being Erected," *DMN*, February 3, 1929.
8. "Highway Crash Is Fatal to Mr. Edgeworth," *DMN*, May 9, 1940; "Soaring Society Renames Carsey," *DMN*, July 8, 1951; "Rites Set," *DMN*, September 13, 1962, sec. 4.
9. "Construction Activities in Dallas and Elsewhere," *DMN*, July 1, 1928.
10. "Fair Band Shell Declared Acme of Such Structures," *DMN*, May 3, 1936; "Monday Rites Slated Here for Architect," *DMN*, February 22, 1953; "Council Selects Architect Firms," *DMN*, May 19, 1964.

11. Christopher Long, "Clarkson, Wiley G.," Handbook of Texas Online, accessed May 1, 2015, http://www.tshaonline.org/handbook/online/articles/fclrg; Capt. B.B. Paddock, ed., "Wiley Gulick Clarkson," *History of Texas, Vol. III: Fort Worth and the Texas Northwest* (Chicago: the Lewis Publishing Company, 1922), 110-111.
12. "Pioneer Texas Builder Dies," *Wichita Daily Times* (Wichita Falls, Texas), July 3, 1955.
13. "Corgan, Jack Murl. AIA 47," in *American Architects Directory*, 3rd ed., ed. John F. Gane, AIA (New York: R.R. Bowker Company, 1970), 180.
14. William J. Moore, interview by Elizabeth Nelson Patrick, August 29, 1981, University of Nevada Oral History Program.
15. "Hubert Hammond Crane AIA," in *American Architects Directory*, 1st ed., ed. George S. Koyl (New York: R.R. Bowker Company, 1955), 118; Judith S. Cohen, "Crane, Hubert Hammond," Handbook of Texas Online, accessed May 25, 2015, http://www.tshaonline.org/handbookonline/articles/fcrss.
16. "Paul Philippe Cret (1876-1945)," Penn Biographies, University Archives & Records Center, accessed October 1, 2016, http://www.archives.upenn.edu/people/1800s/cret_paul.html.
17. "Danna, John B. AIA," in *American Architects Directory*, 2nd ed., ed. George S. Koyl (New York: R.R. Bowker Company, 1962), 153.
18. Architects' Roster Questionnaire for Everett V. Welch (January 26, 1953), American Institute of Architects, accessed July 27, 2016, http://public.aia.org/sites/hdoaa/wiki/AIA%20scans/Rosters/WelchEverettV_roster.pdf.
19. "Senior Engineers: James Black Davies, Jr., B.A., B.S. in E.E., E.E.," *The Cactus 1916: the Year Book Published by the Student Body of the University of Texas* (Kansas City, Missouri: Union Bank Note Company, 1916), 97; Architects' Roster Questionnaire for James B. Davies (October 3, 1927), American Institute of Architects, accessed July 31, 2016, http://public.aia.org/sites/hdoaa/wiki/AIA%20scans/Rosters/DaviesJamesB_roster.pdf; "Death Notices: Davies," *FWST*, January 20, 1966, sec. 3. Researching Davies can be confusing. When his father, J.B. Davies Sr., died in 1917, James Black Davies Jr. dropped the suffix from his name. When his own son was born in 1922, the architect adopted the name James B. Davies, Sr. and named his son James B. Davies Jr.
20. Delos Smith, "Blame Faulty Heating System for Explosion," *Berkeley* (California) *Daily Gazette*, March 20, 1937. The Texas historical marker for the Gaston Public School Complex listed one of the architects as "Howard DeFee." Subsequent research by Texas Historical Commission staff revealed his actual name to be Marvin E. DeFee.
21. "Contract Let for Garage Building and New Ice House," *Eagle Lake* (Texas) *Headlight*, August 2, 1924; "Government Men Here on Courthouse Project," *Meridian* (Texas) *Times*, March 22, 1935.
22. "Obituary: Emory S. White," *San Jacinto News* (Shepherd, Texas), January 9, 1973.
23. Stanley Marcus, *Minding the Store: a Memoir* (Denton, Texas: University of North Texas Press, 1974), 92-94; "Roscoe Plimpton DeWitt (1894-1975)," The Monuments Men, accessed August 18, 2011, http://www.monumentsmenfoundation.org/biophp?id=72.
24. "For Licensing of Architects," *DMN*, October 16, 1928; "Architects of Dallas Will Enter Display in Southern Exposition," *DMN*, September 29, 1929; "Dallasite Sails to Be Architect at Trinidad Base," *DMN*, July 24, 1941.
25. "Charles Stevens Dilbeck Drawings, 1929-1969," Alexander Architectural Archive, University of Texas Libraries, University of Texas at Austin, accessed January 2, 2016, http://www.lib.utexas.edu/taro/utaaa/00110/aaa-00110.html.
26. *Polk's Sherman City Directory 1923* (Sioux City, Iowa: R.L. Polk & Co., Publishers, 1923), 99, 170; "Blast Blamed upon Faulty Heat System," *El Paso Herald-Post*, March 20, 1937; "J. Loftin Downing Succumbs at 63," *DMN*, December 20, 1954, sec. 3.
27. Ernest Langford, *The First Fifty Years of Architectural Education at the Agricultural and Mechanical College of Texas* (College Station, Texas: College Archive, Agricultural and Mechanical College of Texas, 1957), 7; "Theatre Designer Dies at Dallas," *Big Spring* (Texas) *Daily Herald*, October 20, 1937.
28. Stephen Fox, "Finn, Alfred Charles," Handbook of Texas Online, accessed July 17, 2016, http://www.tshaonline.org/handbook/online/articles/ffi32.
29. "Dallas Had Hard Fight to Get Zoning Power," *DMN*, October 1, 1935; "Lester N. Flint, Architect, Dies Suddenly at Home," *DMN*, January 19, 1938; "Former Parisian Dies in Dallas Tuesday Morning," *Paris News* (*PN*), January 18, 1938; Rachel Stone, "Residential Resurrection: an Oak Cliff Family Finds Its Next Home in an Old Commercial Building," *Oak Cliff Advocate*, April 2014.
30. "City Thrills to Aviation Glory in Love Field Ceremony," *DMN*, October 6, 1940; "Donald S. Nelson: an Inventory of His Architectural Records, Drawings, and Photographs, 1910-1975," Alexander Architectural Archive, University of Texas Libraries, University of Texas at Austin, accessed May 30, 2015, http://www.lib.utexas.edu/taro/utaaa/00042/aaa-00042.html.
31. "Fooshee and Cheek: an Inventory of Their Drawings and Records, 1930-1966," Alexander Architectural Archive, University of Texas Libraries, University of Texas at Austin, accessed January 2, 2016, http://www.lib.utexas.edu/taro/utaaa/00017/aaa-00017.html.
32. E. D. Alexander, "Flying Architect Keeps Quitman Man Eyeing Air," *FWST*, January 7, 1950.
33. "Preston M. Geren: an Inventory of his Drawings, 1937-1969," Alexander Architectural Archive, University of Texas Libraries, University of Texas at Austin, accessed July 23, 2016, https://www.lib.utexas.edu/taro/utaaa/00012/aaa-00012.html.
34. "Architect Began Career While Still in School," *DMN*, February 26, 1950; "Otto H. Lang and William J. Lang Announce" (advertisement), *DMN*, February 22, 1942; "Gill Gets Highest AIA Honor," *DMN*, April 24, 1967.
35. "Architects' Firm Formed," *DMN*, February 19, 1928.
36. "Architect of Texas University Projects Succumbs in Chicago," *DMN*, February 9, 1932; Walter T. Rolfe, "Architecture of UT Tells Simple Story," *DMN*, January 2, 1943.
37. "Architects' Firm Formed", *DMN*, February 19, 1928; "Prominent Architect E.B. LaRoche Passes," *DMN*, April 19, 1944.
38. Biographical sketch, Architects and Artists box, Centennial Collection, Dallas Historical Society; Christopher Long, "Dahl, George Leighton," Handbook of Texas Online, accessed August 11, 2011, http://www.tshaonline.org/handbook/online/articles/fda86.
39. "C.H. Griesenbeck" in *The Encyclopedia of Texas, Vol. 2*, ed. Ellis Arthur Davis and Edwin H. Grobe (Dallas: Texas Development Bureau, 1922), 694-695.
40. "S.B. Haynes, Architect, Dies: Rites Pend Here," *Lubbock Avalanche-Journal* (*LAJ*), January 27, 1970.
41. "Kirby, L(averne) H(owe) (AIA)," in *American Architects Directory*, 1st ed., op. cit., 302; "Rites

Scheduled For L.H. Kirby," *LAJ*, October 27, 1972.

42. Weinman and Smith, op. cit.

43. David Van Zanten, Ashley Elizabeth Dunn and Leslie Coburn, *Drawing the Future: Chicago Architecture on the International Stage* (Chicago: Northwestern University Press, 2013), 25; "P(ierre) R(ichard) L(eonard) Hogner (AIA, Emeritus)," in *American Architects Directory*, 1st ed., op. cit., 252; Laura Hughes and Laura Trieschmann, "Embassy Gulf Service Station," National Register of Historic Places Registration Form (Chevy Chase, Maryland: Traceries, August 16, 1993).

44. W. Hawkins Ferry, *The Legacy of Albert Kahn* (Detroit: Wayne State University Press, 1987), 8-11; "Albert Kahn (March 21, 1869-Dec. 8, 1942)," HistoricDetroit.org, accessed January 29, 2017, http://historicdetroit.org/architect/albert-kahn; "Albert Kahn, Architect," Ford Motor Car Company History, accessed January 29, 2017, http://fordmotorhistory.com/factories/long_beach/kahn.phpl; "Albert Kahn, World Famous Architect, Dies," *Chicago Daily Tribune*, December 9, 1942.

45. "Anton Korn, Architect, Dies at Waco," *DMN*, August 24, 1942; "Anton F. Korn, Jr." in *The Encyclopedia of Texas, Vol. 2*, op. cit., 544.

46. "Veteran Architect Who Added To Dallas Skyline to Retire," *DMN*, February 22, 1942; "Pioneer Dallas Architect, Otto H. Lang, Dies at 82," *DMN*, October 19, 1947.

47. "Frank O. Witchell Dies, Designed Many Buildings," *DMN*, April 24, 1958.

48. "C.H. Leinbach" in *The Encyclopedia of Texas, Vol. 1*, ed. Ellis Arthur Davis and Edwin H. Grobe (Dallas: Texas Development Bureau, 1922), 311; *Manufacturers Record* (Baltimore: Manufacturers Record Publishing Co., May 25, 1922), 67; Edward A. Blackburn, *Wanted: Historic County Jails of Texas* (College Station, Texas: Texas A&M University Press, 2006), 123.

49. "Architect Lemmon Dies at 86," *DMN*, December 23, 1975; Frank Thrower and Marian Ann J. Montgomery, "Mark Lemmon: Dallas Architect of Community Churches," *Legacies: a History Journal for Dallas and North Central Texas* Vol. 17, No. 2 (Fall 2005), 54-56.

50. *Draft Registration Cards for Fourth Registration for New York State, 04/27/1942-04/27/1942*, NAI No. *2555973* (St. Louis, Missouri: the National Archives at St. Louis); Paul Goldberger, "Architecture: a William Lescaze Retrospective," *New York Times*, August 21, 1984; D. J. Huppatz, "Whatever Happened to William Lescaze?" Critical Cities, accessed January 29, 2017, http://djhuppatz.blogspot.com/2010/04/whatever-happened-to-william-lescaze_29.html; Stanley Marcus, *Minding the Store: a Memoir* (Denton, Texas: University of North Texas Press, 1974), 91.

51. "Colonial Home Used: Architect Explains Style of New Funeral Home Here," *PN*, June 1, 1951; Jay C. Henry, *Architecture in Texas: 1895-1945* (Austin: University of Texas Press, 1993), 200.

52. "Theo S. Maffitt and Theodore S. Maffitt: an Inventory of Their Drawings, c. 1914-1981," Alexander Architectural Archive, University of Texas Libraries, University of Texas at Austin, accessed June 5, 2016, http://www.lib.utexas.edu/taro/utaaa/00017/aaa-00017.html.

53. Carolyn Hughes Toft, "John Lawrence Mauran, FAIA (1866-1933)," Landmarks Association of St. Louis, accessed July 30, 2016, http://www.landmarks-stl.org/architects/bio/john_lawrence_mauran/.

54. "Howard R. Meyer Collection, 1924-1986, 2011," Alexander Architectural Archive, University of Texas Libraries, University of Texas at Austin, accessed October 11, 2016, http://www.lib.utexas.edu/taro/utaaa/00006/aaa-00006.html.

55. Margaret Truman, *Bess W. Truman* (New York: Macmillan Publishing Company, 1986); Neild, Edward F., Dictionary of Louisiana, accessed July 29, 2016, www.lahistory.org/site14.php.

56. "Somdal, Dewey Andersen AIA 39, FAIA 48," in *American Architects Directory*, 2nd ed., op. cit., 661; "Cornerstone to Be Laid at Tech Main Mon.," *Ruston* (Louisiana) *Daily Leader*, November 28, 1936; "Social Center Planned for Louisiana Tech," *Monroe* (Louisiana) *Morning World*, June 6, 1937.

57. Biographical sketch, Architects and Artists box, Centennial Collection, Dallas Historical Society; Christopher Long, "Donald Siegfried Nelson," Handbook of Texas Online, accessed August 10, 2011, http://www.tshaonline.org/handbook/online/articles/fnejz.

58. "Gaylord Noftsger, Architect, Dies," *Daily Oklahoman* (Oklahoma City), August 21, 1979; "Noftsger, B. Gaylord AIA 37," in *American Architects Directory*, 3rd ed., op. cit., 670.

59. "Patterson, Joseph Julian. AIA 45, FAIA 62," in *American Architects Directory*, 2nd ed., op. cit., 537.

60. "Teague, James Calloway," Biographical Dictionary of Architects in Canada, 1800-1950, accessed July 3, 2015, http://dictionaryofarchitectsincanada.org; *Journal of the American Institute of Architects*, Vol. 1 (January 1913-December 1913): 94.

61. "Pelich, Joseph (Roman) (AIA)," in *American Architects Directory*, 1st ed., op. cit., 427; Judith S. Cohen, "Pelich, Joseph Roman," Handbook of Texas Online, accessed July 28, 2016, https://tshaonline.org/handbook/online/articles/fpepv.

62. "Perkins, John Astin, AIA 45", in *American Architects Directory*, 2nd ed., op. cit., 545.

63. "Maurice Peterman" (obituary), *DMN*, September 26, 1971.

64. "About People of the Theater," *Motion Picture Herald: Better Theaters* (March 4, 1939): 14; Nancy Hopkins Reily, *Georgia O'Keeffe, a Private Friendship, Part II: Walking the Abiquiu and Ghost Ranch Land* (Santa Fe, New Mexico: Sunstone Press, 2006), 46-48; "John Worley and H.F. Pettigrew," *Brownsville Herald*, August 17, 1949; "Dallas-Built Houses Provided Homes for Atom Bomb Makers," *DMN*, September 24, 1945; "Boom in Building Swamps Arlington," *DMN*, February 3, 1952.

65. "H.F. Pettigrew" (obituary), *DMN*, August 16, 1976; "Builder John Worley Given Prather Award," *DMN*, October 3, 1970.

66. "Architect Phelps Dies," *San Antonio Light*, October 9, 1958.

67. "Dewees, Dahl AIA," in *American Architects Directory*, 1st ed., op. cit., 135; "Henry T. Phelps, Architect, Found Dead in His Apartment," *San Antonio Express*, December 6, 1944.

68. "Simmons, Colonel Clifton (AIA)," in *American Architects Directory*, 1st ed., op. cit., 436.

69. "Pitts, Llewellyn William (AIA)," in *American Architects Directory*, 1st ed., op. cit., 507.

70. "Current News," *The American Architect* (January-June 1921): 190; "Rites Set Today for Architect," *DMN*, October 13, 1972.

71. "Well-Known Texas Architect Roy E. Lane Dies at Age 72," *DMN*, August 8, 1956, sec. 3; "ALICO Since 1910," American Amicable, accessed September 30, 2016, http://www.alicobuilding.com/heritage.

72. David Minor, "Humphrey, TX," Handbook of Texas Online, accessed July 7, 2015, http://www.tshaonline.org/handbook/online/articles/hvhar; "Rita Theater Opens Doors to Public Today," *Greenville (TX) Evening Banner (GEB)*, March 16, 1933; "Dallas Firm to Construct Auditorium for $148,700; 180 Days Is Time Limit," *GEB*, December 31, 1938; "Chamber's New Home Approved," *Greenville (TX) Banner (GB)*, January

8, 1954; "Open House at New Library Slated for Sunday," *GB*, June 9, 1954.

73. "Ray, S(idney) W(illiam) AIA," in *American Architects Directory*, 2nd ed., op. cit., 575; Robert M. Hayes, "East Texas Notebook," *DMN*, March 18, 1960.
74. "Why Conceal the Facts?" (advertisement), *DMN*, October 9, 1927; "Funeral Set Monday for L.E. Sadler," *DMN*, December 26, 1965.
75. "Company Headed by Tech Alumni to Work on New Air Academy," *Georgia Tech Alumnus* (September-October 1954): 22; "Architect Firm 'Favored,'" *Kansas City* (Missouri) *Times*, March 21, 1968.
76. "Sibbert, Edward F(rederick)," in *American Architects Directory*, 2nd ed., op. cit., 641.
77. Diane Elizabeth Williams, "Azalea Residential Historic District," National Register of Historic Places Registration Form (Tyler, Texas: City of Tyler/Historic Tyler, Inc., July 31, 2002).
78. "Hoke Smith Passes after Long Illness," *DMN*, February 4, 1943.
79. "New Theater Is Begun at Fort Worth, One at Taylor Being Remodeled," *DMN*, November 19, 1939; "Smith, Raymond F. AIA 38," in *American Architects Directory*, 3rd ed., op. cit., 854.
80. Howard Barnstone, "Staub, John Fanz," Handbook of Texas Online, accessed August 3, 2016, https://tshaonline.org/handbook/online/articles/fst94.
81. *The Archi of Alpha Rho Chi*, Vol. XVII, No. 4 (April 1936): 20; "Buys Dallas Chain of Grocery Stores," *DMN*, April 15, 1931; "A Quarter-Century of Progress: We Honor These 25-Year Employees" (advertisement), *DMN*, April 12, 1956; "Kroger Food Chain Now 75 Years Old," *DMN*, August 20, 1958; "Stueber Retires as Architect of Wyatt Stores," *DMN*, January 22, 1961; "Alumni 'Specs,'" *The Alpha Ro Chi Letter* (January 1985): 5.
82. Jay Firsching, "511 Akard Building," National Register of Historic Places Registration Form (Dallas: Architexas, July 25, 2013).
83. "Thomas, Arthur E(lliott) (FAIA)," in *American Architects Directory*, 2nd ed., op. cit., 302.
84. Brad Russell, "Hall of Honor," *The Structural Engineer* (Spring 2012): 12.
85. "Merrill, W(alter) Ralph, AIA," in *American Architects Directory*, 2nd ed., op. cit., 478.
86. "Irving Timlin Dies, Retired Architect for Telephone Co.," *St. Louis Post-Dispatch*, October 19, 1955; "Timlin, Irvin Ray AIA, Emeritus," in *American Architects Directory*, 1st ed., op. cit., 580.
87. "Herbert Voelcker," in *The Encyclopedia of Texas, Vol. 2*, op. cit., 560-561; "Voelcker, Herbert R(udolph) AIA 42," in *American Architects Directory*, 2nd ed., op. cit., 727; Gregory Smith, "Jack County Courthouse," National Register of Historic Places Registration Form (Austin: Texas Historical Commission, 2012).
88. "Architect Here Dies at Age 74," *Wichita Falls Times*, November 16, 1962.
89. Karen Kingsley, "Emile Weil," KnowLA Encyclopedia of Louisiana, accessed September 10, 2016, http://knowla.org/entry/795.
90. Robert Leighninger, "Weiss, Dreyfous and Seiferth," KnowLA Encyclopedia of Louisiana, accessed July 29, 1016, http://knowla.org/entry/502; "Dreyfous, Felix Julius (AIA)," in *American Architects Directory*, 1st ed., op. cit., 144; "Seiferth, Solis (AIA)," op. cit., 497.
91. "Typical Modernized Colonial Home," *FWST*, May 3, 1937; "Laurel House Sold," *Citizen* (Houston), November 28, 1947; "This All Ceramic Home," *Houston Chronicle*, August 20, 1950; Ben Koush, "The Angelo and Lillian Minella House," City of Houston Protected Landmark Designation Report (Houston, February 13, 2006).
92. "Architects Form State Society," *DMN*, June 11, 1939.
93. "New Menard Hotel Formally Opened," *Laredo Daily Times*, May 7, 1928.
94. Christopher Long, "Withers, Elmer George," Handbook of Texas Online, accessed August 16, 2015, http://www.tshaonline.org/handbook/online/articles/fwirl; Peter Ketter with Wagner and Klein, Inc., "Menard County Courthouse," National Register of Historic Places Registration Form (Austin: Texas Historical Commission, March 5, 2003).
95. "Woltz, Robert P. Jr. AIA 39," in *American Architects Directory*, 2nd ed., op. cit., 775.
96. "P(ercy) E(dward) Zimmerman," in *American Architects Directory*, 3rd ed., op. cit., 790; "Artistic Work On Bank Annex Is Masterpiece," *LDN*, July 17, 1931.
97. "Here 'n' There," *LDN*, December 12, 1941 and January 22, 1942; James Gast, *The Astrodome: Building an American Spectacle* (Boston: the Aspinwall Press, 2014), 50.
98. "Peters, Strange and Bradshaw Is Busy Local Firm," *Sunday Avalanche-Journal* (Lubbock, Texas), September 22, 1929; "Peters, Noah Linton," American Institute of Architects membership file, accessed September 2, 2016, http://public.aia.org/sites/hdoaa/wiki/AIA%20scans/M-P/PetersNoahLinton.pdf.
99. "Strange, William Thomas, Jr. AIA 37," in *American Architects Directory*, 3rd ed., op. cit., 888.
100. "Epstein A(braham) (AIA)," in *American Architects Directory*, 1st ed., op. cit., 159; "We're 94!," Epstein-What's New? (July 14, 2015), accessed August 2, 2016, http://www.epsteinglobal.com/whats-new/2015/were-94.
101. "Construction News," the *Construction News* (May 29, 1913): 10; "News from Various Sources," the *American Architect* (September 15, 1920): 366.
102. E. D. Alexander, "Self-Taught Engineer 'Figured out' Many Things in Career," *FWST*, December 17, 1961, sec. 2; "Charles Davis, Ex-Engineer, Dies at 90; Rites Tuesday," *FWST*, October 28, 1974.
103. Alexander, "Self-Taught Engineer 'Figured out' Many Things in Career," op. cit.; Judith Singer Cohen, *Cowtown Moderne: Art Deco Architecture of Fort Worth, Texas* (College Station, Texas: Texas A&M University Press, 1988), 100-101.
104. "Everett Lee Frazior, Sr." (obituary), *FWST*, accessed September 26, 2009, http://www.legacy.com/obituaries/dfw/obituary.aspx?pid=136054504; Calvin Sutton, "About Stamps," *FWST*, May 28, 1961, sec. 3.
105. Henry, *Architecture in Texas*, op. cit., 311; "Dudley Green, Architect, Dies," *DMN*, July 29, 1948.
106. "Corsicana Student in Rice Institute Wins Scholarship," *Corsicana Daily Sun*, June 19, 1931; "King, A(rthur) George (AIA)," in *American Architects Directory*, 1st ed., op. cit., 299; "Obituaries: A. George King, architect," *FWST*, January 6, 1984.
107. Weinman and Smith, op. cit.
108. "H. Plunkett Rites Slated for Saturday," *Tyler Morning Telegram*.
109. "Attend Open House, Denton's Most Modernistic Dwelling," *Denton Record-Chronicle*, August 16, 1935; "Name Ex-Abilenian to Rural Aid Post," *Abilene* (Texas) *Reporter-News*, January 7, 1937; "Hilton Shepherd to Be Buried Today," *FWST*, April 29, 1976; "Dr. Everett Shepherd dies," *PN*, August 10, 1983.
110. "Walter Dorwin Teague, FIDSA," Industrial Designers Society of America, accessed May 28, 2017, http://www.idsa.org/content/walter-dorwin-teague; Rebecca Gross, "A Dandy of a

Camera," Cooper Hewitt, Smithsonian Design Museum, accessed May 28, 2017, https://www.cooperhewitt.org/2015/02/07/a-dandy-of-a-camera; Geoffrey Hacker, "Walter Dorwin Teague Designs First All Plastic Truck: Clues July-August, 1955," Forgotten Fiberglass, accessed May 28, 2017, http://www.forgottenfiberglass.com/fiberglass-car-marques/one-offs/walter-dorwin-teague-designs-plastic-truck-clues-july-august-1955; Sarah C. Rich, "The 86-Year-Old Company That Still Designs Your In-Flight Experience," Smithsonian.com, accessed May 28, 2017, http://www.smithsonianmag.com/arts-culture/the-86-year-old-company-that-still-designs-your-in-flight-experience-101934583.

111. Anne-Laure Garrec, "Bourdelle, Pierre," French Sculpture Census, accessed January 30, 2017, http://frenchsculpture.org/en/artist/bourdelle-pierre; "The Texas Exposition," *Daily Capital News* (Jefferson City, Missouri), November 12, 1936; "War Restricts Use of Largest Liner Ever Built in U.S.," *Port Arthur* (Texas) *News,* May 10, 1940; John Gaines, "Marine Log: Visitors Touring Savannah See Merchant Fleet Future," *Galveston* (Texas) *News,* February 8, 1963.

112. Francine Carraro, "Bywaters, Williamson Gerald [Jerry]," Handbook of Texas Online, accessed December 13, 2011, http://www.tshaonline.org/handbook/online/articles/fby14.

113. "Herring Coe," Medallic Art Collector, accessed January 25, 2017, http://medallicartcollector.com/herring-coe_biography.html; "Coe Bas Reliefs," Houston Parks and Recreation Department, accessed January 25, 2017, http://www.houstontx.gov/parks/artinparks/herringcoebasreliefs.html.

114. "All around Club Is Entertained at Stewart Home," *Zanesville* (Ohio) *Signal*, November 26, 1932; "Local Artists Complete Series of Authentic Murals," *Sunday Times-Signal* (Zanesville, Ohio), May 30, 1937, sec. 2; "Floor Tile Made Here Is Still in Use Nationwide," *Sunday Times Recorder* (Zanesville, Ohio), May 28, 1972.

115. Philip Parisi, *The Texas Post Office Murals: Art for the People* (College Station, Texas: Texas A&M University Press, 2004), 156-157.

116. Lea Rosson DeLong, "Hogue, Alexandre," Handbook of Texas Online, accessed May 27, 2017, http://www.tshaonline.org/handbook/online/articles/fhoad; "Alexandre Hogue," Smithsonian American Art Museum Renwick Gallery, accessed May 27, 2017, http://americanart.si.edu/collections/search/artist/?id=2265; "Alexandre Hogue: The Erosion Series," Dallas Museum of Art, accessed May 27, 2017, https://www.dma.org/art/exhibitions/alexandre-hogue-erosion-series; Susie Kalil, *Alexandre Hogue: An American Visionary* (College Station, Texas: Texas A&M University Press, 2011), 130-151.

117. "Dwight C. Holmes Is Exhibiting Art Here," *Fort Stockton* (Texas) *Pioneer,* October 19, 1969.

118. "Peter Hurd, American Painter," *Encyclopædia Britannica*, accessed May 27, 2017, https://www.britannica.com/biography/Peter-Hurd; "Peter Hurd, Painter of Southwest," *NYT*, July 10, 1984; "Southwest Artist Peter Hurd Dies in New Mexico," *Washington Post*, July 10, 1984.

119. Biographical sketch, Architects and Artists box, Centennial Collection, Dallas Historical Society.

120. Steven R. Butler, "Raoul Josset and Jose Martin: a Tale of Two Artists," *Legacies: a History Journal for Dallas and North Central Texas* Vol. 23, No. 2 (Fall 2011): 24.

121. Alan S. Mason, "McIntosh, Roger D., House," National Register of Historic Places Registration Form (Dallas, July 1, 1982); Tracy Lewis, "Living in Glass Houses," *Texas Monthly*, December 1977, 128.

122. "Frank A. Mechau," John Simon Guggenheim Memorial Foundation Fellows, accessed October 29, 2016, http://www.gf.org/fellows/all-fellows/frank-a-mechau.

123. Biographical sketch, Architects and Artists box, Centennial Collection, Dallas Historical Society (DHS); "Alma Mater, 1932," Museum Without Walls, accessed January 29, 2017, http://www.culturenow.org/entry&permalink=09107&seo=Alma-Mater_Alma-Mater-and-Yale-University; *Murals at Ariel Rios Federal Building 1935-2006* (Washington: US General Services Administration, 2006), accessed January 29, 2017, https://www.gsa.gov/graphics/pbs/Ariel_Rios_Brochure_Final2.pdf.

124. "Guide to the Evaline Sellors Papers," The Old Jail Art Center, Albany, Texas, Texas Archival Resources Online, accessed July 13, 2015, http://www.lib.utexas.edu/taro/ojac/00003/ojac-00003.html.

125. Patricia Peck, "At the Museums: Thomas Stell Joins Art Faculty of Texas University," *DMN*, February 9, 1945; Kendall Curlee, "Stell, Thomas Matthew, Jr.," Handbook of Texas Online, accessed September 25, 2016, http://www.tshaonline.org/handbook/online/articles/ftsbe.

126. *Draft Registration Cards for Fourth Registration for California, 04/27/1942-04/27/1942,* NAI No. 603155 (St. Louis, Missouri: the National Archives at St. Louis); Biographical sketch, Architects and Artists box, Centennial Collection, DHS; Edward Lebow, "The Amazing Colossal Sculptor," *Phoenix New Times*, October 31, 1996.

127. Biographical sketch, Architects and Artists box, Centennial Collection, Dallas Historical Society; Kendall Curlee, "Tennant, Allie Victoria," Handbook of Texas Online, accessed August 9, 2011, http://www.tshaonline.org/handbook/online/articles/fte37.

Bibliography

Frank Carter Adams, ed., *The State of Texas Building* (Austin: Steck, 1937).

Michael Andrews, *Historic Texas Courthouses* (Albany, Texas: Bright Sky Press, 2006).

Michael A. Bernstein, *The Great Depression: Delayed Recovery and Economic Change in America, 1929-1939* (New York: Cambridge University Press, 1989).

Edward A. Blackburn, *Wanted: Historic County Jails of Texas* (College Station, Texas: Texas A&M University Press, 2006).

Alfred C. Bossom, *Building to the Sky: The Romance of the Skyscraper* (London: Studio, 1934).

James H. Bruns, *Great American Post Offices* (New York: John Wiley & Sons, Inc., 1998).

Steven R. Butler, "Henry 'Dad' Garrett: the Wizard of Dallas, Texas," *Legacies: A History Journal for Dallas and North Central Texas* Vol. 22, No. 1 (Spring 2010)

Steven R. Butler, "Raoul Josset and Jose Martin: a Tale of Two Artists," *Legacies: A History Journal for Dallas and North Central Texas* Vol. 23, No. 2 (Fall 2011).

Chronicles of Smith County, Texas (Tyler, Texas: Smith County Historical Society, 1962-2008).

City of Fort Worth, Texas: Municipal Life, 1931-1937 (Fort Worth: City of Fort Worth Bureau of Municipal Research, August 1937).

Jerome Cochran, ed., *Texas General Contractors Association Monthly Bulletin* (Houston: Texas General Contractors Association, 1929-1937).

Judith Singer Cohen *Cowtown Moderne: Art Deco Architecture of Fort Worth, Texas* (College Station, Texas: Texas A&M University Press, 1988).

Van Craddock, Jr., with Eric Dabney and Scott Williams, *Historic Gregg County: An Illustrated History* (San Antonio: Historical Publishing Network, 2006).

Ellis Arthur Davis and Edwin H. Grobe, eds., *The Encyclopedia of Texas* (Dallas: Texas Development Bureau, 1922).

David Dillon, *Dallas Architecture: 1936-1986* (Austin: Texas Monthly Press, 1985).

Al Eason, *Boom Town: Kilgore, Texas* (Kilgore, Texas: Kilgore Chamber of Commerce, 1969).

Fort Worth Citywide Historic Preservation Plan (Princeton, New Jersey: Looney Ricks Kiss, 2003).

Stephen Fox, *The Country Houses of John F. Staub* (College Station, Texas: Texas A&M University Press, 2007).

Allen Freeman, "A Hard Fight Waged Over 1949 Soft-Drink Headquarters," *Historic Preservation News* (July 1, 1993).

Michael V. Hazel, "Building the Westminster Abbey of the New World," *Legacies: A History Journal for Dallas and North Central Texas* Vol. 23, No. 1 (Spring 2011).

Jay C. Henry, *Architecture in Texas: 1895-1945* (Austin: University of Texas Press, 1993).

Herbert M. Hinckley, Jr., *Under the Dome* (New York: Carlton Press, 1968).

Maxine Holmes and Gerald D. Saxon, eds., *WPA Guide and History: Written and compiled from 1936 to 1942 by the workers of the Writers' Program of the Work Projects Administration in the City of Dallas* (Dallas: Dallas Public Library, Texas Center for the Book and University of North Texas Press, 1992).

Marjorie Ingle, *Mayan Revival Style: Art Deco Mayan Fantasy* (Salt Lake City: Peregrine Smith Books, 1984).

W. Dwayne Jones, *A Field Guide to Gas Stations in Texas* (Austin: Texas Department of Transportation, Environmental Affairs Division, Historical Studies Branch, 2003).

Journal of the American Institute of Architects, Volume 1, January 1913-December 1913 (Washington, D.C.: The American Institute of Architects, 1913).

Susan Allen Kline, *Eight Decades of School Construction: Historic Resources of the Fort Worth Independent School District, 1892-1961* (Fort Worth: City of Fort Worth, 2003).

Ernest Langford, *The First Fifty Years of Architectural Education at the Agricultural and Mechanical College of Texas* (College Station, Texas: College Archive, Agricultural and Mechanical College of Texas, 1957).

Antoinette J. Lee, *Architects to the Nation: The Rise and Decline of the Supervising Architect's Office* (New York: Oxford University Press, 2000).

Debbie M. Liles, *Will Rogers Coliseum* (Charleston, South Carolina: Arcadia Publishing, 2012).

Carol Morris Little, *A Comprehensive Guide to Outdoor Sculpture in Texas* (Austin: University of Texas Press, 1996).

Virginia Savage McAlester, Willis Cecil Winters and Prudence Mackintosh, *Great American Suburbs: The Homes of the Park Cities, Dallas* (New York: Abbeville Press, 2008).

William D. Moore, *Masonic Temples: Freemasonry, Ritual Architecture and Masculine Archetypes* (Knoxville, Tennessee: The University of Tennessee Press, 2006).

Jacob W. Olmstead, "From Old South to Modern West: Fort Worth's Celebration of the Texas State Centennial and the Shaping of an Urban Identity and Image" (doctoral thesis, Texas Christian University, 2011).

Capt. B.B. Paddock, *History of Texas, Volume III: Fort Worth and the Texas Northwest* (Chicago: The Lewis Publishing Company, 1922).

Philip Parisi, *The Texas Post Office Murals: Art for the People* (College Station, Texas: Texas A&M University Press, 2004).

Richard Pells, *Modernist America: Art, Music, Movies and the Globalization of American Culture* (New Haven, Connecticut: Yale University Press, 2011).

Michael Phillips, *White Metropolis: Race, Ethnicity, and Religion in Dallas, 1841-2001* (Austin: University of Texas Press, 2006).

Caleb Pirtle III and Terry Stembridge, *Echoes from Forgotten Streets: Memories of Kilgore, Texas, Oil Capital of America* (Berkeley Heights, New Jersey: London Square Media, 2009).

Kenneth D. Ragsdale, *Centennial '36: The Year America Discovered Texas* (College Station, Texas: Texas A&M University Press, 1987).

Carol Roark and Byrd Williams, *Fort Worth's Legendary Landmarks* (Fort Worth: TCU Press, 1995).

Harry Rucker, "Film Row: From Vaudeville to the VCR," *Legacies: A History Journal for Dallas and North Central Texas* Vol. 10, No. 1 (Spring 1998).

C.W. Short and R. Stanley Brown, *Public Buildings: A Survey of Architecture of Projects Constructed by Federal and Other Governmental Bodies between the Years 1933 and 1939 with the Assistance of the Public Works Administration* (Washington, D.C.: United States Government Printing Office, 1939).

Tarrant County Historic Resources Survey (Fort Worth: Historic Preservation Council for Tarrant County, Texas, 1985-1988).

Jesse O. Thomas, *Negro Participation in the Texas Centennial Exposition* (Boston: The Christopher Publishing House, 1938).

Frank Thrower and Marian Ann J. Montgomery, "Mark Lemmon: Dallas Architect of Community Churches," *Legacies: A History Journal for Dallas and North Central Texas* Vol. 17, No. 2 (Fall 2005).

Mark Weiner, "Consumer Culture and Participatory Democracy: The Story of Coca-Cola During World War II," *Food and Foodways: Explorations in the History and Culture of Human Nourishment* Vol. 6, Issue 2 (1996).

Dorman H. Winfrey, *A History of Rusk County, Texas* (Waco, Texas: Texian Press, 1961).

Willis Cecil Winters, *Fair Park* (Charleston, South Carolina: Arcadia Publishung, 2010).

Willis Winters, "The Ford Motor Company at the Texas Centennial Exposition," *Legacies: A History Journal for Dallas and North Central Texas* Vol. 23, No. 1 (Spring 2011).

Writers' Program of the Works Projects Administration in the State of Texas, *Texas: A Guide to the Lone Star State* (New York: Hastings House, 1940).

Digital newspaper archives were invaluable for quickly locating detailed information from primary sources: NewsBank (http://www.newsbank.com) provided access to historic issues of the *Dallas Morning News* and the *Fort Worth Star-Telegram,* while NewspaperArchive (http://newspaperarchive.com) and Newspapers.com (https://www.newspapers.com) were important tools for searching regional and national newspapers.

Ancestry.com (http://home.ancestry.com), Find A Grave (http://www.findagrave.com) and Heritage Quest Online (http://www.ancestryheritagequest.com/HQA) provided biographical information from census records, city directories, obituaries, and death certificates.

The American Institute of Architects (AIA) Historical Directory of American Architects (http://public.aia.org/sites/hdoaa/wiki) was a valuable source of biographical information about architects.

The Texas Historical Commission's Texas Historic Sites Atlas (http://atlas.thc.state.tx.us) includes data on Texas properties listed on the National Register of Historic Places and information from state historical markers. The National Park Service's NPGallery (https://npgallery.nps.gov) includes similar information on National Register-listed properties outside Texas.

The Texas Historical Association's Handbook of Texas Online (https://tshaonline.org/handbook) contains biographies of significant individuals, including architects, builders, and business leaders, as well as accounts of important events in Texas history.

The University of North Texas Libraries' Portal to Texas History (https://texashistory.unt.edu) includes historical newspapers, documents, publications, and primary sources related to Texas history.

The Alexander Architectural Archive, University of Texas Libraries, The University of Texas at Austin (http://www.lib.utexas.edu/apl/aaa), includes biographical information about a number of architects; its online catalog of architectural drawings sorts building documentation by architect.

Illustration Credits

HISTORIC PHOTOGRAPHS

Archives of the Smith County Historical Society
Tyler, Texas
Mother Frances Hospital, entrance
Union Bus Depot

CHRISTUS Trinity Mother Frances Health System
Tyler, Texas
Mother Frances Hospital, overall

Dallas Historical Society
Contemporary House

Dallas Municipal Archives
02011_2D1DC, Dealey Plaza site plan
02011_2D1DC, Dealey Plaza rendering
99003_4_7004b, Dallas City Hall mural, railroad
99003_4_7006b, Dallas City Hall mural, water
99003_4_7008b, Dallas City Hall mural, radio police cars
99003_4_7010b, Dallas City Hall mural, viaducts

Dallas Public Library
Dallas History & Archives Division
MA82-2-29, Paul Laurence Dunbar Branch Library
PA76-1/4884.2, Gaston Building (c. 1952)
PA-76-1-30024-6, The Highlander
PA-76-1-35036, Dallas YMCA
PA76-1-35053, LaMode
PA76-1-35505, Lone Star Gas Co. Building
PA81-00238, Southwestern Bell Telephone Co. Long Distance Building
PA81-00318, Dallas Power & Light Co. Building
PA81-00357, Cokesbury Bookstore
PA83-13-8, Terminal and Administration Building, Love Field
PA83-34/90, Gaston Building (1895)
PA83-42-1977-12-7-2, Dal-Hi Stadium relief
PA85-16-35, Harlem Theater
PA20000-3-1283, Dr. Pepper Bottling Co. headquarters

Denton County Office of History and Culture
Denton, Texas
312 Marietta Street, Denton

Gregg County Historical Museum
Longview, Texas
C002424, Hurst Clinic
BK016, Longview National Bank
BX010, Longview News & Journal Building
BX032, Longview Coca-Cola Bottling Co.

Houston Public Library
Houston Metropolitan Research Center
Alfred C. Finn Collection
The People's National Bank Building
MSS-19-551, Entrance
MSS-19-554, Banking Hall
MSS-19-559, Exterior

National Automotive History Collection
Detroit Public Library
Packard-Dallas, Inc.

State Fair of Texas Archives
Texas Centennial Exposition
1936kc.00360, Hall of Negro Life
1936kc.00022, Portland Cement House rendering
1936.00061, Aerial view of exposition grounds
1939.00030, Esplanade of State
No number, Ford Motor Co. Building

Texas State Library and Archives
1972/11-29, "Esplanade and Reflection Basin at Night," postcard

University of Texas at Arlington Libraries
Special Collections
10001518, Sinclair Building
100000325, Passenger waiting room, Texas and Pacific Railway station
Courtesy, *Fort Worth Star-Telegram* Collection, Special Collections, The University of Texas at Arlington Libraries, Arlington, Texas
10015267, Equitable Building & Loan Association
AR407-2-3, Blackstone Hotel
AR407-9-49, Terminal and Administration Building, Meacham Field
Courtesy, Jack White Photograph Collection, Special Collections, The University of Texas at Arlington Libraries, Arlington, Texas
10015371, Marshall Kennady House, rear façade
10015374, Marshall Kennady House, front façade
10004035, Aviation Building
AR430-41-0-6, Fort Worth City Hall
AR430-41-75-2, Fort Worth Public Library
AR430-44-528-2, United States Court House, Fort Worth
AR430-44-804-1, W.T. Grant Store
AR430-45-833-36, Bowen Bus Center
AR430-48-185-19, Gas Building, Fort Worth
AR430-49-1-15, Palace Theater, Fort Worth
AR430-49-20-55, Fort Worth Dr. Pepper Bottling Co.
AR430-49-256-1, City-County Hospital, Fort Worth
AR430-49-610-1, Harris Clinic
AR430-74-207-1, "Wild & Whoo-pee" electric sign
Courtesy, W.D. Smith Commercial Photography Collection, Special Collections, The University of Texas at Arlington Libraries, Arlington, Texas

Historic postcards
from the authors' collections

ORIGINAL PHOTOGRAPHS

Steve Clicque
4401 Beverly Drive, Highland Park
4637 Mockingbird Lane, Highland Park
4512 Potomac Avenue, University Park

Lovita Irby
Circle Theater, Dallas

All other original photography by Jim Parsons and David Bush

Index